CATTLE

COTTON

CORN

CATTLE COTTON CORN

A HISTORY OF CENTRAL
TEXAS MIDDLE-CLASS
RANCHES, 1880–1930

W. C. ARNOLD

TEXAS TECH UNIVERSITY PRESS

This book is typeset in Adobe Caslon Pro. The paper used in this book meets
the minimum requirements of ANSI/NISO Z39.48-1992 (R1997). ♾

Designed by Hannah Gaskamp; cover design by Hannah Gaskamp

Library of Congress Cataloging-in-Publication Data

Names: Arnold, W. C., 1945– author. Title: Cattle, Cotton, Corn: A History of
Central Texas Middle-class Ranches, 1880–1930 / W. C. Arnold. Description:
Lubbock, Texas: Texas Tech University Press, [2022] | Includes bibliograph-
ical references and index. | Summary: "An account of the lived experiences of
four small Central Texas family ranches drawn from oral histories and fam-
ily records"—Provided by publisher. Identifiers: LCCN 2021050054 (print) |
LCCN 2021050055 (ebook) |
ISBN 978-1-68283-128-1 (cloth) | ISBN 978-1-68283-135-9 (ebook)
Subjects: LCSH: Ranches—Texas—Blacklands—History. | Ranches—
Texas—Blacklands—Social life and customs. | Ranch life—Texas—Blacklands.
Classification: LCC F392.B546 A76 2022 (print) | LCC F392.B546 (ebook)
| DDC 976.4/26—dc23
LC record available at https://lccn.loc.gov/2021050054
LC ebook record available at https://lccn.loc.gov/2021050055

Printed in the United States of America
22 23 24 25 26 27 28 29 30/ 9 8 7 6 5 4 3 2 1

Texas Tech University Press
Box 41037
Lubbock, Texas 79409-1037 USA
800.832.4042
ttup@ttu.edu
www.ttupress.org

This book is dedicated to my wife, Tricia, and my two boys, Thomas and Philip.

Contents

Acknowledgments

THIS BOOK HAS BEEN PART OF A LONG AND ARDUOUS process beginning in 1995 and now finished almost thirty years later. My professors, family, colleagues at work, and friends have had incredible patience and endurance in following me through this ordeal. I began to take history courses for pleasure, enjoying the seminars, reading books, and discussing them with bright young graduate students. I am still having fun.

I came to history rather late in life. When I began to retire from medicine, my wife told me I needed something to keep busy. Since I was the first among my siblings to retire, my father told me he wanted me to take over managing the family ranch. He wanted to cut back but also wanted to keep the income, so I would direct things for no reimbursement. I took ranch management courses to prepare to oversee the ranch.

About the same time, a physician friend encouraged me to take history courses at the nearby university (Texas Christian University). Many local professionals were taking classes there. That plan appealed to me, because I had grown up listening to the stories from my great-grandmother and other family members about growing up on the frontier. I enjoyed taking courses for several semesters, enrolling in classes on my afternoons off, since I did not play golf.

One afternoon, the departmental secretary asked me to drop by the chairman's office after class. I thought I had hurt another student's feelings when I had expressed myself in a rather straightforward manner. So I was prepared to be admonished. Instead, the chairman said the faculty had been discussing me and they wanted me to "get serious" about history. He told me to go see Dr. Ben Procter, who would explain. Well, I knew Dr. Procter's tough reputation, so I knocked on his door rather hesitantly. A booming voice told me to come in. There sat this bear of a man, his glasses on top of his bald head as he sized me up. I gave him my name and he told me he knew who I was. My heart sank. I was sure I was going to be expelled from class. I told him the chairman had sent me to talk to him. He told me to sit down. He lowered his glasses to look me over more closely.

Procter explained that the faculty wanted me to enroll in a degree program. I responded that I already had lots of degrees and was not sure I needed another. He frowned and said I needed to get a "real doctorate" rather than the "trade school degree" I had at that time. I immediately decided I liked this man.

This marked the beginning of my path to a doctorate in history. Procter and I bargained over credit earned for my previous studies and then he told me I would have to write a dissertation. I asked what that entailed. Was it like a giant book report on some obscure subject? He bellowed, "No!" It was—or would be in my case—finding information in diaries and letters that had never been discussed before. I had no idea what that meant and how I could accomplish what he wanted. So I was going to be expelled after all.

The next weekend I drove to the ranch and, in my capacity of managing partner, met with my father and his cousin, Cavitt Caufield. I wanted to reorient the cattle pastures around a central barn as we had been taught in ranch management. But Cavitt told me that the fences would "wash" if put in certain places "like they did in '88." I remarked that I did not remember any flooding in 1988. He looked at me and said, "No—1888. Granddaddy told us all about it." I later asked him how he knew all that stuff he was telling me. He said it was in the ranch records. When I asked which ones he was referring to, he told me about the records on the sleeping porch of the old house built in 1880 by my great-grandparents.

My great-uncle Monty, who managed the ranches before my father, had an office on that porch. He had been exiled to this remote area by his wife (my great-aunt Eula) and his mother (my great-grandmother Kate) because he smoked and chewed cigars. I remember him sitting in an old leather chair, which still smells like Uncle Monty's cigars, as he worked at an old rolltop desk. On the porch were several old lopsided wooden file cabinets. I straightened the cabinets so their drawers would open. Inside I found bundles of letters and ledgers, ranch records from the 1850s, and records from Boligee, Alabama, beginning about 1820. The mother lode!

As I continued my research, my cousin Cavitt Caufield continued to give me support and advice. He gave me access to papers he had at his house from his father, George Caufield, and uncle, Josephus Cavitt. Cavitt had saved several leather file boxes of their business records, including carbon copies of correspondence. He had copies and originals of the letters between his great-grandfather Henry and Henry's brother Watson Caufield, and other members of their family going back to the 1820s. These were in Watson Caufield's trunk when he died.

Cavitt later took me to meet some distant cousins, the Foote family, in Coryell County. They had kept the records of the Foote ranch from the 1870s in several trunks in an old chicken hatchery building behind their family home. They had recorded business records annually in small ledger books from daybooks they kept in their shirt pockets. They had also preserved several hundred letters in Army ammunition boxes and had large ledgers containing the business records of Henry and Watson Caufield's brother-in-law William Ewing Young and his sheep ranch. This was an incredible amount of economic data detailing the finances of these families covering decades.

Because the paper was fragile, I photocopied all the information and carefully returned it to the owners. My father and Cavitt furnished their own tax records, including expenses and crop income. I recorded interviews with several family members who remembered the last six decades. These are the primary sources upon which this book is based.

Of course, I must thank my principal professor, Dr. Ben Procter. He probably did not realize what a task he took on by accepting me as one of his graduate students. But neither did I. After my first day at one of his writing seminars, where the discussion centered on topic sentences or "Mother Hubbards" (an expression for covering all the information under a topic sentence's wide skirt) and passive voice, the other graduate students took pity on me and explained what Dr. Procter was talking about. Mark Barringer and Mark Beasley became my permanent friends that day and they have continued to help me since. Mary Kelley and Bart Pointer joined them later. I owe all of them a great debt of gratitude.

Other relatives brought me additional records. Roberta Powell, Frankie Glaze, and Dr. Speegle, all descendants of William Young, gave me additional records and encouraged me. I photocopied their records and added them to my growing collection. I am appreciative of their efforts. I made a trip to Boligee, Alabama, and the Greene County Courthouse in Eutaw, where I found old wills, notes, and newspapers. I added them to my archive. In addition, Cavitt, my father, and Sonny Foote spent many hours talking to me about the "old days." I recorded many of our conversations. Those three men helped me a great deal. I cannot thank them enough.

Finally, I need to thank my family, especially my wife, Tricia, who has been extremely patient and supportive. When I told my two sons, Thomas and Philip, that I was going to get a doctorate in history, they shot me that *You gotta be kidding* look teenagers give you when you do something really embarrassing. After a while they accepted that their dad was just a bit odd and let it go. Now, having graduated from college, they actually seem to enjoy reading my writings. I guess things really do change over time.

CATTLE

COTTON

CORN

Introduction

THE NORTH AMERICAN COLONIES WERE AN AGRICUL-tural society and remained so for several generations. Poor roads connected small subsistence farms to port towns containing populations that today are designated "small towns." Even as the country grew, the population largely remained rural and formed the basis of Thomas Jefferson's idea of an educated, landowning, democratic society. Farmers built their own homes, wove their own clothing, and raised enough to feed their families.

The Industrial Revolution and railroads changed all that. Urban populations grew as immigrants and farmers moved to the cities to work in factories. Farmers had to raise enough not only to feed their families but to sell for cash to buy manufactured goods such as shoes, clothing, and farm implements. The railroads made urban areas more accessible, as passengers could avoid the terrible roads. Farmers now had a market for their excess production. They purchased more land and raised more crops with the new farm equipment.

By the end of the nineteenth century, the Industrial Revolution began to mechanize agriculture and revolutionize American farms. Agricultural productivity increased rapidly, forcing more farmers into the cities. By the beginning of the twentieth century, the urban population exceeded that in rural areas.

The rapid changes caught farmers in the middle. Their prosperity decreased and land that had once supported large families now could no longer produce enough income for necessities. Eighty acres would not support a family. Farms consolidated, pushing the displaced families into the urban areas for work. Unrest led to the Populist Era as farmers attempted to gain control of their futures. But farmers were soon outvoted by the urban populations, and agriculture as a way of life began to slowly decline. Many lost their land and became sharecroppers. Eventually the Great Depression ended the small farms.

For several decades after the Texas Revolution, Central Texas on the edge of the Blackland Prairies—the area roughly delineated by McLennan, Bell, Coryell, and Falls Counties—remained the outer edge of the frontier. In the late 1840s and early 1850s a few individuals began to raise cattle in the area and to start subsistence farming. Waco Village was founded along the Brazos River. Yet, by the Civil War, the northwestern portion of McLennan County, Coryell County, and Bosque County remained sparsely populated, containing fewer than one hundred families.

This changed rapidly in 1882 when the railroads pushed through the western portion of McLennan County. With access to markets for their crops, immigrants, particularly Germans, began to buy farms, fence the land, and raise cotton. The Industrial Revolution brought barbed wire as well as deep water-well drilling equipment and windmills, which made farming—even away from surface water sources—profitable. The new settlers left ranchers with the choice of moving west to continue raising cattle or fencing their property and changing to specialized livestock and/or cotton farming. Henry Caufield did both, purchasing ranches in Shackleford County and Mexico, also fencing his McLennan County holdings to raise mules and Shetland ponies and upgrading his cattle. He began to farm by fencing some of his pastures and planting cotton.

By 1890, northwestern McLennan County had entered a new era and cotton was king. In 1910, McLennan County was the largest cotton-producing county in the state of Texas, raising 80,000 bales annually, and Texas was the largest cotton-producing state in the United States.

By managing the commodities produced on the local farms, small towns flourished, especially along the rail lines. With most of their land now planted in cotton and managed by sharecroppers or tenant farmers, Henry Caufield and his children moved to the nearby town of McGregor and began to invest in local businesses. Railroads also pulled people from the small villages into towns with utilities and other luxuries.

The increased use of mechanization on farms, particularly tractors and harvesters, allowed a single family to farm ever larger acreage. After World War I, mechanization displaced farmworkers and sharecroppers. They moved to the cities for work in factories and services. The smallest towns slowly languished. Life drifted along until drought and the Great Depression hit the farmers with poor crops and low prices. At that point the cotton empire began to collapse.

After World War II, the introduction of the mechanical cotton picker drove the remainder of farmworkers into the cities, and the small towns began to die. The price of cotton never made a total resurgence after the Depression, and local farmers began to switch to raising grains—corn, wheat, and milo. Those who did not adapt to the changes were left behind in poverty.

Prosperous ranchers and farmers constituted the middle class of agrarian America during the latter part of the eighteenth until the early twentieth centuries. Over the preceding hundred years, the Industrial Revolution had changed manufacturing and labor in small factories across England and the United States. Now over a fifty-year period from 1880 to 1930, the agricultural portion of the American economy underwent dramatic alterations. At the middle of the nineteenth century the majority of Americans lived on farms, made their living from the soil, and prospered. By the beginning of the twentieth century, America had become an urban society. The farming population had shrunk to a minority of Americans, and many farmers lived on the edge of poverty.

While most historical works have concentrated on the wealthy and famous or, more recently, on women or the poor and oppressed, few works have detailed the lives of Middle America—the vast middle class of prosperous Americans who form the backbone of the country and the economy. Prior to the Great Depression, most of the middle class lived on farms and owned their own land, but many were doctors, lawyers, small planters, and merchants living nearby in small communities. They were neither rich nor famous. This literate and cultured portion of society kept records, especially letters that detailed their lives. This work tells the story of these Middle Americans—how they lived, the issues they embraced, how they spent their money, how they planned and invested, and what happened to them during the transition from an agricultural to an urban society.

This book is not a family history but rather relates how several related families responded during the transition of the United States from an agricultural-based to an industrial-based economy. Because these families often worked together as an economic unit, the individual members are described so that the reader can follow their actions. Some description of personalities also clarifies why they made certain choices.

The Caufield, Cavitt, Young, and Foote families were not particularly unique: they were not rich, famous, or powerful; they did not hold high elected offices; nor did they command armies or militias. Rather they were quite ordinary people—prosperous immigrant yeomen farmers—whose lives were swept up by the events of American history. The Caufields were remarkable not only for being literate—both men and women could write—but because they wrote hundreds of letters to each other and other members of their clan as well as saved their papers: letters, receipts, ledgers, journals, etc. As a result, their correspondence and records provide a documentary window into the mid-nineteenth century as experienced by a middle-class Texas family.

What follows is the story of how the Caufields progressed from farming on the Texas frontier to cattle ranching. Then, when pressed by farmers fencing the free grass that they had enjoyed for half a century, they switched to cotton, which became their life for the next fifty years. Their children moved off the farms into the neighboring small towns to enjoy the benefits of a more urban life. But the Great Depression and other factors doomed cotton farming. They struggled until after the Second World War. When cotton farming remained unprofitable, they switched yet again. This time they began to raise corn as their main crop. Now, fifty years later, many are switching once more, this time back to livestock.

The agricultural revolution that occurred between 1880 and 1930 changed the life of the rural middle class and the four related families. The Caufields—Henry John Caufield and his sister Mary Jane Caufield—had moved with their families to the frontier of Central Texas, where they established flourishing agriculture-based businesses. H. J. Caufield prospered in free-range cattle ranching and Mary Jane Caufield Young and her husband, William Ewing Young, prospered raising sheep in a more arid region.

When the frontier moved farther west over the next thirty years, the building of the railroads, the encroachment of farms, the fencing of the range, and the decline in the value of livestock spurred a change to raising pedigreed livestock and later a switch to cotton production. After the Depression cotton never again became a reliably profitable crop, and the families shifted from cotton to corn and other grains, which are now the main products of the business. They moved from cattle to cotton to corn.

During the latter part of the nineteenth century, their children began to move into the small towns and nearby cities. Henry

Caufield's daughter Mary (or "Mollie," sometimes spelled "Molly") married Josephus Cavitt, who leveraged numerous small-town agribusinesses off the income from his family's cotton production. At times Josephus Cavitt was involved in too many projects and businesses to present in chronological order. Instead, this book uses a topical format focusing on each business and following it through the period. Mary Jane Young's daughter Mary Ann married Frederick Foote, who continued to raise sheep on his ranch and only cautiously entered other fields.

The first generation's successes will be examined briefly with a comparison in the prices of manufactured goods and agricultural commodities. The sources of income and expenses for the second generation will be presented in more detail. The influences, politics, and economic forces that affected each generation's decisions—right or wrong—will be explored.

Each family experienced a different fate. The Cavitts lived lavishly and neglected their holdings. They sold most of their land during the agricultural slump preceding the Great Depression of 1929 to continue their lavish lifestyle. The Young family carefully guarded their investments and distributed them to the next generation. The Footes continued to hold their land, using their income from livestock to offset losses in cotton.

The Caufields suffered a mixed fate. Henry Caufield passed his land on to his children. Most of them moved to the city, became absentee landlords, and eventually lost their land. Those who continued to live on their farms or who closely supervised their tenant farmers endured and still own their land. When cotton prices fell, Joe Cavitt and George Caufield were unable to pay the debts they had amassed and went bankrupt. The Foote family, who had little debt, hunkered down and survived with their land intact. However, none of the members of these families enjoyed the prosperity of their parents.

The period from 1880 to 1930 was a time of rapid change in agriculture. Mechanization decreased the amount of human labor needed to raise crops and increased productivity. When crop prices fell, those who had not mechanized or who had borrowed money were unable to meet their note payments and lost their land. Farmers who could not support their families on the land moved to small towns or industrialized urban areas. But farmers who lived modestly, who lived and worked on their land, and who avoided debt survived.

This book presents the detailed records kept by four related families: the Caufields and Cavitts who switched from cattle to cotton and the Young and Foote families who primarily engaged in raising sheep and later cotton. Beginning in the 1850s, these families kept exhaustive records. Their lives, marriages, adaptation to changes, success and failures, entertainments, educations, and deaths are detailed through letters written over several generations and are like those of many thousands of other families. These records also provide an interesting window into this period in American history. They provide a view of the adaptability of the rural agricultural population and illustrate how these hardworking Scotch-Irish immigrants adapted to the mechanization that overwhelmed them and yet managed to thrive.

Several characteristic values marked these middle-class farming families. First, education played a significant role in their lives. Church and family were also important. Thrift and living within one's means formed a core value. Borrowing as little money as possible and paying it back as quickly as possible was a basic tenet of the older generation. Those who breached these social and economic values did so at their own risk and with the families' disapproval.

Education was a valued commodity in these four families, and all the children were encouraged to attend college. The original immigrants from Northern Ireland—both men and women— could read and write, placing them in a small minority. The second and third generations attended college: the Cavitts went to

Washington and Lee College; the Youngs went to Daniel Baker College and Vanderbilt University; and the Caufields went to Presbyterian College in Chattanooga. This emphasis on education occurred in a period when less than 3 percent of the American population up until and including that time attended any college, making these families an exception to the norm.

Each generation achieved varying degrees of prosperity by their elder years and, on their deaths, left their children real goods—land, furnishings, and household goods—rather than cash inheritances. Some of their children prospered while others lost their inheritance.

The prices of commodities, of livestock, then of cotton and wool from 1850 to 1940 determined their standard of living. The comparable prices of these commodities never rose as high after World War II as they had been in the "glory years" during the first decades of the twentieth century. The purchasing power of the dollar remained relatively stable for the first ninety years (from 1850 to 1940). After World War II, however, inflation drove down the value of the dollar. To estimate the relative worth of various expenses into today's dollars, multiply the price paid in those years by 50 to determine the approximate value in 2021 dollars. For example, Henry Foote was trying to earn $46 in 1887 to return home by rail. That does not sound like a lot of money until converted into present-day dollars, which makes that ticket worth $1,150. The relative prosperity of these families thus decreased as inflation increased the price of durable goods.[1]

Finally, throughout this period, mechanization decreased the quantity of rural workforce needed to raise the crops. Each farmer was able to work more acreage in the same amount of time, but the increased cost of raising crops, factoring in expenses such as machine purchases, repair, and replacement, gasoline, etc., made the profitability about the same.

After World War II, cotton produced less income than grain crops. The boll weevil, cotton root rot, and the prolonged drought of the 1950s made cotton a difficult crop to raise in Central Texas in sufficient quantities to make a constant profit. Mechanization helped only a little: although it decreased labor costs, the crops remained small. Gradually the local farmers changed their crops to a rotation of corn, maize, and wheat. As commodity prices remained low over the next decades, farmers began to shift their cornfields into pasture and the raising of cattle. A driver through East and Central Texas sees almost no fields planted in cotton. Instead, cattle now graze on fields that formerly were planted in cotton.

I

Cattle—
The Beginning,
1820–1860

THE CAUFIELD FAMILY ARRIVED IN THE UNITED STATES in 1820 as part of the diaspora of Scotch-Irish fleeing economic repression. British economic policy devastated the economy of Northern Ireland when the English government applied the Corn Laws to the region. The laws forced the products of Northern Ireland or Ulster to be shipped first to England before being exported to other countries. The resulting tariffs, fees, and commissions enriched the English merchants but made the prices for Irish goods noncompetitive on the world market. When the landlords began to raise land rents, even the substantial merchants and small landowners began to emigrate.[1]

The Scotch-Irish had originally settled in Northern Ireland in the seventeenth century during the English Civil War and the

Puritan Wars of 1600–1650 against Catholic-Irish rebellions. Oliver Cromwell and King William IV planted Protestant immigrants from England and Scotland in the region to ensure that a reliable and loyal populace inhabited Ireland. The Protestants shipped to Northern Ireland were often among the most acrimonious adherents to various Presbyterian sects—those whom Cromwell most wished to deport from England to keep peace in the countryside. The settlers were usually poor Scottish tenant farmers who moved with the promise of free land.

Initially, the land granted to each family in Ireland was generous and ample. Over the ensuing generations, however, overpopulation and division of farming plots between heirs reduced the land available into small plots barely able to sustain a family. The reduction in prices from the Corn Laws for their produce and handmade linen made subsistence precarious. When the large feudal estates refused to sell additional land and enclosed much of the commons, even the small landowners began to leave. Henry Fullerton, a small landholder and Caufield ancestor, who remained in Northern Ireland, lamented the departure of his son William to America, noting, "I cannot understand why he is leaving. I will leave him twenty-seven acres for his family."[2]

As a result, beginning in the mid-eighteenth century, young Irishmen began to immigrate to the United States, where land was available and cheap. Between 1730 and 1820 over 500,000 people left Northern Ireland, and the population decreased by more than 50 percent throughout the rural areas. Additionally, many young families moved to urban areas where jobs were to be had. The countryside was virtually depopulated, with only parents and perhaps one child left on each farm.[3]

Upon arriving in the United States, Irish immigrants brought with them a land hunger that had a profound effect on the western frontier expansion of the new American nation. In their experience, land represented wealth and security. Thus, the Scotch-Irish immigrants sought to own as much land as possible. And they moved quickly and relentlessly to satisfy their hunger.[4]

The Scotch-Irish immigration began in earnest around 1730 through the port of Philadelphia. The new immigrants found land available on the frontier beyond the previously founded Quaker and German communities, and they settled heavily in Western Pennsylvania. Initially, blocked by the Allegheny Mountains to the west, they flowed south, down the eastern mountain valleys, through the Shenandoah Valley, into North Carolina, and then across the Cumberland Gap westward into Kentucky and Tennessee. Later immigrants arrived through the port town of Charleston, South Carolina, and moved along the newly constructed National Road (or Cumberland Road) into Georgia and Alabama.

Generally, the Scotch-Irish immigrated in large, extended family groups. Although they left Ireland later than most of the Scotch-Irish immigrants, the Caufields were no different. The first group, consisting of two single males, arrived in the United States in 1820 through Charleston. Two years later a second wave of relatives arrived aboard the transport ship *Celebes*, also through the port of Charlestown. The ship's registry contained twelve close family members: children, cousins, in-laws, brothers, and sisters. Included in the list were Watsons, Dunns, Fullertons, Johnstons, and Caufields. They met other relatives in Charleston; one was George Hays, who gave them employment on the plantations he managed. For the next two years they recovered from their trip and adjusted to their new country.[5]

The Caufields followed a similar pattern of chain migration to the Blackland Prairie of Alabama. The forced resettlement of the Choctaw Indians from Alabama and Mississippi to Oklahoma had opened a vast amount of land for settlement. There was plenty of land for everyone. An assortment of relatives, including John Dunn and George Hays, scouted the land recently released by the

Indians. In Greene County, Alabama Territory, they found soil similar to that on their old farms in Londonderry, Ireland. The young males scouted the new land and, after crops were planted and houses built, a second wave containing their wives and children and older parents and relatives joined them, traveling along the National Road from South Carolina to Alabama.

From 1822 to 1824, the Caufields and their relatives purchased land around the town of Boligee, Greene County, about eleven miles from the county seat at Eutaw. The families settled on land between the Tombigbee and Black Warrior Rivers in Alabama. By 1824 they had secured title to their new farms, built cabins, and planted crops.

The largest group arrived in the fall of 1824. They were joined by the Johnsons, Dunns, and Fullertons, who had married Caufield sisters; the Watsons, whose sister was married to a Caufield; the Henrys, who were married to a Johnston; and other relatives, including the McAlpines, McLemores, Hayses, and Castles. Boligee came to be known as an "Irish" settlement, and census records document that almost all the inhabitants were related. The voting tally sheets for Boligee in 1840 recorded twenty-six male voters, nineteen of whom were kin. Other scattered relatives arrived during the next twenty years, some to stay, some on their way to opportunities farther west.[6]

One of the first duties for these immigrants was to build a church. These families belonged to a peculiar sect called the Brethren, a group of "freethinking" strict Presbyterians who refused to accept direction from the Anglican Church of England. They had settled together in Antrim, in Northern Ireland, and they immigrated together to the United States. By 1825 they had built their first church at Boligee, which stands to this day. Consistent with their beliefs, the building was a simple small wooden structure containing wooden pews without cushions. (One did not go to church to be comfortable.) There was no elevation for the parson.

(Preachers were no better than anyone else.) The building contained no ornaments ("papist" relics). Church records documented the same close kinship patterns, with nine family members out of thirteen children listed in church school. The cemetery around the church contained the first and second generations of the same families. Those families who stayed behind after the migration to Texas continue to use the burial site to this day. Their descendants built very similar churches in Texas on Dunn's Prairie near Dunn's Fort, Wheelock Prairie near Wheelock, and at Harris Creek on the South Bosque River.[7]

In early 1833, several family members traveled to the recently opened lands in Texas to look for new opportunities. They liked what they saw and encouraged the families to move to Texas. In December 1833, the second generation of the Scotch-Irish families began another chain migration from Alabama to Texas. Following the Federal Road through to Vicksburg and Natchitoches and on to the Sabine River, they crossed the Sabine and followed the Camino Real, the Old San Antonio Road, westward through San Augustine and Nacogdoches.

The travelers left in a long train of wagons, oxcarts, and carryalls. Traveling six days a week, they rested their teams and attended religious services on Sundays. Hugh Henry, John Fullerton, James Dunn, and James Young led the caravan. Also in the wagon train were Henry and Sarah Caufield Fullerton; William and Mary Fullerton Henry; Elizabeth McMillan; Ann McMillan and her children; Edward and Mary Young McMillan; Leticia Caufield Ellis; James and Isabell Caufield Dunn; James and Mary Dunn Young; and William Ewing Young and sons John and William. Thomas Caufield and his children stayed behind because his wife, Nancy Watson Caufield, was unable to withstand the difficulties of a trip due to her illness. She was terminally ill with tuberculosis.

The first wave laid their land grants about Wheelock in Robertson's Colony and began to build new lives. James Dunn determined the exact site of their settlement when his wagon bogged down on the Old San Antonio Road. Riding about while the families camped for the night, he crossed an area of open prairie and decided to place his claim there. His kin settled together in the wooded area bordering that open prairie between the Trinity and Brazos Rivers that came to be called Dunn's Prairie. James Dunn built a fort on the highest part of his land to serve both as a protection from Indian raids and as a site for political and family gatherings. The group placed their cemetery behind the fort.

The settlers set their headrights near each other along Peach and Cedar Creeks in what is now Robertson County, established a village they called Staggers Point, built their churches, and began their new lives on the Texas frontier. They placed their leagues farther out on the frontier, which was often not safe from Indian depredations for several decades. Other relatives from Alabama would join them over the next ten years.[8]

The Scotch-Irish families brought their folkways and their religion with them to Texas. Religion was of great importance to fundamentalist Presbyterians. Isabell Caufield Dunn (Aunt Bell), shortly after arriving in the Robertson grant, established the first Presbyterian church—the "Old Irish Church"—in a log cabin on the Red Top Prairie between Staggers Point and Dunn's Fort. Soon the Reverend Peter Hunter Fullenwider began preaching a strict Presbyterian creed from the podium of the church. They started a school in the church to provide the education the Scots valued so much.

Shortly after his arrival in Texas, William Ewing Young Jr. began to correspond with his cousin and close friend Henry J. Caufield, who had remained behind in Alabama with his family. Young encouraged Caufield to join them in Texas. In March 1848, Young wrote from near Wheelock, Texas, that "the grass [is] up very pretty over the prairie. . . . The cattle are beginning to fatten up and look slick." Knowing that Henry liked to hunt he added, "I was out hunting an ox when we came across a drove of old gobblers. . . . I can tell you its fine sport to get after an old gobbler with your cow whip." When Henry's mother's illness and death left Henry lonely and unhappy, Young commiserated, saying, "Henry I'm sorry your [sic] left so lonely back in Old Greene."[9]

In 1849, twenty-one-year-old Henry Caufield and his twenty-three-year-old sister Mary Jane joined their aunts and cousins at Wheelock. They emigrated from Boligee a year after their mother's death from tuberculosis and several months after their father remarried a widow with two daughters. They left two younger siblings, sixteen-year-old George and twelve-year-old Elizabeth, at home with their father and stepmother. An older brother, Watson, had left earlier in the year for the California goldfields. The older siblings did not get along with their stepmother and believed she had forced them from their home, but they remained devoted to their father.

Henry and Mary Jane Caufield traveled overland to New Orleans, then by steamer to Galveston, and by stagecoach to Wheelock where their aunts, Isabell "Bell" Caufield Dunn, Sarah Caufield Fullerton, and Letitia Caufield Ellis, lived and began their new lives. Mary Jane moved in with her aunts and cousins and lived with them until her marriage to William Young. She became a companion for her aunts, particularly Bell, who suffered from rheumatism and traveled from spa to spa to "take the waters." Aunt Bell spent several months each year at Centerville, which specialized in hot-water baths. She usually took Mary Jane along for company.

Henry went to work for his first cousin, Josephus Cavitt, driving oxcarts and freighting cotton, lumber, and produce. The oxen traveled about ten miles a day on the two-hundred-mile route to Houston, which took about six weeks round trip. In the port city Henry purchased supplies and took them back to the Cavitt store in Wheelock. In Houston, wagon yards specialized in buying wagons and livestock. Sometimes he sold his wagon and oxen and rode home on horseback. On other trips he freighted his purchases back. In addition, he drove the carts between the Cavitt farm, the cotton gin, and the docks on the Brazos River where steamships freighted the cotton crop to the port of Galveston.

Andrew Cavitt had investigated the newly opened Texas lands with his friend James Coryell in 1832. After negotiations with the owners of the Robertson grant in Nashville, Cavitt and Coryell decided to immigrate to that area. Cavitt and Coryell placed their leagues side by side along the Leon River in what is now Coryell County.

The Cavitts migrated from Tennessee to the Robinson grant in 1835 in a train of twenty wagons, more than twenty slaves, and their entire household goods. They arrived just in time to become part of the "Runaway Scrape," the flight of Texas families to the Louisiana border ahead of Santa Anna's invading Mexican armies. Andrew Cavitt, the father of seven sons, died during the evacuation and was buried along the roadside near Millican.

After Andrew Cavitt's death, James Coryell became the family protector until his death in an Indian attack while hunting for a bee tree. One of the Cavitt boys was scheduled to go on the bee hunting trip, but his participation was vetoed by his mother that morning.

Ann Cavett, wife and second cousin of Andrew Cavitt, remarried another cousin, Cavitt Armstrong, and established the family on their lands around Wheelock in Robertson County. The seven boys, Josephus, Volney, Sheridan, Richard, Andrew, James, and William, married into other well-established pioneer families, including the Dunns, the Caufields, the Sparkses, and the Robertsons. In 1862, Josephus Cavitt purchased 8,000 acres in Coryell, Bosque, and Hamilton Counties for $10,000. He continued to add to his holdings, and eventually the Cavitt family owned extensive tracts of land in East Texas, around San Angelo, and in Coryell County.

By the Civil War, the Cavitts had been in Texas for a generation and a half, and their wealth and marriages made them one of the predominant families in eastern Central Texas. In his petition to President Andrew Johnson to obtain amnesty after the Civil War, Volney Cavitt listed assets of 10,000 acres, 1,500 sheep, 2,000 cattle, and 100 horses, with a net worth of more than $40,000.[10]

The Cavitt and the Caufield families were close relatives and partners in business over the next generations. Josephus Cavitt, Volney's brother and the second son of Andrew Cavitt, married Isabell Dunn, whose mother, Isabell Caufield Dunn, was Mary Jane and Henry Caufield's aunt Bell. Volney Cavitt's eldest son, Josephus ("Joe"), would marry Henry Caufield's daughter Mollie. Other, more distant cousins intermarried, and the families would work together for over a hundred years.[11]

In 1850, Caufield went into partnership with the elder Josephus Cavitt and took six hundred head of cattle to the Cavitt league on the Leon River in Coryell County. In return for his labor, he was to receive one-fourth of the increase in the herd. Caufield said later that "the land was too brushy and there were too many Indians." He slowly drifted the herd to the South Bosque River, about ten miles away, where he settled in a pecan grove on a slight rise above the river. The cattle grazed on several hundred thousand acres of Blackland Prairie bounded by the Leon, South Bosque, and Middle Bosque Rivers. Henry Caufield soon had a large herd containing both his and his cousin's cattle.[12]

Over the next several years, Henry grew his herds. Anglo settlements had forced the Indians west of Gatesville, and they occasionally depredated into McLennan County during the next decade. He was alone on what was the frontier at that time, with only a few neighbors who lived miles from his new base. But "batching it" did not seem to bother Henry. He explained in a letter to his brother that he felt "like a lord over all that I see. I am alone with my horses and dogs." Caufield built a small cabin with cedar logs

obtained at the Cavitt league on the Leon River. He set up house-
keeping and began to meet his neighbors. At that time only a few
families lived in the vicinity, among them the Neil McLennan
family and several families—including the Crains, Joneses, and
Sandefers—clustered at a crossing of the South Bosque River.
He soon had a band of young single male friends, including Neil
McLennan and Wylie Jones, who lived nearby. The trio rode
together across the Central Texas prairie gathering their cattle,
chasing wild horses, camping, and hunting, and became lifelong
friends. They served together in the Civil War. Henry married
Wylie Jones's sister, and Henry's oldest son, Watson, would marry
Neil McLennan's oldest daughter, Kathrine.[13]

On January 24, 1848, James W. Marshall discovered gold in Sutter's
millrace on the south fork of the American River. News of the
strike swept with an ever-increasing crescendo across the nation. In
California the word spread slowly at first, and as late as April 1 the
San Francisco *California Star* made light of the discovery. However,
by June 1848, the local residents began to swarm into the new goldfields, and by the end of summer the population of San Francisco
had decreased by half; ships lay in the harbor abandoned for lack
of sailors, and the city's land prices crashed. In August, the *New
York Herald* became the first Eastern newspaper to announce the
discovery of gold in California, and by September the New Orleans
Picayune echoed the news. On December 5, 1848, President James
Polk officially announced the discovery of gold in California. Gold
fever gripped the nation as men began to leave their homes to make
their fortunes in the foothills of the Sierra Nevada.

Only a few first-person accounts of the trip to California still
exist. Most are letters written to local newspapers or included as
part of travelers' guides. Many prospectors were illiterate; most

did not keep records; and some of those accounts were lost. The trip was long, hazardous, and inconvenient. Once in the goldfields, most miners encountered appalling conditions. Many died, others returned home, still others stayed in the new state, but almost everyone, after a few months or years, had little to show for their efforts. One account that survived is a series of letters written by the Caufield family in Alabama and Texas.[14]

In fall 1848, the Caufields in Boligee, Greene County, Alabama, read of the discovery through their subscription to the weekly *Boston Statesman* and caught the California gold fever. While the Caufield siblings were settling in Texas, the oldest brother, Watson, after a falling-out with his stepmother, decided to join the gold rush along with some of his friends. It took them several months to prepare for the trip, settle their debts, and say their goodbyes; thus, Caufield and his group did not leave Alabama until the middle of March.[15] His adventure would last six years.

A pioneer in 1849 could travel by three routes to the California goldfields, all of which were dangerous. The trip across the continental United States, although shorter in miles and cheaper, was more dangerous and took several weeks longer than the oceanic routes. One could walk all the way to California, and many did. Those using the overland route endured rain, snow, hostile Indians, deserts, poor food, and exorbitant prices. The cheapest and safest route was a six-month journey by sea down the east coast of south America, either around Cape Horn or through the Strait of Magellan, up the west coast of the continent, and on to San Francisco Bay. This circuit was subject to the uncertainties of wind and water. A quicker way was to go by sea to Panama, cross the isthmus, and resume sailing up the Pacific coast. Disease was the principal danger involved in the overland route across Panama. Whatever the means of passage, every trip to the goldfields took from three to six months. The Alabama group decided to travel over the Isthmus of Panama to California.[16]

The Forty-Niners commonly banded together into larger groups for protection, economy, and succor in case of illness. Although vowing everlasting friendship and pledging to work together in the goldfields, these new companies rarely survived arrival at San Francisco. Like others when they reached New Orleans by boat from Mobile, Watson Caufield and his companions from Alabama joined a group led by a Dr. Gaile. "There are eight of them," he wrote, "and they are a fine company." On April 14, seven days after their arrival, they sailed from New Orleans on the *General Stanton* for Chagres, Panama.[17]

Shortly leaving New Orleans, the Alabamans found that the cholera epidemic that was raging in the city had followed the party onto their boat. The run to Chagres, which the sixty-five passengers expected to take seven days, actually lasted seventeen days. Caufield wrote to his father, "About the ninth day we were out at sea, sickness commenced. I assure you it was a serious sight. About every two days a death. It was nothing else but cholera here and cholera there. There were seven deaths on board before we got to Chagres. Some of them died in four or five hours after being taken ill. It was awful to sit there and see a man in perfect health taken away so soon." Caufield and his group did not contract cholera and remained healthy.[18]

The trip across the Isthmus of Panama followed a route developed by the Spanish centuries before and began with the landing on the steamy, tropical Caribbean coast at the squalid port city of Chagres, continuing up the malaria-ridden Chagres River and over the mountains on narrow, wet trails before ending on the Pacific coast at shabby Panama City. This was not an easy journey, but the Spanish had made the route a well-known and frequently traveled trail. The first wave of Americans had staggered ashore in Panama in January 1849 to take a quick trans-isthmus route to the Pacific Ocean. By the end of May 1849, some fifty-nine vessels had discharged their passengers at Chagres. Thousands more were to follow along the old Spanish treasure trail.

Caufield and his party arrived on April 22, 1849. After waiting three days in Chagres, they traveled three days by canoe up the turbid Chagres River, each traveler paying native porters $6 and arriving at the small village of Gargona forty miles from the mouth of the river. By the end of 1849, this price had increased to $10 per person for canoes capable of carrying four or five passengers. Caufield noted that "the natives are hard working people and very kind. They have little. All the way up the river most of them have some liquors for sale and coffee and fruits plenty. We were advised not to eat any of their fruits as they were not healthy in this warm climate."[19]

While contracting for mules, the party waited two days at Gargona in vermin-infested native huts, crossing the mountains overland on a twisting jungle path barely three feet wide. Another traveler, John Letts, noted that "two miles out of Gargona you enter a mule path running through a dense forest. . . . You sometimes pass through gullies in the side of the mountain sufficiently wide at the bottom to admit the mule and its rider, and looking up you find yourself in a chasm with perpendicular sides into which the sun has never shone." Caufield wrote, "It rains here every day. There is nothing but a small trail from Gargona to Panama winding round the mountains. The distance is 24 miles. A right hard matter to walk it up and down the same day." The mules cost Caufield $9, and his share of provisions for the entire ten-day trip across the isthmus was $14. By the middle of the summer the cost of a pack mule had risen to $30 and the cost of the entire trip had risen to as much as $40.[20]

The weather and food were but two hazards of the trip. The isthmus was notoriously unhealthy. Malaria, cholera, yellow fever, and food-borne diarrhea were common maladies afflicting the travelers. Having avoided cholera in New Orleans and on their ship, the group remained in good health until they experienced an epidemic of dysentery while in the mountains. Caufield wrote his father, "I am sorry to inform you that we lost one of our men since we came here." He noted the death of one of his Alabama cousins: "John Mawhinny was unwell coming up the river and the first night we stopped he was taken with a cramp in his stomach and he liked to died but got over it. When we arrived at Gargona he was still unwell, so we hired a horse for him to ride over to Panama, which he went in care of Dr. Gaile. The second day after arrival he was taken with fits. He only lived through the day. We buried him at the American Burying Ground. There were fourteen graves there."[21]

After crossing the isthmus, Caufield and his party arrived rain-soaked, hollow-eyed, and hungry on the Pacific coast, where the crowded conditions and poor sanitation at Panama City shocked the travelers. They "stopped some miles out from Panama City on account of water and wood. We think it is healthier here than in town." Caufield noted that 3,500 Americans were awaiting the arrival of ships for San Francisco. "About half of them have stayed here until they get enough money to go to San Francisco. A great many of them are gambling and would kill for money."

The last leg of the trip to California was by ship up the Pacific coast to San Francisco. Because of a lack of passenger vessels on the Pacific side, a bottleneck had developed in Panama City that did not ease until the shipping companies established regular steamship service in 1851. John Letts and his friends resorted to renting a berth on a "fast sailing schooner" so crowded that the captain abandoned the ship when the passengers protested.[22]

Seven days after his arrival at Panama City, Caufield and his companions secured passage with 305 other travelers on the *Panama*, one of the first steamers to make the California–Panama run. When they left for San Francisco on May 18, they considered themselves fortunate, for "men have been here three months and are not off yet. There have been three vessels leave for San Francisco. No steamers have arrived yet." As he closed his letter home, Caufield voiced a common feeling among the Forty-Niners: "I am tired of this. I have got this far and am anxious to go on. My good friends do not fret yourselves about the gold mines for they are not the thing that they are cracked up to be."[23]

Caufield kept meticulous records of his travel expenses, thus offering an accounting of his journey. The trip from Boligee in Greene County, Alabama, overland and down the Tombigbee River to Mobile on the coast cost $3, and $2 for board; passage from Mobile to New Orleans by steamer cost $2 plus $6 for board; passage by sail from New Orleans to Chagres, Panama, cost $45; the ten-day trip across the isthmus cost $29; and the steamer from Panama City to San Francisco cost $165. The total expense for the three-month trip, then, was $252. The return passage five years later, using the trans-isthmus railroad, cost only $175 to New York and lasted about five weeks. The new railroad took just six hours and charged only $25—a vast improvement over the outward-bound journey.[24]

In California, the miners were far from their families and often lonesome. They desired to learn about friends and relatives back home and grumbled about their lot in California. Watson Caufield was no exception and complained constantly about the lack of letters from home.

By 1851, Caufield had abandoned mining and was running a sawmill "between the south and middle fork of the American River, twelve miles from Coloma and about two from Auburn on the opposite side of the river."[25]

As so often happened to companies formed for the gold rush, Watson's original group had scattered, and he knew the location of only one of his former comrades. "I rec'd a few lines from Frisbie. He is well and speaks of returning home this fall." In letters written from "Brooks and Cooks Sawmill" to his younger sister who had remained in Greene County, Alabama, with her father and stepmother, Caufield asked about mutual friends and for the latest gossip from home: "Sister, you have no idea how much I think about home and how I would like to be there to see you all. . . . Say to some of the family they might write to a person, as they have no idea how I would like to hear from them." In addition, Caufield included another common Forty-Niner lament in a letter to his folks back home. "I am really tired of hard work as I have done so much of it since California. . . . The health of this country is good, but mining is poor and times dull."[26]

In the goldfields, entertainment and medical care were expensive and difficult to obtain. On October 19, 1854, a ticket to a dance cost $10. Because "quite a number of ladies [were] present" with whom to dance, the proprietor sold seventy tickets. Evidently Caufield did not attend, remarking, "I think it would be rather expensive to attend such parties for amusement."[27]

Health was important to the miners, because illness meant either death or extraordinary expenses. Although suffering from colds and bruised ribs from an accident, Caufield remained fit. "Dear Sister, my health has not been good for some time on account of a very bad cold and also a fall that I got off a log which came very near breaking three or four ribs but I escaped pretty lucky," he wrote, adding that "above all things keep me from being sick in this Country as there are no accommodations here for the sick. A physician would not come to see one for less than 25–30 dollars which counts up in a few calls." Another miner related, "We found that sickness prevailed to an alarming extent, particularly land scurvy, owing to the constant use of salt and greasy provisions without vegetables. . . . There was also rheumatism simple and acute, sciatica, fever, and ague."[28]

The distance apart for the members of a close family was often trying, especially when disaster occurred. Fifteen-year-old Elizabeth, or "Lizzie," the youngest of the Caufield children—she was thirteen when her siblings left Alabama—had kept a constant correspondence with her older siblings. She corresponded with her older sister Mary Jane most frequently; they wrote about every three months. The letters took one to two months to reach the recipient. In 1850, shortly after her brother and sister left Alabama, she wrote Mary Jane that "I have just got four [letters] from you and two from brother. Tell him he is too stingy to pay the postage." She then goes into a long description of what everyone they knew had been doing. In a later letter she described her boarding school in Eutaw: "I never had time to write, I had to work on Saturdays and go to church on Sundays. I don't expect I will go up this session. . . . I was learning very fast at school. I was studying grammar, history, geography, arithmetic and writing." Three years later she wrote, "I am still going to school and getting along with my studies very well." She then covered all the local news as usual.[29]

The trip home was as hazardous as the outward-bound journey. Caufield noted that "quite a number of steam vessels have been lost on the Pacific side. The *Yankee Blade* is lost and a large number of passengers bound homewards on the 2nd of this month and half a million in money. It is rather risky to travel on them." The passengers on this vessel, happy about leaving California, had engaged in a drunken riot that contributed to, if not actually caused, the losses aboard the ship.[30]

Watson Caufield left California to return to Alabama on April 16, 1855, with $1,500, his profits for five years of hard labor. Upon securing his passage home via the Panama railroad and the steamer *Atlantic* to New York, Caufield sent his father a note containing his plans as well as copies of his itinerary: "Father, I write to inform you that I leave tomorrow for New York. Fare is $175 dollars [*sic*] including the railroad on the isthmus. I write this in order if I should get lost or shipwreck at sea you may know that I have left Cal." In addition, rather than carry cash on the trip, he took the precaution of sending to Alabama a copy of an exchange draft for $500 drawn on the Wells Fargo office in Coloma, California.

In New York, Caufield had visited a friend and owner of the sawmill where he had worked in California and who had left a year earlier, leaving Caufield to sell the business. After visiting New York, Caufield traveled to Boston, where he visited friends, including the former sawmill owner. He then traveled down the Ohio and Mississippi Rivers to his home in Alabama.[31]

By June 1855, Watson Caufield had reached his home in Alabama, and his brother Henry and sister Mary Jane in Texas invited him to join them in a new adventure. "We will look for you out in the fall. I hope you intend to remain here when you come. I would be glad you would live with Henry," Mary Jane wrote in an 1855 letter, while Henry wrote five days later, "Wat, we are doing well. The land is rich, and cattle grow with a minimum of care. I hope you will join us here soon."[32]

When Henry and Mary Jane Caufield departed Alabama for Texas, they left two younger siblings, Elizabeth ("Lizzie") and David, at home. Watson, their other brother, had left for California the year before. Although far apart, the family stayed in close contact through their letters. Mary Jane and Lizzie seemed to have been particularly close. They exchanged a series of letters over the years that show a young girl growing into womanhood. "I heard from you all and want to go to Texas very bad." Lizzie attended a local finishing school and wrote an excellent letter with perfect penmanship, spelling, and grammar. She wrote, "Mrs. Lawrence from Tuscaloosa is boarding here. She is teaching school but has not been teaching for three weeks. She . . . sprained her ankle. Today is the first time she has been downstairs. She has got about twenty scholars." The next year she wrote, "I don't think Miss Gresswoler will stay any longer. She has about twenty-five scholars this cession [*sic*]." She began to sign her letters "E. Caufield." David was a poor writer. Watson, Henry, and especially Mary Jane wrote their sister frequently. In the fall of 1854, just as she completed her education and began to entertain suitors for marriage, Elizabeth Caufield died of quinsy, a complication of acute tonsillitis.[33]

Streptococcal infections had become serious during this period prior to antibiotics, particularly in young adults. The infection manifested itself in several ways. Erysipelas, a skin infection that spread rapidly as a red rash, could result from lesions as simple as a mosquito bite. Once it spread, erysipelas could evolve into sepsis, with systemic symptoms such as fever, and might be fatal. Another common complaint, strep throat, could spread into the tissues in the back of the throat, causing a peritonsillar abscess; the swelling closed the airway. This condition was called quinsy and could result in death. The patient often suffered a sore throat, seemed to recover, then became acutely ill and died. Lizzie Caufield appears to have died of strep throat and quinsy. The family, particularly Mary Jane, was devastated.[34]

A series of letters crossed in the mail, including ones from Mary Jane's brothers in Texas and California. Shortly afterward, she received a letter from her aunt Isabell notifying her of sister Lizzie's death and begging her to come home. Their father, Thomas Caufield, wrote to his sons about the tragic news in December 1854. "I expect before you receive this you have received information of your sister Lizey [sic]. She died 25 of October three days after you wrote her. She was confined to her bed for eleven days. Jack Johnston attended to her." (Johnston was a cousin whose medical education at Princeton and Philadelphia Thomas Caufield had helped subsidize.) "He came every day for nine days. The morning before she died, we all thought she was better. Jack stayed all night then left. I came home about fifteen minutes before she died." This letter seems to have been the impetus that started Watson on his way home to his family in Alabama.[35]

The family was to experience one more tragedy. The youngest brother, George David, had stayed at home when his older siblings left. While in his freshman year at Transylvania University in Kentucky, George contracted tuberculosis. Many young men contracted tuberculosis while living in the close quarters of college rooming houses or, more likely in this case, from milk from tubercular cows.

No cure existed, but the treatment of the time was to send the afflicted to a new climate. George was sent to Texas to stay with his brother and sister. Watson brought his brother to visit his aunt Isabell at Centerville, a resort community known for hot springs, and stayed to care for him.

George was much sicker than the family had thought. He had contracted scrofula, a tubercular infection of the cervical lymph glands. Scrofula was usually contracted from ingesting the milk from a cow infected with tuberculosis. It did not usually involve the lungs. The pulmonary type of tubercular infection was contracted from close contact with other humans and oral secretions. In the course of scrofula, the glands in the neck became swollen and, quite often, soft from necrosis or liquefaction of the gland tissue. One treatment was to drain the glands by opening the overlying skin. This was not the best method and usually led to chronic drainage of yellow, cheese-like secretions. These secretions were usually very infectious to others.

The costs of George's treatment were carefully recorded by Watson. George had his gland drained by a local Texas physician for $25. The cost of board for George and his horse by the doctor was an additional $26. Watson did not approve and took him to another physician, a Dr. W. Brooks, who stated the glands should never have been drained. But the damage had already been done. George's health slowly degenerated until he was bedridden. He was treated with weekly bleeding and calomel enemas twice weekly. After a five-month confinement in Centerville, he improved somewhat and moved to Wheelock. His care in Wheelock cost $3.50 for doctor's visits twice weekly. Medications, including expectorants, quinine, and brandy, cost $49.50. Bleeding was $1 and enemas were $1.50.

George's disease resumed its downward course and the tuber-culosis spread to his lungs. Alerted to his brother's rapid decline, Henry and his wife visited George in Wheelock. George David Caufield died in 1857 from miliary tuberculosis or the "galloping consumption." Josephus Cavitt paid $34 for his coffin and buried him in the Cavitt cemetery.[36]

Over the years, while his brother Watson was in California, Henry Caufield had begun to build his ranch, buying land and increasing his cattle and horse herds. By 1855, he began hauling lumber by oxcart from Houston. He had had no income for the last two years and needed cash to get married.

Ranchers used brands to mark their livestock, and Henry Caufield began to mark his cattle with his own brand, HC, and the Cavitts' cattle with JC or VC. Earmarks delineated the prog-eny of the cow and the inheritance of the owner's children. In 1863, he purchased the IXL brand for his horses and mules. For fifty years Caufield continued to use the same brands, paying Josephus Cavitt, his brother Volney Cavitt, or their children a pro-rated share of any sales.[37]

Once settled into the area along the South Bosque, Henry Caufield began to establish a ranch of his own. He initially con-centrated on raising cattle and horses, grazing them across the unfenced open prairie around his homestead. In 1853, the gentle-man who owned the land on which Caufield was squatting drove up to the cabin. He offered to sell the land. Henry quickly took him up on the proposal and gave him a deposit. Later, Henry fretted that the man might not have been the actual owner. But, after several months, the gentleman returned, and they negotiated a price of $2 an acre for 320 acres. The note carried an interest rate of 10 percent a month. Henry hurried to his aunts in Centerville and Wheelock, refinanced the note for 5 percent annually, and paid off the original owner. He continued to increase his land. In 1886, H. J. Caufield purchased 240 acres for $2,340, or $19.75 an acre, from John Darragh, assignee for David Leneham's Bounty Warrant #694, patent #875, from the State of Texas, dated 1850.

Henry began to consider marriage. While riding about one day, Wylie Jones's younger sister, Martha, and her friends dropped by to meet their new neighbor. Caufield was not at his cabin, but the girls went in and noted that it was quite a mess. Martha cleaned the cabin and they rode on. Several days later, Henry went by the Jones's house to thank the ladies for the cleaning job, met Martha, and fell in love.[38]

On July 20, 1856, Henry Caufield married Martha Jones, the seventeen-year-old daughter of his nearest neighbor, Aquilla Jones, at her parents' home at South Bosque. Mary Jane Caufield Young and Watson Caufield were present for the wedding.

Family tradition says that Wiley Jones and Neil McLennan prepared a barbecue to celebrate the wedding. All the neighbors—the Crains, the Joneses, and the Cavitts—in addition to Watson and Mary Jane, were invited. As the meat simmered over the open pit, a group of Waco Indians, a rather motley tribe, camping on Caufield Creek about half a mile away, smelled the roasting meat and walked over. Frightened by the Indians and revolted by their smell and dirtiness, the crowd allowed them to eat as much as they wished, which was quite a lot. Full, greasy, and flatulent, the chief belched and blessed the marriage, then wandered back to their camp. This has led to a family tradition of giving a ranch barbecue when a family member marries and having a ceremonial Indian wedding.[39]

The couple immediately began to raise a family on their new ranch. Their children included Elizabeth (Lizzie), born 1857; Wiley Watson (Wat), born 1860; Thomas Aquilla, born 1863; Martin Cavitt (Mart), born 1865; Mary (Molly), born 1869; George Henry, born 1875; and Minnie Dee (Deedie), born 1877.

Over the years, Henry built a wooden house, slowly adding rooms. Sending oxcarts to Houston to get milled lumber, Caufield added a room to the original structure each time they had a child. The house became a long L-shaped structure of nineteen rooms with outside hallways and porches connecting the rooms.

The early settlers thought that the Blackland Prairies were suited only for livestock, due to the lack of water and the dense black clay soil that was difficult for plows to penetrate. They believed that soil that would not grow trees would not support crops, either. But subsistence farming to provide for the needs of family and stock became a necessity among Central Texas ranchers because of their isolation, the absence of roads, and the long distances to mercantile establishments. Waco, fifteen miles away, was the primary source of supplies. Later a store in South Bosque offered food and finished goods.

Initially, Caufield "raised no crops. I am altogether on the range." About 1856, after starting a family, he changed his thinking. He plowed his first fields to produce a garden and grain to feed his growing family and livestock. He protected his crops with plank fencing and bois d'arc hedges. To his brother Watson he announced, "I intend sowing about four acres of wheat, planting six acres in corn, [and] sowing my little truck patch in oats. I aim to make enough bread and horse feed to do me this season." Each year Henry increased his cropland, concentrating on corn, wheat, and oats. At first his plowed fields lay on flat river bottom land near his house. The oat patch and the garden were close to the creek, and he cut a small irrigation ditch to provide a dependable water supply. Neil McLennan, watching his good friend and neighbor plowing the virgin land, remarked that "no good can come of this."[40]

In 1857, Henry branded 480 calves, with about 50 more to bring in. He had a herd of 1,500 head and 50 horses "running at large on the prairie." That year he sold 50 steers for $16 each; ten of the steers were his. By the end of the year, he had branded 700 calves and sold another 100 head for $12 each. In 1858, Caufield stopped branding in early July because the screwworms were so bad. By then he had branded 525 calves and still had 40 to 60 head in the brush. His 25 mares had 15 colts, a poor return. In 1859, he branded 400 head on Deer Creek and 300 on Elm Creek. Joe Cavitt added 20 horses to the herds.[41]

As Central Texas moved from unsettled frontier to becoming more populated, grazing cattle became the main business of the Caufield Ranch, and they sought ways to market their livestock. In 1855, Shapley Ross led a cattle drive to Independence, Missouri, on the Shawnee Trail. The Shawnee Trail ran from Central Texas, through Dallas along the Preston Highway, through Oklahoma, to Missouri, where it met the railheads at Shawnee, Missouri.

Following this lead, Henry organized several cattle drives over the Shawnee Trail to Chicago. He began to trail his cattle to this new market as early as 1858 when Henry's brother-in-law Wiley Jones and James Black, one of the Caufield Ranch hands, drove a herd to Missouri.

Finding too many cattle—more than 45,000 head—for sale in Missouri and the price too low, they moved on to Illinois, wintering south of Chicago. In May, Henry noted that "Jim Black is not back yet." By June, word came that they were returning and had reached the Mississippi. Jones and Black returned a month later. Henry noted in July that "Wylie has returned from the north and Jim is hunting deer." They kept a daybook of the drive, recording the daily mileage the herd covered, the expenses, and events each day. The trip had taken more than eight months—they left in October and returned in July—with little return for the length of the drive. The records fail to show if the ranch made a profit on this venture.[42]

After a few years, the Missouri farmers noticed that their cattle began to die after the Texas herds passed and began to bar cattle from crossing their farms. This was due to the ticks that fell from the longhorns and attached themselves to the local cows. The livestock caught a viral disease now called "Texas fever." Longhorn cattle were immune to the disease. Texas fever would plague the Texas cattle for the next several decades. As a result, the local Missouri farmers began to oppose the cattle drives and forced the herds back to Texas. The Caufield drive seemed to have sidestepped the problem.

After the Civil War, the cattle drive to Abilene on the new Chisholm Trail, which did not pass near farms, offered an alternate and safer route to the railroads. Unfortunately, the Kansas settlers began to move westward and to farm near the cattle drives. They forced the cattle drives farther west, toward Dodge City. In the 1890s, when cattlemen discovered Texas fever was caused by ticks, they began an intensive dipping program that eliminated the ticks and made Texas longhorns safe to be around other cows.[43]

Henry's brother Watson frequently visited the Texas ranch, and they were in constant contact by letter over the next several decades. Watson had periodically sent his brother money from his California business to invest in cattle and land. Henry had invested the money wisely, and Watson eventually moved to live with his brother.

Every Texan is familiar with the three icons of the Texas economy: oil, cotton, and cattle. However, Texas has a fourth major agriculture product that is often overlooked: the sheep industry. Sheep and wool were a major factor in the Texas economy before oil or cotton became important. The Spanish missions along the San Antonio River listed thousands of sheep in their inventories during the seventeenth century. During the eighteenth century, sheep and wool were a main pillar of the Mexican economy. Today, wool and mutton continue to be important agricultural products in Texas and throughout the Southwest.

Although the mission herds had been gone for a century, shortly after Texas Independence, several Anglo families began to experiment with sheep in East Texas. Among these families were the Cavitts and Youngs. Other groups had noted that large areas in Texas, especially the Hill Country, were ideally suited for sheep, and by 1860 several million sheep roamed the Texas grasslands.

When Caufields and Cavitts moved to Central Texas in the 1840s and began to raise cattle and cotton, the Young and Foote families followed a different path, moving to Coryell County and beginning to raise sheep. They realized that the best products for their land were sheep and wool. Wool was fetching high prices on the local and international markets.

While Henry Caufield was building a ranch in McLennan County, in 1856, Henry's sister, Mary Jane, married their childhood friend William Young. They began their married lives with relatives in East Texas raising sheep. Initially the couple lived in Young's mother's house near Franklin while William and his brother George farmed and ranched in partnership. Later they settled in the Wheelock area on Young family land, where their first two children were born. There they continued to farm and raise livestock. In 1858 they purchased their first land. Young reported that "I have bought a piece of land from Cousin Josephus Cavitt. I got the piece of prairie in front of Mother's tract from here to the San Antonio road containing two hundred acres and then I got a piece above Mother's field for a building place, including the Black Jack Grove at the side of the field. It contains about eighteen acres and then I got fifty from Mother and forty-three acres from George Dunn." The land cost $600.[44]

The couple kept careful records of their income, expenses, and sheep in a series of ledgers and noted important events in letters to their relatives. William and Mary Jane made money in whatever way they could. Mary Jane wrote her brother: "I have some two hundred fifty or three hundred pounds of butter put up to sell when the weather gets cool so I can send it to market. . . . We have had as many as a hundred [of our milk cows] up. We did not milk more than thirty of them."

Accounts for their 1859–1860 flock of sheep showed costs of $4.70 a head, with a total investment of $1,939. In 1859–1860, Young "sold his wool in Houston for $749." This amount compared favorably with the income of $881 that William's father-in-law Thomas Caufield in Alabama derived from cotton and the $800 that brother-in-law Henry Caufield earned on his cattle ranch in McLennan County. (A summary of their sheep business is provided in tabular form in appendix A.)[45]

Looking for opportunity, Young expanded his livestock herds and ventured into raising sheep and wool with his brother George and cousin, Josephus Cavitt. In 1850, he cautiously purchased a small number of animals. By 1858, Young wrote: "Brother George and I are farming and sheep herding in partnership. . . . We have about two hundred and sixty of an increase." They initially purchased the locally available Spanish Churro breed favored by the Mexicans. They soon realized that the greatest income could be derived from wool. Although known for their hardiness and good-flavored meat, this strain produced wool fleeces weighing an average of only five pounds. Mary Jane wrote her brother that "William has commenced shearing. . . . He weighs the fleeces as he shears them. The lightest was one pound and three quarters and the heaviest was nine and three quarters. They generally weigh from three to eight pounds. Some of them are very fine wool."

In order to increase their wool production, the brothers decided to crossbreed their sheep with the Merino variety, known to produce fleeces of twenty pounds or more. Merino sheep also had a strong herding instinct, which prevented scattering of the flocks, and to tolerate drought and scanty forage.[46]

However, Merino stock was hard to come by. The Merino, a breed developed and prized by the Spanish, produced extremely fine wool. To protect their monopoly on this product, the Spanish monarchy had forbidden the export of any Merino, even to their American colonies. Fortunately, on the ascension of a Bourbon to the Spanish throne in the mid-eighteenth century, the new monarch gave his cousin, the French king, a herd of Spanish Merino, which the French raised on the royal farms at Rambouillet. The French had no qualms about exporting their new acquisitions.

About 1840, Americans, eager to obtain breeding stock, began to import the French Merino—the Rambouillet strain. The Americans paid large premiums for full-blooded stock, which they prized for their fine fleeces, suitable for making dress goods that demanded high prices in the marketplace. These French Merinos were available to the Texas sheepmen, but they were expensive. The Youngs sought to purchase crossbreeds that were more available and less expensive.[47]

Young, his brother, and Joe Cavitt combined their efforts to obtain Merino breeding stock to upgrade their flocks. The weather thwarted their initial attempt to obtain Merino crossbreeds. In 1858, Young wrote that "Cousin Josephus went out to Arkansas this spring to purchase a lot of sheep, but the water courses were so high he did not buy at $1.50 for grown sheep and 75 cents for lambs," because he could not get the animals across the rivers. Finally, in late 1858, Cavitt and Young succeeded in purchasing purebred Merino rams in Arkansas for $200 each and began to interbreed the animals with their existing stock, significantly increasing the wool yield from their flocks. Young noted that the animals yielded fleeces of twenty and twenty-two pounds.[48]

Their joint venture was quite successful, and by 1859 Cavitt had 1,100 crossbred sheep, and Young and his brother had about the same number. Young recounted his business to Watson Caufield: "You wanted to know how our sheep were doing. We bought at first 470 head—$1.70/head first cost and all expenses up till January 1, 1859 was $1,939.12. Credit on sheep till January 1, 1859, was $598.76. We had on first of January 740 head. A net increase of 270 head. Our keep costs about 3 [and] one fourth dollars per head. . . . We have this spring already 317 lambs. Now about 1057 head. Our wool netted 23 one/third cents a pound. I have engaged it this year at 25 cents/pound, to be delivered in Houston. Last year they averaged 5 lbs/head." They transported the wool on oxcarts to Houston for the Boston market, as did most Texas sheepmen of the day. They had no net income for 1857, using the wool money to build sheds and fences. In 1859, Young purchased an additional 240 head for $1,000.[49]

To upgrade their flocks further, in 1860, Young traveled to Pennsylvania, Virginia, and Arkansas, purchasing and driving a herd of crossbred Merino back to Texas. He wrote: "We had a very rough trip from Virginia with our sheep. I started with 250 head and I have 240 head here—ten were sold. We have been eight weeks on the road." Later he wrote, "We have a rather short crop from our stock this year. We have about 310 lambs from our home stock. We now have about 100 lambs from [the new sheep]." Young purchased the 250 mixed-breed sheep for a total of $1,045.30. Additional expenses included the cost of transport on the railroad to Mississippi ($1.59 a head, or $394 total), a horse to herd the animals for $30, and feed for $52. For about $6 a head, the partners had successfully increased their herd size, obtained strains that produced more wool, and crossbred the new animals with their existing animals.[50]

Unfortunately, the new sheep did not continue to thrive in East Texas, resulting in a move by Young to his family league in Coryell County. In 1858, Mary Jane wrote: "Our sheep are doing very well. We have had about two hundred and sixty of an increase." But by the next year, during a severe drought, she wrote, "Our sheep have not done well this summer. They suffer for both grass and water. . . . The black tongue [bluetongue, a virus found chiefly in sheep] has been among the stock. The range was too small for the number that was on it and William has started to move his sheep upon the Middle Bosque."

The immediate cause of Young's move to the family league in Coryell County was a prolonged drought in East Texas and the resultant overgrazing of his land. But experience had also taught that the East Texas sheepman must get away from the humid coast. In the hot and humid climate of East Texas, the Merino suffered from insect infestations and infections in the redundant skin and wool around their necks.

About 1854, Young and his new family moved to the Young family league in Coryell County. Henry Caufield noted, "W. E. Young and family have moved up to the country about 25 miles above me." There he built his family a fortified wooden house able to withstand Indian attacks on a knoll beside the Middle Bosque River. The two-room log cabin with dirt floors served until 1870 when he built a much larger home. Mary Jane Caufield Young transferred her two infant children to her new residence in the summer of 1860 with a note to her brother Henry: "William has started to move his sheep up upon Middle Bosque. He has been up to look at the country and likes it so well that he intends to pack up all his moveable goods and chattels and leave this area as soon as he conveniently can." That year they purchased the initial 393 acres and began a partnership in sheep and land acquisition.[51]

In 1853, the Texas legislature sectioned Coryell County out of Bell County. Although Fort Gates had been closed and the fort moved farther west in 1852, the area, particularly around Gatesville, had attracted enough population to become reasonably safe from Indian attacks. In 1854, the 300 residents organized a county government; however, the area remained scantily populated, with Gatesville having a population of only 434 people in 1880. Turnersville, originally known as Buchanan Springs, was not organized as a township until after the Civil War, but by 1880 it had a population of more than 200 souls. Young and his family moved to the northwestern corner of the county near Turnersville. William built his new home on a hill beside a spring next to the Middle Bosque River.[52]

In the more arid acreage in the Cross Timbers region of Coryell County, twenty miles northwest of Gatesville, the sheep herds thrived. From the initial 393 acres he now owned, Young ranged his sheep over the unfenced adjacent grazing land, building his herds to more than 3,000 sheep by 1888. He eventually owned more than 4,000 acres and was the largest taxpayer (after Mr. Pancake) in Coryell County.[53]

The Civil War, the collapse of the frontier defenses, and pressure from the Comanche Indians forced the Youngs back to East Texas for the duration of the war. When the war ended, they returned to their homestead and restarted their sheep-raising program.

The Civil War, 1860–1865

IN THE MONTHS PRIOR TO THE START OF THE CIVIL War, the brothers did not seem to approve of slavery nor of secession, although they were guarded in expressing such views in their letters. They did comment on politics, Sam Houston, and the Know Nothing Party. Henry wrote, "Texas is going to secede if they do not get some Constitutional Guaranty from the administration. You can see the Lone Star up in every town and every business House."[1]

As Texas moved toward secession, Henry and his sister urged Watson to join them in Texas. Money was in short supply, and Henry wrote, "I would like to have about 200 of your loose change if I knew I would ever replace it. I don't think that there is 200 in circulation in this county at this time. Bring it with you." Watson came shortly afterward.[2]

Slavery was a difficult issue for the Caufields. They expressed no abhorrence of the practice, but they owned no slaves until their father's death. Thomas Caufield, the siblings' father, died in Alabama in 1858. Watson, who was living at Boligee at the time, nursed his father during his final illness and settled his estate. Dividing the estate took over a year, as Watson had to reach an agreement with their widowed stepmother.

Thomas Caufield had purchased about one hundred acres for each of his children. When they failed to return home, he purchased a married pair of slaves to live on and farm each plot. This made him a wealthy man with four hundred acres and six slaves. He produced a bale of cotton on every six acres, or about sixty bales a year, selling at $0.20 a pound—an income of about $6,000 a year, or about $600,000 in today's dollars. On his death, each of the three remaining children inherited not only their acreage but also the slaves who farmed the land.

Disposing of the land was relatively simple. Watson sold their father's land and house and kept meticulous notes as he settled outstanding debts and sold household items. He eventually divided the estate, giving the cash from the sale of his father's farm to his stepmother. Mary Jane and Henry and Martha traveled to Alabama in January of 1859 for the final settlement of Thomas Caufield's estate.

Watson Caufield and two helpers had farmed his share of the land for the two years preceding his father's death. With the old man's death and the selling of the land, there was no place for the slaves. The family felt responsible for the couples and asked them if they wished to continue to live in Alabama and be sold to other owners or if they preferred to move to Texas. They chose to move to Texas.

Henry and Mary Jane brought the three couples to Texas when they returned from Boligee after the settlement of the estate. While Watson's brother and sister returned to Texas, Watson stayed behind in Alabama to sell his farm. He eventually went to Texas in 1860 with the farm still unsold. Dr. Mayes, a cousin, managed to rent the land and later sell it to a Mr. Timmons. This sale was to torment Watson Caufield for a decade, as Mr. Timmons protested every change to better the terms of the sale to his advantage.

On the return trip, Henry, his wife, and his sister stopped in Mobile, went by ship to New Orleans, then went to Houston, traveling overland in a buggy to Hempstead, by stage to Wheelock, and by wagon to South Bosque. Henry followed overland from Hempstead on foot with the slaves and wagons. By March 5 they were back in Texas. The biggest loss on the trip for Henry was the death of his favorite dog. He asked his brother to send him a replacement.[3]

Unfortunately, the Black couples did not like Texas. The slaves missed the familiarity of Alabama and its people. On the frontier they were isolated and exposed to a new, lonely, and frightening environment. In western McLennan County, the nearest Black people were five to ten miles away. Men were expected to join in the ranching culture, riding roundup, branding cattle, and fixing fences. There was no cotton to care for.

The siblings' letters were full of the complaints and illnesses of the new slaves. As Henry wrote his brother, "Lige is the most trifling fellow I have ever seen. He is of no use on the ranch. He is afraid of horses and cannot or will not ride. He cannot work cattle and is too afraid of Indians to do us a favor and run off. . . . I have assigned him to plant an oat patch, mind the garden, and help around the house."

Lige's wife was also unhappy and afraid of Indians. She complained of a variety of illnesses and did little work. She became the cook and housekeeper, caring for the small children. Watson and his sister began to rent their slaves to relatives in East Texas, where they lived in more familiar surroundings. Henry wrote Watson that "Tom Caufield was here . . . and got Steve about the first of the month." Watson traveled frequently to check on the slaves' well-being and on one occasion brought them home rather than have them continue to work under an abusive overseer. This solution worked for the next decade until the end of the war.[4]

When slavery was abolished, the family freed their slaves with a great deal of relief. At the end of the Civil War, Henry wrote his brother Watson that "I heard that Garrison [sic] had freed the Negros at Galveston. As soon as I got the word, I had Lige and Hester up to the house, told them they were free." They gave them some acreage and a couple of mules for their own and sent them on their way.[5]

With the war upon them, Henry Caufield, young enough for the draft at thirty-seven years of age, volunteered for Cook's Battalion in the Texas State Militia, serving for two years protecting Galveston. During his service, Henry and his battalion was sent on guard duty with "150 Yankee officers captured at Galveston" to Camp Ford near Tyler and on to Shreveport. Watson, although too old for the draft at fifty-two years of age, faced local peer pressure to join the Confederate forces. Patience Crain Black wrote her husband, Caufield Ranch hand Jim Black, a volunteer in Henry Caufield's battalion, "People are talking that Watson Caufield still has not joined the army." Watson eventually joined the Subsistence Bureau, scouting for cattle. He later avoided active duty because of a fistula-in-ano (anal abscess), which kept him from riding horses. But by 1863, when the Confederacy was desperate for more men for their armies and the age for the draft was extended to fifty years of age, Watson was called back for another physical, was found fit for service, and finished the war in the Subsistence Bureau. When Henry's two-year enlistment was up, he returned to McLennan County, joined his brother, and reenlisted, this time in the Subsistence Bureau.[6]

On October 11, 1862, recognizing the increasing importance of obtaining food for their armies, the Confederate Congress had passed a statute exempting from the draft individuals engaged in raising stock—one male for every five hundred head of cattle. Both

Henry and Watson Caufield met those criteria. They received certificates from General Edmund Kirby Smith certifying them as
herdsmen.[7]

Watson became an active letter writer to his friends in the Army
and took care of their affairs along the South Bosque. James Duke
from South Bosque, married to one of the Jones girls, Martha Jones
Caufield's first cousin, wrote several times from Louisiana, where he
fought with Colonel J. W. Speight's Brigade under General Richard
Taylor. Duke owed a J. Haley $40 to pay for "new axles on his
wagon." Duke thanked Caufield for paying the debt and told him
to collect a yoke of oxen from Dr. Drury to pull the wagon. Duke
gave his approval for the wagon to go to Mexico for trading goods.[8]

South and West Texas experienced a severe drought, especially during the latter years of the Civil War, making trailing to
Mexican markets difficult. Nevertheless, some ranchers attempted
to drive small herds of cattle south to sell in Mexico through
Matamoros, without much success. Generally, the Mexican market was unprofitable to Central Texas ranchers due to arid conditions along the trail, the ready availability of native Mexican cattle,
and the low prices paid for beef in Mexico.[9]

Watson Caufield engaged a local man too old for the draft to
take the wagon full of cotton with a small herd of cattle to Mexico.
The wagon joined a train of wagons traveling to Laredo, where
they sold the cotton but had trouble selling the cattle because of
the drought and low prices in the area. The gentleman returned via
the King Ranch, bringing coffee, needles, and other much-needed
supplies to the South Bosque area. Duke was later killed at the
battle of Mansfield, Louisiana.[10]

Watson frequently wrote his two first cousins, William and
Henry Caufield, who were in the Confederate Army. William
joined the Greene County Greys, Colonel Nicholas C. Gould's
Twenty-third Texas Cavalry. He and his brother died in the siege
of Richmond near the end of the war.[11]

During the war, virtually all the external markets for Texas cattle were closed, and local ranchers were unable to sell their herds. Prior to the Civil War, Texans had driven small numbers of cattle overland to New Orleans or to Kansas and Missouri over the Shawnee Trail. At the outbreak of the war, Lincoln had not only ordered a blockade of the Confederate coast but also outlawed overland trade with the South, thus cutting off the Midwestern markets for Texas cattle. Other antebellum Texas herds had trailed through Alexandria, Louisiana, to New Orleans. The Federal occupation of New Orleans cut that market. By the end of 1862, Union forces had occupied or successfully blockaded Galveston, Indianola, and most other Texas ports. The export of hides, tallow, and beef, essential to the economies of the ranches of the Coastal Plains and South Texas, also ceased.[12]

As the war progressed, Texas and Florida, relatively untouched by the conflict, became important suppliers of livestock to the Southern armies, and the Subsistence Bureau began to collect and drive thousands of head of cattle through East Texas to the army depots. Although the activity of Federal gunboats made the river crossing dangerous, the Confederates still attempted to swim small numbers of cattle across the Mississippi River to feed General Joseph E. Johnston's army in Mississippi and Alabama. Eventually the fall of Vicksburg interrupted the supply of Texas livestock to the eastern Confederate armies.

In Texas, cattle glutted the market, and the Trans-Mississippi armies became the primary market for the herds. Both the Confederate Army and the state militias authorized competing units to buy livestock. Before the war, Texas cattle sold for $15 to $17 a head. By late 1864, William White, the Confederate government commissary and subsistence agent in Texas, was offering stockmen only $25 in Confederate currency (about $6 in US currency) for cattle "four years old and upward" and only if the animals were rounded up and delivered to local depots. He offered

$22 (about $5 in US currency) per head for cattle "collected at the expense of the Government."[13]

The Confederate Subsistence Bureau remained responsible for obtaining beef for the Southern troops, while the state of Texas was responsible for obtaining supplies for the state militia. The Confederacy also gave the Subsistence Bureau the responsibility for collecting "payment in kind," a 10 percent tax to the Confederate government.

The McLennan County Subsistence squad was typical of a Confederate Army Subsistence Bureau beef procurement unit. The officers consisted of Major R. A. Howard, commanding; Major Wiley Jones; and Captain F. M. Harris, the local collection agent in Waco. Herders held rank in the Confederate Army and included Neil McLennan, H. J. Caufield, and Watson Caufield. These men were more than forty years of age (some were in their fifties) and all were local ranchers, landowners, neighbors, and relatives from the same settlement on the South Bosque River. As in most procurement units, these men initially had served in other military units before being detached to serve as herders. Some men received certificates of exemption from conscription and others received special orders with written authorization to travel to buy livestock. Special Order #78, written from the headquarters of the Trans-Mississippi Department, detailed Watson Caufield and Neil McLennan as herders to report to Captain Harris as agent for the Subsistence Department under Major Howard in Waco.[14]

From these units a procedure was established for gathering Texas beef to feed the Confederate armies. The men were organized into companies, consisting of an active-duty army major who coordinated with the regular command structure; a local agent or captain stationed in urban areas and responsible for purchasing, financing, branding, storing, and transshipping the animals; and procurement agents who went into the countryside to purchase, gather, and drive cattle to the pens. At the pens, the local agents

branded the livestock with a Confederate Army trail brand, and
when enough cattle had been gathered, a different set of herders
drove the cattle from the urban depots to army headquarters.[15]

Agents gathered cattle into herds, which they consigned to
groups of five to eight men who drove 1,000 to 2,000 head of cattle to market, traveling about fifteen to twenty miles a day. Rain,
flood, stampedes, and illness were the most common problems
they encountered.

This pattern of extended kinship groups commanded by older
and more prosperous ranchers entering the subsistence corps was
common throughout the South during the Civil War. These older
men not only had the funds to buy livestock but also could afford
to await reimbursement by the Confederacy. They had the stature
to buy or requisition cattle without offending the local population, the knowledge to recognize good cattle, and the skills to
drive them to central holding pens. The work was hard and stren-
uous for the older men, requiring long days in the saddle, but their
numbers were augmented by energetic teenagers too young for the
draft and by temporarily wounded or disabled soldiers. In the recollections collected by the Texas Trail Drivers Association, many
of the cowboys, by then quite elderly, mentioned obtaining their
first cattle-trailing experience during the Civil War driving cattle
with their older relatives.[16]

With the onset of the Civil War and the withdrawal of Federal
troops from the Texas frontier forts, Indian depredations began
to increase, and the boundary of safety receded to a line just west
of Gatesville. Because of the increased threat from Indian raids,
William Ewing Young moved his family and flocks back to East
Texas for the duration of the war. However, he remained in Coryell
County, close to his remaining livestock, and served in the local
militia, the Frontier Battalion, scouting the frontier areas around
Gatesville. Young kept a diary of his daily activities, the weather,
and his daily work from 1860 to 1868.[17]

During the war, the state legislature of Texas divided the frontier into three districts, placing a field officer of the state militia in charge of each. George Erath received command of the Central District headquartered in Gatesville. Erath was a family friend of the Caufields' and lived down the South Bosque from Henry Caufield. Erath recalled that "the frontier was also unprotected, and the legislature passed a law calling out the militia in the frontier counties. They were to act on the minute plan, that is some few to be always scouting, the rest to be in readiness at any time called. They were to furnish themselves everything, except, perhaps, ammunition." William Young was part of this militia.

The Frontier Battalion consisted of older men and those not eligible for Confederate service. Because he did not approve of slavery, Young had to "keep his head down" and joined the Frontier Battalion with Erath as his commander. Erath wrote, "This service was in the shape of local protection. Only in case of invasion were the men to be taken out of their counties." Young spent most of his time at home, minding his animals, but occasionally he "scouted about" for several weeks at a time. While gone, he employed young boys to watch his herds. In 1863, he hauled his wool to Houston, only to have it confiscated by the Confederate Subsistence Bureau to make uniforms for the army. Union forces had blockaded Galveston, closed the ports, and blocked shipping.[18]

Like many Texans Young sent a friend, S. Mayfield, to Mexico in 1863 with a wagonload of wool to buy goods. Mayfield brought back needed supplies, including eighty-two pounds of coffee, fifty pounds of sugar, salt, rope, and fabric for clothes. The pair split the cost of the trip, with Young paying $21.32 as his share.

During these turbulent times, settlers engaged in little commerce. The Confederate currency was quickly devalued and useful only to pay taxes, which rapidly increased as the Confederate cause failed. As the value of the currency fell, William had to barter his cattle and sheep.

But his purchases were minimal also: less than $200 annually. In 1863, Young paid $28.84 in Confederate taxes ($8.67 in US currency) and $20.17 in state and local taxes. By 1864, Confederate taxes had increased to $150.35 and state and local taxes to $103, paid in Confederate scrip or in "in kind"—crops or livestock. The Confederate war tax rose from $45 in 1863 to $131 in 1864 to $350 in 1865. By the end of the war, Young, who had started with cash reserves of over $4,000 in 1861, had $125 in cash—$48 new issue Confederate currency, $15 in state issue, and $65 in Bank of New Orleans notes. In 1864, Young received his final payment of $100 on his Confederate war bond—in Confederate currency. In other words, he was broke. He had to start all over again . . . but he had his land and his livestock.[19]

In the aftermath of the Civil War, Watson Caufield encountered a difficult situation. Just prior to secession, after Watson had moved to Texas, his local agent, Dr. Mayes, sold his Alabama farm to a Mr. Timmons. The initial deed of sale was in United States dollars. Watson Caufield held the note, which called for an annual payment. After the Confederacy was established, payments had to be in Confederate dollars on a one-to-one par with the federal currency. As the war wound down, the Confederate dollar became virtually worthless, but Timmons, the buyer, insisted on paying in the deflated Confederate dollars and even tried to pay off the balance of the note in Confederate currency. He begged off several years of note payments because of crop loss due to war and weather.

After the war, when US currency was reestablished in the South, Timmons claimed he did not owe any balance because it had been changed into Confederate currency, which was now legally worthless. Finally, when faced with eviction, Timmons began to claim that the property had a defective title because one of the Caufield cousins, who had been killed in the war in Virginia, had failed to sign a note payment for repairs made to the house. Of course, since the boy was dead, he could not co-sign the note.

However, Timmons wanted to be paid in US dollars for the improvements he had made to the dwelling during the war years. Watson returned to Boligee after the war, planning to eject Timmons from the property. Unfortunately, Timmons died, and it took almost a year to settle his estate before Timmons's widow could be evicted and the property resold.[20]

3

Ranching in Central Texas, 1865–1885

WHEN THE WAR ENDED, HENRY CAUFIELD RETURNED to his ranch and began to rebuild his herds. The war had depleted his livestock, but the land was still open and the grass free. Unbranded cattle roamed the prairie, and many of Henry's neighbors had used his unbranded cattle for food and to pay their taxes. Henry and Watson hired James Black and other returning veterans, gathered the cattle, and branded them. He paid the workers with a quarter of beef every Saturday or an occasional dairy cow that was captured. Family lore says that when the war was over, the brothers had several hundred head of cattle that they had gathered for the Confederate government. They added those cattle to their own herds.

The next years were quiet and prosperous. This would change with the building of the Gulf, Colorado, and Santa Fe Railroad through McLennan County in 1882 and the founding of McGregor only ten miles away.

Watson and Henry Caufield personally led several cattle drives to Abilene consisting of livestock gathered from local ranches. On one drive, in 1868, Henry reputedly returned with $45,000 in cash in his saddlebags. Because Central Texas ranchers did not have the large herds later raised on the Panhandle range, they gathered cattle from neighbors and hired local young men to drive the herds under the supervision of several older ranchers. The men would form a "cow-catching" group in the early summer, bringing in all the cattle they could find. They carefully recorded each brand and earmark and notified local owners, who could either come and get their animals or send them to market with the rest. They advertised for the owners of unclaimed animals.[1]

In addition to his sheep, Young, in partnership with his brother-in-law and friend Henry Caufield, raised cattle, horses, and mules. Caufield and Young began a close cooperation with their livestock and other economic and family events. Caufield concentrated on cattle and later cotton, while Young specialized in sheep and later in some cotton on his more arid land. Caufield established his ranch in McLennan County, about twenty-five miles away from Young's sheep operation, and usually marketed Young's livestock with his own. They moved livestock between their lands in response to drought and other conditions. Cattle, horses, and sheep—all showed a profit in the hands of these entrepreneurs.

In 1874, W. E. Young took a herd of cattle north to the Kansas markets, including cattle for Henry Caufield. But, by 1880, Caufield and Young had stopped leading the drives themselves and begun to send their cattle to market overland by professional herd masters such as W. A. Poage. They would give the herd master a list of their cattle and a letter of ownership and branded the animals with a trail brand. This strategy proved to be equally lucrative without the danger and responsibility of leading the drives.[2]

Henry Caufield continued to increase development of his ranch after the Civil War by fencing his property. Because of a lack of trees for wooden posts, fences to control livestock were difficult to build on the treeless Great Plains. Farmers and ranchers initially used hedges, usually Osage orange (bois d'arc or horse apple), to prevent stock from reaching crops. They built fences of stone or planks to keep the cattle out of gardens and to corral horses in pastures in the immediate vicinity of their houses.[3]

Henry Caufield built their first wire and plank fence about 1872 to enclose the horse and mule pastures and to keep the cattle out of the garden and oat patches. Later, hired hands plowed an eighty-acre fenced field in front of the main ranch house, planting oats for livestock forage. Caufield tore down a plank fence and planted bois d'arc hedges to protect this larger acreage. As they plowed land for cotton cultivation in the late 1880s, they built fences of barbed wire, and the hedges in turn were cut down. A half-mile remnant of the hedge remains along the north side of the field next to Caufield Creek, and a bois d'arc lane is still visible separating the Harris Creek pastures from a tenant's home and garden.[4]

Changes came rapidly to Central Texas in the 1880s. Late in the nineteenth century, two inventions of Yankee ingenuity—barbed wire and the windmill—changed the ranching industry. Several other factors contributed to the ending of the range cattle business in Central Texas, including overgrazing, low prices, the expansion of railroads across the plains, and the demands from Northern markets for a higher grade of beef.

Joseph Glidden of DeKalb, Illinois, received a patent for improved barbed wire in 1874. Initially, the wire cost 18 cents a pound to make, and Glidden could produce 10,000 pounds of wire a day. By 1880, Glidden had sold 80 million pounds of wire, and the price for wire fell from $20 a roll in 1870 to $4 a roll in 1890. With the decrease in the cost of wire, ranchers began to fence their pastures to separate the cattle.

Barbed wire changed the management of the cattle range. Any improvement in the quality of Texas cattle depended on fencing pastures to separate blooded animals from common range stock. Previously there were no fences: the cattle roamed freely across the open prairie and cattle from neighboring ranches mingled over the large area between the South and Middle Bosque Rivers, grazing and breeding haphazardly. Barbed wire allowed ranchers to fence large areas with a minimal number of wooded posts.

Barbed wire was cheap, durable, and easy to use and maintain in fence construction. Barbed wire fences helped delineate the boundaries of the owners' property and kept neighboring cattle from entering their fields, but the fences also cut up the free grazing areas, forcing ranchers to move their herds farther west in search of unfenced open ranges. The landowners' economic well-being now demanded intensive rather than extensive land use, and the profits realized from farming soon made land too valuable for grazing. The Caufields chose to do both.[5]

Because horses have thinner skin than cattle, Henry Caufield believed that barbed wire scarred the horses' hides and allowed screwworms to infest the sores. His fences initially consisted of four strands of smooth wire strung through holes bored in the fence posts. According to family history, Watson Caufield bored these holes with a hand auger, while hired hands placed the fence posts and strung the wire. Each day he took a drill, a stool, and a jug of whiskey and drilled holes until he fell off his seat. The ranch hands then took him home, where he napped on his cabin porch for the rest of the day.[6]

Although barbed wire first appeared in Texas in the late 1870s, the Caufields only began to use it extensively about 1882, stringing it along the boundaries of their property to protect their new cotton fields. Over the next decades, they plowed the fertile sections of land along the South Bosque river bottom first, fencing their crops from the livestock while allowing the cattle to graze over large areas of unfenced, open prairie. The river bottom fields were treeless, well watered, and fertile, ideally suited to cotton. Initially the fences were intended to keep cattle out of the crops, but later the family used fences to contain livestock within certain areas.

Farmers and ranchers had always depended upon regular rainfall and sought relief from nature's fickle ways. They were at the mercy of forces beyond their control—rain, drought, snow, and storms—that determined the fate of their crops and livestock. They sought ways to control the availability of water. Letters written by these early pioneers referred to the weather and its effects. In 1855, Watson Caufield indicated that "we have a very dry summer in Texas and but little prospects of making any crops. The grass is all dryed [sic] up in the prairies and no water for stock without going miles." In 1857, Mary Jane Caufield wrote, "Cotton is small." Yet, the following year Henry Caufield recorded that "our ground is too wet to plow." In another letter he went on to state that "our cane and wheat crops look fine. Grass is splendid and cows and horses fat."[7]

Caufield built his original ranch house on a slight rise above the flood level of the South Bosque River at the junction of Caufield Creek and beside a deep pool. As early as 1860, during a severe draught, Henry wrote, "We have had no rain this year. . . . My spring failed." After he dug a well behind the house he said, "I have got plenty of water [now]." But, as the need for water became critical later that year, Caufield had to trail his cattle to Hog Creek and the North Bosque River to find enough water.[8]

Water had always been a precious commodity and now became even more important. Because potable water was necessary both for settlers and their domestic animals, farmers built most of their dwellings close to ready water sources—either springs or streams. Crops depended on natural rainfall, but livestock needed a constant supply of fresh water. Limited rainfall, fewer streams, and long distances between springs and streams limited the usefulness

of large areas of the Blackland Prairie. As fencing began to prevent free-roaming stock from reaching water, access to streams
became a source of contention in many areas. The technology
already existed to drill water wells, but they needed a way to pump
water to the surface. Windmills filled that need.

The development of drilling equipment and windmills to pump
water changed the pattern of cattle ranching and accelerated the
switch to intensive livestock raising and better beef cattle breeds.
Windmills gave ranchers a continuous supply of water even in
times of drought and allowed farmers to live closer to their fields
and away from rivers and creeks. By 1880, Caufield used windmills placed on his ranch's existing wells to supply stock tanks
in pastures without natural water sources. A well dug at the Wat
Caufield house about 1880 has been in continuous use for more
than one hundred years and is typical of the time and region. It is
about fifty feet deep, lined with limestone blocks, and connected
to a windmill.

Water and windmills became important elements in the development of the cotton-sharecropper cycle. On the higher, water-
less Blackland Prairie, the Caufields began to plant cotton. They
placed the sharecropper cabins next to the fields that the croppers
worked. Near most of the tenant houses they dug wells and placed
a windmill to pump water for the tenants' family. Windmills
filled elevated water tanks alongside each house and allowed for
indoor plumbing.

Henry Caufield invested his profits in land. There was little
unclaimed land in McLennan County, as most had been assigned
through various land warrants and grants from the Republic and
state governments. But many of the owners did not live on their
land; they often resided in distant towns or even out of state. When
they died, their descendants saw no need to pay taxes on nonpro-
ductive, isolated tracts. Henry continued to purchase land as it
became available, usually at county auctions for failure to pay taxes.

Determining the boundaries of a piece of property and the place for fences was often difficult, as Caufield tried to clear the titles on his own and his newly purchased plots. Because the early surveys were inaccurate, with descriptions consisting of "a line running from a large oak tree" to "a mound of flat rocks," litigants often determined disputed boundary lines by detecting on which side of the post the owner had placed the wire or where rows of trees had grown. (The wire went on the same side of the post as the cattle; this kept the fence from pulling apart when cattle leaned on the strands.) Small trades of land or payouts of cash for overlapping boundaries and gaps from poor surveys slowly cleared the titles. Eventually, fence lines became delineated on the treeless prairie by rows of hackberry trees that had sprouted from the droppings of birds sitting on the fence wire.[9]

In Central Texas, access to large areas of previously free open range became ever more restricted. Population growth, railroad development, and the increase in commercial agriculture caused a rapid rise in land values, making the purchase of additional grazing land too expensive. Livestock owners soon faced the choice of either selling their herds and becoming farmers or selling their lands and moving their cattle to the open range of West Texas. With the prairies fenced in Central Texas, many local ranchers moved their free-range livestock production farther west. In 1876, the Caufields purchased 6,500 acres of insane-asylum and deaf-asylum land and leased an additional 10,000 acres in Shackleford County. They moved their beef cattle operation to that area and sent a son, Mart Caufield, to manage that ranch. Watson Caufield began to manage the local ranch.[10]

On their McLennan County ranch, the Caufields made the choice to switch from free-range stock to more intensive stock raising, moving to Shetland ponies and mules. They fenced the wooded river bottoms that were unsuited for crops and placed their livestock there. They planted row crops on the flat

Blackland Prairie where their land was plowed and planted with cotton.

The Foote family had resided near New Berlin in western New York State for several generations. After serving as a major in the Union Army during the Civil War, Adrian Foote and his wife moved to Ashland, Massachusetts, a town of about 1,000 located one hundred miles west of Boston. There he became the general manager and treasurer of Warren Thread Company, a wool factory owned by Jordan Marsh Company, a group of Boston investors. Adrian Foote had served in the same Union regiment as Marsh. His proximity to and familiarity with the wool markets in Boston would be a major benefit to his son's sheep ranches.

Adrian Foote was a good businessman. He ran the mills with an iron hand. He knew what was correct and how to handle any situation, and he expected everyone, including his family members, to obey his wishes. He was paid well for his efforts: $5,000 annually by the Warren mill. Foote managed another business acquired by the Jordan Marsh Company, the Dwight Printing Company. E. D. Jordan served as president and Adrian Foote as manager. Adrian also owned several tenement apartments and office buildings himself. In 1884, local voters elected him selectman for Ashland. In 1886, the Cleveland administration appointed Foote postmaster for Ashland as a reward for his longtime support of the Democratic Party. The position paid $1,000 annually. After he posted bond, Adrian moved the office to a building that he owned, then subleased the job at half the salary to a friend.[11]

Soon Adrian focused his energy on finding a new superintendent for the mill, which he continued to manage until his retirement. He was successful in reviving the business, and in 1887 the mill sold $200,000 of thread.

The Footes were a rather tight-knit family. Adrian's two bachelor brothers—Andrew who worked as chief teller (equivalent today to senior vice president) for a bank in Sterling, Illinois, and John who remained on the family dairy farm in New Berlin, Chenango County, New York—kept in close contact with each other. Adrian married Mary Caroline Beardslee, who had also been raised in New Berlin. Her mother, her aunt Cornelia, and her great-uncle Cyril Beardslee continued to live in New Berlin and manage the Beardslee family farms. When Mary's father died, he left her and her sister each half interest in land he owned in Texas. Her mother also left each daughter half interest in the Beardslee family farm, which Great-uncle Cyril continued to manage for them. Adrian and Mary Foote had four children: Frederick, Frances, Jessie, and Henry. Frederick moved to Texas to manage his mother's land. Frances married and moved to Ord, Nebraska, with her husband, William Barstow. The other children stayed in Ashland. Jessie never married and took care of her father and brother Henry until 1892, when he married. Henry and his wife, Cora, had several children.[12]

During the economic depression of 1873–1875, Frederick Foote found opportunities in Ashland limited and decided to travel to Texas to investigate the land his mother had inherited. Foote family history claims that Frederick's grandfather Jesse Beardslee had won several sections of land in Coryell County, Texas, during a poker game in New Orleans prior to the Civil War. Actually, what happened was that his uncle Cyril Beardslee, who had lived in Texas between 1830 and 1850, speculated in land with a partner, John Adriance, a prominent Republic of Texas attorney. Cyril induced his brother Jesse, Fred Foote's maternal grandfather, to invest in Texas land warrants. The brothers placed their warrants near each other in the northeast corner of what is now Coryell County. This is the land that Mary Caroline Beardslee Foote had inherited at her father's death.[13]

The other family members also suffered from the lack of prospects in the one-mill town. Brother Henry, who was deaf and seemed to have had a wild streak, wandered about looking for just the right opportunity. He drank a good bit, did not like hard work, and preferred the comforts of home. Henry lived in Ashland with and worked for his father until he married a local girl and raised a family. He died in 1931.

Thus, in September 1875, twenty-year-old Frederick Foote left Ashland and traveled to Texas to determine the value and best use of this land. Fred developed pneumonia shortly after his arrival in Waco and was nursed back to health by a local Black nurse who fed and cared for him until he could repay her. Foote worked in and around Waco for several years, learning about the local people and economy. He herded cattle on Henry Caufield's ranch before moving on to Coryell County, where he herded sheep for Ezra Morse, a neighbor and family friend in Ashland. On the advice of William Young, his neighbor in Coryell County, Fred decided to raise sheep on his family's rocky land. Initially he raised sheep on shares with Ezra Morse, who owned a nearby ranch. This was the traditional way for a young, ambitious man to begin his own herds: raising stock for a more established landowner and receiving one-third of the increase as partial payment. Most employees elected to receive livestock instead of cash for the rest of their salaries. Cattle require a larger initial investment, and they mature more slowly, while sheep can be raised cheaply on unclaimed, overgrazed range with rapid returns. In 1879, Fred Foote began purchasing sheep in partnership with his father, Adrian, and eventually built a large sheep ranch of his own.[14]

The Foote land was located in the northwestern corner of Coryell County and was an excellent habitat for sheep. Coryell County had been created from the western portion of Bell County in 1854. Previously, titles and taxes had been recorded in Bell County. Gatesville (population 1,400 in 1888) was twenty miles from the Foote ranch and served as county seat for the new county. Nearby Turnersville (population 200 in 1888) was only five miles from the ranch house but over muddy or dusty dirt roads. The land was located in a semiarid and rocky portion of the Cross Timbers area, which had been overgrazed by cattle the previous decade. But sheep thrive on the weeds and forbs that grow in overgrazed areas. They eat grass as a last choice during the winter months, so the Foote land was ideal for sheep. Cattle, on the other hand, must have grass in order to thrive. The two make ideal companions on the same land as long as there is sufficient forage for both during the winter.[15]

Although raising sheep had become a major business in western Coryell County, it constituted only a small portion of the state sheep production. In 1888, local sheepmen owned 40,675 head of sheep out of the state total of 3.8 million head. They produced 271,270 pounds of wool valued at $41,434 (about $1 gross income per animal) compared to 18 million pounds statewide worth $2.9 million. Foote and Young did not become the largest sheepmen in Texas, but they had chosen well. The land they owned was ideally suited for sheep and could hold about 2,000 head without supplemental feeding; that was also the number of sheep that one herder could handle without help.[16]

Back in Ashland, the entire Foote family took great interest in Frederick's sheep ranch, and eventually every member of his family joined the venture. In 1880, Henry Foote spent several months with Fred as he expanded his sheep herds, built sheds, and enclosed pastures. All of Fred's uncles—maternal and paternal—invested or tried to invest in the operation. Uncles John and Andrew Foote invested in both land and sheep. Great-uncle Cyril Beardslee purchased sheep and rented land to the ranch operation.[17]

However, only brother Henry and Uncle John Foote actually visited or worked on the ranch. In January 1882, John Foote visited the ranch for several weeks, stopping in Kansas on his way home. Uncle John warned he was coming to visit soon, probably January or December. He was traveling with a group from New Berlin on their way to take the waters at Hot Springs, Arkansas. Uncle John wanted to be picked up at the train station in Waco on December 27, 1881. He arrived, stayed at the ranch for several weeks, and returned via Newton, Kansas, in January 1882. John Foote, Adrian Foote's bachelor brother from New Berlin, invested in sheep with the family and by 1886 had 550 head on the place. Foote earned half the wool clip and half the lambs for his labor supervising John's herds. Additional labor for herding and clipping John's herd cost $260 annually. The size of Uncle John's herd grew until he sold 220 head in 1892. Even by 1896, John Foote still had a considerable number of animals on the Foote ranch, including 96 ewes and 60 lambs valued at $106. That year the wool clip on the animals yielded $59 and the sale of 140 head brought an additional $132 of income.

Sisters Frances and Jessie Foote also sent small sums to buy additional sheep. Frances was teaching school in Westchester and sent $30 of her earnings to Fred to purchase five ewes and a ram. In 1883, she made $5 on her sheep (a 16 percent annual income on her investment). By 1885, she owned twenty head. The next year she asked Fred to sell the animals and send her the money to buy cattle at her new home in Nebraska.[18]

The Foote family were prodigious letter writers. Several hundred letters flowed from all family members to Texas over the next decades. Frederick Foote never suffered from a lack of advice from those who would supervise his business from afar. Father, mother, uncles, sisters, and brother Henry all wrote regularly. Father Adrian Foote was particularly punctual in his letters, writing sometimes twice weekly with advice.

Adrian, as the patriarch of the family, was a font of suggestions—wanted or not. He attempted to control all aspects of the ranch, as he did his family in Ashland. He subscribed to livestock

journals and a Galveston newspaper—the only one worth reading, according to Adrian Foote—and invested heavily in the farm,
pledging his salary for years in advance to ensure the operation's
success. He combed the local Massachusetts sheep farms for
equipment and animals to enhance the infrastructure and stock.

Adrian Foote could also be a bit overwhelming. During the
week of December 20, 1886, he wrote several letters pressing his
son to personally attend to surveying the boundaries of their land
in Hamilton County for taxes. Back home he was looking for
surveying chains and instruments. On December 24, he began
a series of letters stressing the importance of drilling water wells,
quoting the exact depth and size of piping to purchase. Shortly
thereafter, he wrote on the importance of building sheep sheds
for the winter and prescribed the size, shape, and structure of the
buildings. The next series of letters contained an in-depth anal-
ysis of the merits of an $800 artesian well-drilling machine. He
included a price list. Adrian recommended splitting the cost with
Fred's neighbors. Fred seems to have allowed distance and time to
dissipate the urgency of his father's prolific free advice.[19]

By 1880, Fred had purchased his own sheep and had begun to
raise livestock in earnest. The correspondence thereafter picked
up pace. He had initially contracted to raise sheep on shares with
Ezra Morse, the Massachusetts neighbor, who owned and lived
part-time on an adjoining ranch. The first years of their partnership were difficult. Initially they lost many of their animals to
freezing weather, wolves, and drought. Several local friends from
Ashland, including G. W. Randell and his son Frank, lived and
worked on the Morse Ranch. G. W. Randell returned the next
year to Ashland to care for his wife, Lucy, who was dying of tuberculosis. Frank Randell continued to work for Fred intermittently
for several years.

In 1879, Fred received a notice from J. R. Franklin, a wool factor
in Waco, soliciting his wool clip, along with that of his neighbor

William Young, and offering prices of 23 to 24 cents a pound. Foote contracted with Franklin to sell his first clip, starting a relationship that lasted several decades.

Meanwhile, back in Ashland, the family was becoming more interested in the prospects of the ranch. Henry Foote, on the way to join Fred, arrived in Waco a few days prior to Christmas 1880, bringing clothes sent by Adrian and Mary Caroline Foote. His round-trip ticket had cost $46. Henry planned to stay and become a full partner in the ranch, but he lasted just six months.[20]

By 1881, the ranch was beginning to make money and activity increased rapidly. The previous year Fred had taken several hundred ewes purchased by Ezra Morse, his neighbor in Massachusetts, to herd with his own sheep and to raise on shares for Morse. Unfortunately, because of a negligent herder, wolves attacked the flocks over several weeks and killed large numbers of the animals. The herder ran off and Foote had to take over the herd himself. Morse lost the majority of his investment and was not happy. Frank Randell, who had also worked for Morse and spent several years working for Fred, returned to Ashland to look after his elderly parents but continued to take a close interest in Fred, Henry, and their sheep.[21]

That year Adrian Foote began a quest to purchase 1,000 ewes. At first, he considered buying them in Michigan. But he decided it was too late in the season to ship pregnant ewes with their heavy winter wool coat, which would pack them too closely in the freight cars and result in unacceptable losses in both ewes and lambs. He recommended buying the animals in Texas and sent $200 to pay for the sheep. He noted that sheep could be purchased at $3 a head for ewes. They purchased five hundred ewes for $2,500, delivered in the spring of 1882. Fred purchased an additional five hundred ewes for $3,000.[22]

Life was not always easy on the isolated sheep ranch. Fire, drought, disease, predators, and low prices took a heavy toll on the herds. Wool prices fluctuated. And the herders disappeared without warning—often with part of the flock. Fred had difficulty obtaining tenants, herders, and families who would cook and wash the hands' clothes. Initially, he lived with Mr. and Mrs. G. W. Lee and their three children in the three-room ranch headquarters. Lee labored as a herder while his wife cooked, cleaned, and laundered for the men. But the crowded quarters forced Fred to camp out in the sheds most of the time. Family lore says he lived in a piano shipping crate for several months.[23]

Fred eventually became infested with lice, resulting in his mother prescribing "Kerosene, a fine comb . . . and boiling his clothes." The treatment recommended by his mother included spreading kerosene over his entire body, then washing himself, all his clothes, and all his bed linens. His hair should be combed with a fine comb and sulfur water applied.

When Fred developed an itch—probably scabies—his mother recommended treatment with topical sulfur and molasses. Father Foote prescribed equal parts of cream of tartar and sulfur mixed in molasses and taken orally. As a child, Adrian had been given this recipe with a little whiskey "until the sulphur came out the pores." The mixture was to be taken by mouth nightly for three nights, then applied topically as a salve for several additional weeks.[24]

Fodder for the animals and food for the herders were an additional expense. In 1881, Foote purchased 135 pounds of cottonseed at 80 cents/pound and 298 pounds of bran to feed his animals. He purchased two horses for $125 and paid $3 to have them shoed and fed. Food for the herders included bacon, sweet potatoes, and butter (6 pounds).[25]

By 1882, Fred Foote was thirty-one years old and had spent nine years on the land without a break. That year he began to make a permanent residence for his family on the ranch. As he settled in, Fred built a house, shed, and wooden fence at his headquarters for $1,185. He bought 4,000 feet of lumber costing $100, part of which was used to build sheds for the sheep. He purchased furniture for $100 and hardware for the doors that cost $23.70. He now had a permanent home.[26]

Scab (scabies), a common complaint among sheep farmers, began to infest the Foote herd in 1882. The highly contagious infestation was carried by mites: the insects dug into the skin, damaging the wool by infesting and weakening the fibers. The itching caused an animal to scrape its sides on trees and poles and scratch off the wool. Then the next animal rubbing against that pole also became infected. Scab was best countered by dipping the sheep in a vat containing either tobacco or sulfur. Adrian shipped forty gallons (one barrel) of Dr. T. W. Langford's "New Sheep Dip" from Little Chambers Co. in Baltimore, Maryland for $76.50 plus $26.50 in shipping costs. Treatment for the scab-infected animals began at once. Father Foote also sent a recipe for scab that suggested using tobacco, sulfur, whiskey, and molasses, a treatment that continued to be used by sheepmen for many decades. In addition, he sent a book on diseases in animals and a book of business forms.[27]

Henry Foote never liked ranching when he was in Texas but always thought he would when he was in Massachusetts. He arrived in the fall of 1880, traveling to Texas on the railroad. His brother Fred met him in Waco and drove him to the ranch. Henry worked on the place about six months, until the spring of 1881, when he left, complaining the ranch was "too lonely, the weather too cold, and the food too bad." Records indicate that he managed to shear only one or two sheep a day—compared with the twenty to fifty the other herders sheared.

Henry returned in the fall of 1881 for nine months but again went home in the spring of 1882. While on the ranch Henry had developed scurvy—a condition resulting from vitamin C deficiency, in this case caused by a lack of green vegetables—and began drinking heavily. He was cured of the scurvy with lime juice. His mother sent oatmeal and dried apples. Henry returned to Massachusetts by train on a ticket costing $46 for a trip from San Antonio to Chicago. He transferred at Sterling, Illinois, where he visited his uncle Andrew Foote, and arrived in Ashland by late spring 1882. Uncle Andrew had offered Henry a job making barbed wire at a local factory at $1.90 a day. The work was not to Henry's liking. In 1888, Henry again traveled to the ranch and this time lasted about six months before returning to Massachusetts. He did not like hard work and was a slacker and a complainer, but he always bragged to his wife and children about how hard he had worked on the ranch. This would later lead to serious discord between Fred's and Henry's children: the latter would maintain that their father had been a major contributor to the success of the enterprise. Despite his contribution of only twelve months' labor over thirty years, Henry always considered himself a full half owner of the ranch.[28]

While Fred and Henry worked through the Texas winter in the windy prairie country, life in Ashland continued to progress peacefully. Sister Jessie wrote they had ice-skated on the local pond, been to several plays, traveled to South Farmington to hear Henry Ward Beecher, and enjoyed Thanksgiving dinner. Sister Frances went to dances and visited friends across New England.[29]

The family correspondence covered more than just ranch matters and also revealed their close interrelationships. Fred's mother never ceased to worry about her son and in 1882 wrote: "I cannot help thinking of the trials and toils of the life you have chosen in that barren country." She sent him a coat for his birthday and several pails of dried apples and cranberries. Jessie, who was thirteen when Fred left in 1875, was now twenty-two years old. Frances was twenty-six and teaching school in Westchester. Mother Foote was fifty-five and would die in three years from cancer. Adrian Foote was sixty and would live until eighty-four years of age, dying in 1906. Sister Frances was a frequent letter writer, averaging a letter a month. Frances also forwarded her copies of various books and magazines, including the *Century*, whose articles were a favorite topic of discussion. Sister Jessie wrote rarely, two or three times a year.

In 1882, the Foote family made a series of decisions to solidify their future investments in Texas and in the sheep industry. First, they purchased additional land, part of the Burns Survey, the 2,300 acres adjacent to their survey. Next, they invested in sheds and fences for their sheep. Last, they agreed to purchase enough sheep to maximize the herd's size at about 2,000 head. Uncle John agreed to invest in the sheep herds, as did sister Frances, father Adrian, and Great-uncle Cyril. Fred Foote was now completely committed to raising sheep in Texas.

In 1883, Frances tactfully returned to Fred the hair chain and silver ring he had given a young lady from a nearby town. She had waited for seven years for Fred to return and now had decided to marry another local boy. Fred seemed to be relieved. Henry's letters came every month or so and were often full of angry recriminations against his father.[30]

During the summer of 1884, Fred finally visited his family in Ashland. His mother was dying from an "internal cancer" that had been diagnosed by a Dr. Herman, who had traveled from Boston to examine her and to review her case. Although she would live another year, Mary Caroline Foote's health and ability to care for herself gradually decreased, and by the summer of 1885 she was "under the influence of opiates most of the time." She died in September 1885.[31]

While windmills and wells provided water to large stretches of the arid land, barbed wire kept the neighbors' stray animals out of the now watered pastures. By 1883, the family began to fence their property at great expense. They needed special fences to keep the sheep and lambs in the pastures. They used six-wire fences of plain wire at 31 cents a rod or the new six-wire barbed fences, which cost 52 cents a rod. The plain wire cost 65 cents a pound while barbed wire cost $7.45 a pound. The cost of the new barbed wire fell over the next decade, and Fred expanded the fencing, as he could afford the expense. But the cost of fencing was tremendous for the day, with the cost of labor reaching $15 per mile and with posts, labor, and wire totaling $150 a mile ($15,000 a mile in 2021 dollars).[32]

This area of Central Texas had experienced little difficulty with fencing. Because the land was semiarid, there were few farmers. But the previous two years a fierce range war had raged between the Pancake/Babb and the Sandefer interests for control of the open range. The result was a great deal of fence cutting. Pancake, who had settled in the county in 1852, had at one time operated a ranch fourteen miles across. Unfortunately, he actually owned only a small portion of the land. When the real landowners fenced their property, Pancake began to lose control of his empire. He fought back vigorously, hiring a notorious outlaw named William Babb and his gang. As Pancake's fortunes continued to deteriorate, he began to drink heavily, and when he died a decade later, neither was his passing mourned nor was his estate large.

Babb was Pancake's son-in-law and had lived in the area for decades, but he became a troublemaker. He turned outlaw when he returned from the Civil War and found his family in distress without help from his neighbors. In 1878, Babb killed Deputy US Marshal John Stull at Turnersville. At trial, he promised to leave the county if acquitted. Although the jury acquitted him, Babb did not leave. The next month, over five hundred citizens gathered and told him he had ten days to leave or they would burn him and his family out. Pancake gave him a trusted blue-gray horse named Grayback to help his getaway.

Babb continued with a gang of outlaws to infest the surrounding counties, especially northern McLennan County, robbing

ranchers of their cattle and horses. In 1883, when the authori-
ties finally drove Babb from the area, he went west to the Texas
Panhandle where he rustled cattle, and then later to South Texas,
where he obtained some respectability.[33]

By 1884, as the Footes enclosed their pastures, the family recognized the increasing need for a more dependable water supply
for their animals and began to drill additional wells around their
holdings. Foote added water wells and windmills in 1883, sending to Massachusetts for water pumps costing $64 and in 1887 a
replacement rubber gasket for one of the pumps.

This gasket caused a bit of contention. Father Foote was living
with brother Henry and Jessica in the large old family residence
with little to keep him busy, so he continued to micromanage the
ranch from Massachusetts. He wrote Fred: "There was not the first
reason for your sending the old rubber to me. All you need to have
done was, with your pencil, make a drawing as near as you could
and on it give the measurements of each space size." He obtained
a replacement for the pump gasket and then fussed to Fred about
how to repair the pump. "I can only say it belongs to the pump
and if you take it apart you will see for what purpose it was used.
When you put in your new rubber, you had better find it and put
in a new one. I would at once saturate the nuts, screws and bolts
as far as you can with kerosene so that the rust may easily give way
when you try to start the motor." Adrian offered in his next two
letters additional advice for managing the pumps. Fred seemed to
have tolerated his father fairly well by taking advantage of time
and distance to ignore the advice he did not need nor agreed with.

As the Footes increased their land over the next two decades,
they continued to ensure that their flocks had access to adequate
water by placing windmills on the new land. The new wells cost
$100 to $250 each, depending on the depth. The wells paid off
after a series of dry years from 1885 to 1888 made water a precious
local commodity. Further improvements in 1898 included three

wells costing $42, $37, and $44 each. The windmills he purchased locally.[34]

Herding sheep, drilling water wells, and building sheds were not the only tasks facing Fred Foote: he needed to obtain clear title to his land, often a prodigious feat in Texas. Cyril Beardslee owned 3,600 acres with John Adriance for over thirty years, including the original Foote grant, purchased about the same time by Cyril's brother, Jesse, Mary Caroline Beardslee Foote's father. Over the next decade, problems proving title, conducting surveys, and delineating the exact area of each land grant consumed a great deal of Fred's time. A typical Texas problem complicated the Foote purchases: the initial land surveys were often very imprecise—with wording like "from a large oak tree . . . to a stack of white rocks"—and sometimes the actual boundaries of adjacent grants overlapped or were not contiguous, leaving unclaimed areas between the boundaries. Before a clear title could be registered, the boundaries had to be resurveyed.[35]

Obtaining a clear title to Texas frontier land was complicated. Although the Beardslee family had patented their land in 1856, numerous squatters had lived on various portions of their grant and all the surrounding ones. Some had paid taxes and some had left "their" land to their children. Several families claimed prior ownership of parts of the Beardslee grant. Each claim had to be cleared.

Back taxes were also a problem. To further cloud the titles, as Texas created new counties, they often failed to survey and delineate their own boundaries. Because Coryell County had been created from Bell County, previous titles had been recorded in the latter, and taxes had been paid there. Hamilton and Bosque Counties had been created about the same time. After the new counties were formed, they had no records of previous tax payments, including those made in Austin. Everyone had to scramble to find decades-old tax receipts.

Adrian Foote, as usual, tried to take charge. He wrote Fred, "I wish to know at once the condition of Uncle Cyril's taxes that you paid and amt. and what years are now due and unpaid. . . . There is only one way to do such matters and that is to do it in season." Fred responded to his father's rudeness by ignoring his orders. Subsequent letters would ask for the same information, which seems to have arrived eventually.[36]

The Foote and Beardslee grants lay at the junction of the three counties with parts in each entity. The amount of land and the exact boundaries for each county varied over the years. Extra taxes had been paid in one county but not in another, or two people paid taxes on the same land in different counties. Each county would often demand taxes on the same piece of land, selling the property for delinquent taxes, even if the taxes had been paid in an adjoining county—creating confusing, overlapping tax debts and contested titles. Hamilton County sold some of the land for nonpayment of taxes. The receipts were in the Austin state land office. Proving tax payments became even more difficult when the Hamilton County courthouse burned on November 26, 1886, destroying all records of past tax payments. The Footes took six years to obtain a clear title to their own land and eight years to clear the title on Uncle Cyril's land.[37]

The Foote land joined that of the Young family league on one side and that of the Dunn family—the Caufield and Young cousins in Wheelock—to the north, which made those boundaries and fence lines somewhat easier to determine. But because numerous children and cousins had inherited undivided portions of the grants, fence lines became a complicated family matter. As fences were built, each family carefully watched the fence line to avoid encroachments. They split the costs according to percentage shares in the whole. But collecting those expenses from all the different family members also complicated matters. Some family members refused to pay their share. To facilitate delineating the boundaries,

Adrian Foote purchased survey tools and a survey chain and sent them to Texas.

As if it were not enough that incomplete, overlapping, or clouded titles complicated the Footes' attempts to secure clear title to Cyril Beardslee's land, they encountered another unique problem while surveying the property. An enterprising gentleman named Harold Hattley found a small strip of unclaimed land between two pre-existing land grant surveys. He placed his bounty warrant there, overlapping with his neighbors', paid taxes on the whole, then waited for the original owners to buy him out to clear their titles.[38]

In 1886, the issue with Hattley came to a head. In 1879, Hattley had placed his overlapping warrant grant between Cyril Beardslee's grant and another in 1879. When forced off the adjacent survey in 1881, he moved his boundaries farther over the line into the Beardslee grant. H. H. Harrington, the family attorney in New Berlin and Cyril Beardslee's son-in-law, began a relentless campaign to have the man thrown off the Beardslee survey as well. Hattley stated he would "shed blood before moving" when the Bosque County sheriff served him papers. The project took eight years and only culminated when Hattley's house burned in 1886 and he moved on to another county—probably to try the same maneuver again.[39]

The family purchased additional land as it became available. In July 1882, the Footes purchased the E. A. Blount land in the Burns Survey, 2,322 acres, for $3 an acre. Blount had also purchased the land with Adriance, using a bounty warrant to obtain the land. Blount and Adriance later split the land, each taking individual ownership of a portion of the original grant. They both had paid the county taxes in their home counties or in Austin, as could be done until 1879. However, after the new counties of Hamilton, Coryell, and Bosque were formed, the new counties had no records of the past tax payments. The amount of land claimed by each county had varied over several different years and extra taxes had been paid in one county but not in another or two persons had paid the taxes in the same county.

In 1884, Blount conveyed his title to Adrian Foote. But it took another eight years to obtain a title clear from all tax encumbrances. For this piece, Adrian and Fred paid one-third in cash and signed notes for the remainder over two years. They later purchased an additional 420 acres in the same survey, leaving the 387 acres owned by another descendant of the original owner undivided until decades later. This allowed the family to graze their sheep for free on the extra pasture. In 1883, they purchased the Logan survey from S. J. Chute, 1,476 acres, for $3,500, giving $1,000 down and giving a note for the rest at 8 percent annually. Adrian Foote borrowed $650 from "Old Mike," an employee in Ashland, and $500 from John Foote to finance the new purchases and to buy six hundred additional sheep to place on the new grazing land.[40]

In 1885, Frederick Foote married Mary Ann Young. They joined the Caufield-Cavitt family as the second generation struggled to establish their livelihood by ranching. After they were married, Fred and Mary Ann Foote's life changed dramatically. Since Mary Ann was no longer invited to singles parties and was now in a set of married couples who were burdened with numerous children and too tired or too busy to visit or go to parties, church became the main source of entertainment for Mary Ann. Only occasional visitors came by the Foote ranch house, which was well off the main highways. She was no longer the center of attention nor able to run into town to buy whatever she wanted. Fred was a quiet, frugal, and steady man. He worked hard on the ranch and went into town several times a week to purchase goods and tend to business, occasionally making monthly trips to Waco and to Gatesville, leaving Mary Ann alone to care for the small children. She chafed under the isolation.

Mary Ann Young's marriage to Fred Foote began a new chapter in her family's long history of sheep ranching. She moved from her family's large comfortable home and her large family to a small cabin twenty miles away, alone with her husband and his herders on a lonely, windswept prairie. Fred had remodeled a ranch house to meet Mary Ann's wishes. All was finished except a new fence for the front yard and garden. The house had originally been built in 1877 as a one-room structure and added on to frequently. On her arrival at her new home, Mary Ann proceeded to scrub everything. She exulted that she "did like to have clean floors." Fred smiled and endured. He was soon in firm control. Shortly afterward, every letter noted in several places that "Fred says" and "Fred went." Their marriage would last over fifty years.

Loneliness was a persistent problem along the frontier. Men and women lived many miles from their nearest neighbor and often went months without seeing a nonfamily member. Women had charge of the home and children, keeping them within a small radius from the house. Men could ride about, visiting with other ranchers or going into town to buy supplies. But isolation on a farm in the nineteenth century was not just about distance, it was also about roads—muddy and impassable in the winter—and transportation: proper women usually had to travel in a buggy, and traveling long distances was daunting, especially when it meant leaving house, animals, and children alone and uncared-for for a day or more.

The Young and the Foote families, because of the number of herders they hired, had a continual human presence on their ranches. In addition, the placement of their homes just off the main highway to the railroad brought a constant stream of visitors. Although Mary Ann was often busy cooking for the workers and caring for the children, she spoke of the loneliness of the open prairie. She related that, prior to her marriage, friends visited almost every weekday. Her early letters contained a constant summary of events in the area, including deaths, marriages, church events, parties, weather, and visits. These continued, although dramatically reduced, on the isolated Foote ranch. For company, the family went into town for church and often stayed overnight with friends or other family members.[41]

The young bride, used to the bustle of her own family and now alone on a secluded ranch with just her new husband, was particularly prone to bouts of loneliness. The unfamiliarity of being by herself, afraid, listening to the wind rustle through the trees or whisper through an unfamiliar house, made the newlywed nervous and depressed. And the wind never stopped blowing on the plains. Fred went to the sheep pens, rode after the animals, visited with the shepherds, or went into town to tend to business, but Mary Ann had to stay home, prepare the meals, and mend and wash the clothes. Her longing for wider social interaction pours from her letters.

With her move to Fred Foote's ranch, Mary's attention turned to her new life, and her letters reflected this new interest. Over the next several decades, Fred Foote assumed leadership of the Young family, which consisted of the four daughters after William Young decided to stay in Tennessee and pursue his career building bridges.

There is nothing romantic about owning and operating a sheep ranch. Mary's duties including providing meals and clean clothes for the herders and other hired hands living on the ranch. For example, in January 1888, there were three herders living in the bunkhouse back of the main house. During shearing and lambing, many more workers stayed at the headquarters, including fourteen workers and three "Norwegians." All those workers had to be fed. Mary had trouble from the beginning with her cooks and maids. Her first maid, Ida, a young unmarried girl away from home for the first time, "would not work but read novels all day." Mary complained, outraged that the girl was receiving "$2 a day plus room and board." Fred fired the girl. The next cook was not much better; she also read romance novels instead of cooking for the hands.[42]

To be sure, life with Mary was not easy for Fred or for Mary herself. Her letters indicate that she was fretful and often ill, with only the hired hands and a young, somewhat truculent cook with whom to talk. There was no one to listen to her complaints.

Fred charged his purchases at the Turnersville Mercantile, a small store owned by R. D. Heathly. The store was typical for the times and supplied a wide variety of merchandise, including groceries and clothing. The store had about two hundred customers, including sharecroppers who purchased goods on credit. Fred seems to have purchased goods about every two weeks, buying two hundred pounds of flour for $8; forty-nine pounds of bacon for $7.45; two pounds of tea for 80 cents; and nine pounds of coffee for $2. Fred usually bought about 100 dollars' worth of goods a month from Heathly. In the first week of October 1888, the store sold $883.27 of goods, $310.75 for cash and $572.52 for credit. Heathly purchased $409 of wholesale goods from fourteen salesmen.

At the end of the year, Turnersville Mercantile collected several hundred bales of cotton the farmers processed at the local gin. Heathly paid an average of 8 cents a pound and resold the crop in the nearby towns of Waco, Gatesville, and Valley Mills for 8.67 to 9.95 cents a pound. Heathly's payment to the farmers went toward the balances of their bills at the store, while Heathly kept the increased value for his own profit. Most farmers received only a small cash balance after the transactions were over. They had little recourse. They had signed a mortgage on their crop to Heathly to obtain credit. He owned the cotton and could do as he wished.[43]

As the size of the Foote herds increased, obtaining sufficient water for the animals in semiarid western Coryell County became an urgent problem. Fred began to drill water wells. Because his neighbors had fenced off his access to surrounding waterways, Foote needed his own year-round water supply. In 1882, he purchased a horse-powered artesian well-drilling machine from H. W. Walburn in Fort Scott, Kansas, for $420. He drilled two shallow water wells close to the main house, at a cost of $33 for one and $20 for the other, providing a stable water supply at the main headquarters for both humans and animals. Wells at that time cost about $1 to $2 a foot to drill, with the windmills an additional expense. A pump for one windmill cost $31, pipe $12, and freight from Henry Stowe, Blacksmith, Boston, cost $13. The arrival of the Cotton Belt Railroad in Gatesville and the Santa Fe at Crawford in 1882 had facilitated the shipping of equipment and lowered the transportation costs as well.[44]

In 1885, Frederick continued to increase the ranch's infrastructure with sheep sheds, outbuildings, and fences. That fall the family invested in an eight-strand barbed wire fence for the lambing fields close to headquarters, ordering the wire from mills in Indiana. Other purchases included a harrow for $49, a sulky plow for $100, a cultivator, a chain for surveying, a planting drill from Fort Scott, Kansas, trunks, clothing, and connections for the windmills. Adrian Foote, as usual, took charge and wrote, "I shall order from the maker at Little Falls, N.Y. to be shipped to you as they wrote to me they could do to Gatesville, Texas, the cultivator."[45]

The winter of 1885 was one of the coldest in American history. The blizzards that swept across the western United States resulted in disastrous losses of livestock across a wide breadth of the nation. On the Great Plains, many cattle firms experienced 80 to 90 percent losses of their animals and faced bankruptcy by spring. Although the winter in Central Texas was also very cold, the losses on the Foote Ranch were not as severe as they were farther west. The animals sheltered in new sheds and were supervised by Foote and the herders to avert disaster. Despite Fred's good work in saving his herds, his father offered scant praise. Instead, Adrian sent a copy of an article in the Dallas newspaper quoting cattle losses of $40,000,000 and admonishments to continue to be careful of the livestock. Regardless, the losses hurt.[46]

A severe drought followed the harsh winter. Water was in short supply in the Turnersville area and throughout the region. There was little water in the creeks and rivers. Cattle and horses suffered the most as the grass began to dry up, and ranchers began supplemental feeding in early fall instead of around January when grass normally ran out. Fortunately, the Foote and Young ranches had already drilled sufficient water wells to survive a prolonged drought as long as the range provided forage for the animals.[47]

By 1886, the basic infrastructure of the ranch was in place. The Foote family, particularly father Adrian, kept a careful watch over the operation, supervising the building of sheds, the cultivation of fodder, and the placement of wells and windmills. Unsure of local quality, they continued to purchase New England equipment for their holdings, including another water pump costing $64.44 (shipping cost more than the pump) made by Henry Stowe in Boston. Later, Fred had to send to Boston for replacement rubber gaskets for the pumps. In his typical manner, Adrian chastised Fred for sending an actual gasket, but later noted that he had needed to have the exact size to order the replacement part. Their foresight paid off in the summer of 1887 when a prolonged drought hit the area. The Foote ranch fared much better than the surrounding area.[48]

Weather has always been the bane of the rancher's and farmer's fortunes. In 1889, the drought became so severe that Hurst Springs near Turnersville on the Young property became one of the few sources of water. William Young had to fence his springs, post a guard, and allot only two gallons a day to each person. But Foote had little trouble, since he no longer depended on surface water supplies. His herds did well. The losses to the other herds, however, were severe.[49]

That same year, a major depression began in New England, shutting down the Ashland mill and throwing most of the town out of work. Adrian, who remained in Ashland with Jessie and Henry, became lonely after his wife's death and contemplated selling the house. Unable to find a buyer because of the economic downturn, he remained there until his death. Jessie wrote Fred that "Ashland is dead." Henry complained and grumbled about just about everything. He continued to work for the mill and his father, and operated a business hauling goods throughout the local area. He employed several drivers and owned several teams and rigs. In 1887, he purchased a matched team of bay horses for $800 and added another wagon. Despite his complaining, he was doing all right for himself. In 1891, Henry visited the ranches one last time for about six months, living with Mary and Fred and their children. He returned to Ashland, convinced that ranching was not for him. He married Cora Elizabeth Cutter in 1892.[50]

Marketing wool from an isolated ranch on the Texas frontier was difficult. Although Augustus Schreiner had developed a market for wool in Kerrville and San Antonio, shipping the wool overland to these markets decreased the profits. The markups by factors as they sold from San Antonio to Houston and then shipped by boat from Houston for resale in Boston further reduced profits for the growers. On the advice of his neighbor, William Young, Fred Foote sent wool samples from his clip of 1881 to J. R. Franklin, a wool factor in Waco. Franklin graded the wool as "medium/clean" and sold the entire clip for 23 to 24 cents a pound. He shipped the wool to Boston by railroad. Franklin would continue to market their wool for the next decade.[51]

In 1883, Fred sold twelve bags of wool (about 6,000 pounds) through Franklin at 20 cents a pound, netting only $485 and depositing the funds in the Waco State Bank. He later sold ten bags of wool for 18 cents a pound. In 1884, trying to find a steady and reliable market for his wool, Franklin traveled through New

England, leaving sample fleeces with various mills. The mills were interested. They wanted a clean and dependable source of quality wool, and direct selling cut out the Texas and Boston middlemen, increasing profits for both the mills and the producers.[52]

With the encouragement of Adrian Foote and Ezra Morse, the local sheepmen tried to ship their wool directly to the market in Boston. In 1885, Foote and Franklin shipped his wool and that of William Young, causing great excitement in the family. Ezra Morse, a former resident of Ashland who owned and operated a sheep ranch near Turnersville with Fred Foote, had arranged to sell all the local wool through the Brown and Williams Company, a prominent Boston wool agent. Fred's wool arrived first and Adrian impatiently awaited the arrival of Morse so the bags could be opened. Adrian made several trips to Boston to look over the newly arrived wool. Morse's and Young's bags arrived several weeks later. Adrian and Henry returned several more times to the Boston market to view the grading and supervise the sale of the clip. The Foote wool was graded as medium and fine. The medium wool paid a premium at twenty-seven cents a pound because it better fit the machinery used in the New England woolen mills. The wool that graded fine sold later for 25 cents a pound. While in New England, Foote supervised the selling of Young's wool which had arrived on the ship *San Marcos* from the port of Galveston insured with the Phoenix Insurance Company of New York where he paid 0.75 percent ($23) to insure $2,882 of wool.

The prices in Boston dropped later that year to 18 cents a pound, and they stored eleven bags to wait for a better price in 1886. Wool at Waco sold at 19 to 21 cents a pound.[53]

On a return trip in 1885, Franklin stopped in Ashland and visited with Adrian Foote, who was also trying to establish an ongoing relationship with one of the New England wool factories. Franklin and Adrian traveled to Stafford Springs, Connecticut, to visit the Riverside Woolen Company, owned by Cyril Johnson and

Richard Beebe. There they attempted to presell their Texas clip to the factory. The owners liked the sample fleeces but were wary of changes in the quality from one year to the next and would not completely commit themselves without looking the wool over each year before purchase. They wanted Foote and Franklin to send ahead five to six fleeces, which the factory would keep. This arrangement, although good for the factory owners who got first right of refusal on quality wool, was not quite so good for the far-away producer. Later the next year, in response to Franklin's inquiries, Riverside Woolen Company sent John Norton to the ranch. Norton stayed at the Menger Hotel in San Antonio, attended the annual wool sale, and corresponded with Fred Foote before visiting the ranch. He traveled via railroad and took a sample fleece back with him. They failed to establish a permanent relationship.[54]

When Adrian discovered he would not have complete control of the proceeds from the sale, he was not happy. Fred had taken a partial advance payment in Waco for 15 cents a pound. Adrian took the remaining balance and repaid several debts, including the $650 loan from "Old Mike," who used the money to set off on a trip back to Ireland. Adrian kept the rest, sending Fred small increments over several months. Fred did not like being treated like brother Henry, with his father controlling every penny. He let Adrian know how he felt quite directly, resulting in strained relations for several months. Still, Fred did not receive the last $75 of the money until January 1887.

In 1886, the Footes and the Youngs again attempted to sell their wool in Boston. This time J. R. Franklin, the wool factor in Waco, visited the ranch and facilitated the shipment. Foote made arrangements to send the wool to Boston via Waco and Houston to Brown and Company. (Brown and Williams had split their business.) There, in the Boston market, the ranch wool was once again graded under the watchful eye of Adrian. Medium-grade wool, the primary product of the Foote herd, once again sold at a slightly higher price than fine wool. That year Fred arranged for the entire amount to be paid in Waco. His father said nothing.[55]

The wool clip for the year of 1886 cost $165 for shearing, $43 for the wool sacks, and $75 for hauling the product to Houston by rail. Young joined Foote and they shipped their wool to Boston on a seven-day steamboat trip from Galveston. Herding for the year cost $700. The wool sold for 24.25 cents a pound, a gross profit on 15,338 pounds of wool of $3719.47, for a net of $2,736.

The next year Fred Foote abandoned shipping directly to eastern markets. The family concluded that the difference in income from selling in Boston was too small to compensate for the increased cost and risk. They decided to sell all future clips in Waco or Houston. Although the Boston wool market offered access to foreign wool merchants and the price was higher, the cost of shipping the wool to Boston was also higher. After paying commissions to the Boston wool factors, the increase to profits was minimal. Paying for hauling the wool to Houston, shipping via steamship to Boston, storage in Boston, and the insurance to protect from losses consumed any potential profit.[56]

Wool sacks were often items of contention for the suppliers. Ranchers packed sheared wool fleeces into large bags of heavy cotton ticking that cost about $3 each. Each bag contained 250 to 500 pounds of wool. The stockmen wanted credit for the bags or to have them returned. The purchasers could resell the bags and considered them a bit of extra profit on their purchase. To add insult to injury, the purchaser deducted three pounds from the total fleece weight for the weight of the bags. Foote eventually bargained for a 1.5-pound deduction and the return of the bags.[57]

The year 1885 brought major changes to the Foote family. Grandmother Beardslee died in New Berlin, New York, in the spring of 1885. She had been living with her daughter Cornelia (Aunt Carrie) and her son-in-law Augustus. In September of that same year Mary Caroline Beardslee Foote died from cancer. Her will left each of the two girls, Jessie and Frances, $500 and half of her New York farm, Meeker Hill. She left each of her sons, Fred and Henry, $500 and half of her Texas land. She left her husband her portion of the house, her $3,000 life insurance, and $500 cash. He was not pleased. His wife had bypassed his control.[58]

When the family finished probating the will in 1886, the land in Texas was passed in joint and undivided ownership so Fred could continue to use the entire ranch. The girls rented Meeker Hill to their uncle John Foote for dairy farming, receiving $200 annually. The will had to be probated in New York, Massachusetts, and Texas, which delayed its completion. Several trunks of goods sent to Fred were his share of the personal inheritance. The shipment included several pictures and frames, pillowcases, sheets, quilts, and blankets. Also included were clothes: hats, stockings, flannel shirts, and a leather coat, among other things. The total value of the goods shipped was less than $80. That amounted to all the personal goods Fred received from his inheritance.[59]

In 1886, a dispute began that was typical of family businesses. It would continue for the next fifty years. When Mary Caroline Foote died in late 1885, she left each son an undivided half interest in her land. In late 1886, Henry Foote wrote his brother Fred that he wanted his half of the "sheep business." What constituted Henry's share of the assets became the subject of generational controversy. Fred Foote had moved to Texas and started the sheep ranch on his mother's 3,200 acres in 1875. He had lived there continuously and personally built all the buildings, drilled the water wells, shepherded the sheep, and married and built his family home on the ranch.

Henry had worked on the ranch for just six months in 1880, returning home because "the work was too hard, the weather too cold, the food too bad, and the country too lonely." Although he had returned in 1881 for another nine months, he went back home once again after an attack of scurvy. He had lived with his father and sisters in the family home free of charge since his return. Meanwhile, father Adrian Foote had sent thousands of dollars to pay for capital expenses and helped finance the purchase of an additional 2,300 acres. He had financed the down payment on other acreage, and father and each brother paid an equal one-third share on some of the notes. Fred and his father had split the cost of others but Fred paid for most of the improvements himself. Henry's share of the note payments had been deducted from his wages by his father because Henry drank and gambled his money away.[60]

Henry wanted to be free from his father's control, but the family was afraid he would lose his share and wanted to protect both Henry and their own investments. Henry was deaf, drank to excess, and tended to squander his money. He was continually looking for a better place and moved from job to job every year or so. He sent monthly letters to Fred complaining about his life and asking for more money as his "share." In 1886 he was working at his father's mill as an independent teamster and managing his father's rental tenements. Adrian continued to manage Henry's money, deducting living expenses and note payments and paying the debts Henry acquired while cavorting about. He kept Henry on a tight string, which Henry greatly resented.

The traditional division of income for such investments, and the contract made with his uncle, stated that Fred, as ranch manager, would receive half of the income from the wool and half the increase in the sheep herd. Fred had kept careful records and accounts, plowing all his income back into the ranch and living on less than $200 a year. Unfortunately, Fred did not keep track of ownership of the sheep that died or where he had invested his personal income. The questions which arose were: What exactly was the value of Henry's "share" and what was Fred's "work equity"? Eventually, Henry, Fred, and Adrian Foote worked out a division—one overly generous to the nonworking Henry. Fred paid Henry $200 a year from the ranch income as land rent but remained in control and owned all the sheep and improvements. They appointed sister Jessie the trustee for Henry, his land, and his income. But, as is so often the case, to his dying day Henry, his widow, and their children believed they had been cheated. Each sued at least once for a larger share but lost every time.[61]

Frances, a schoolteacher in neighboring Westchester, had stayed home to take care of their mother. In 1885, with her mother dead, Frances was now free to marry her fiancé, Will Barstow. Will had moved to Ord, Nebraska, where he worked in the wholesale grain and cattle business. Frances visited at least once to find and furnish a house. They finally married on November 30, 1886, "quietly and at home." She left with her new husband by train for Nebraska the first week in December. On the way, they stopped to visit Uncle Andrew in Illinois. Frances had her first child in 1887 and by 1890 had two children, a girl named Eileen and a boy named Adrian. Frances was not overly fond of the prairie, writing to Fred that "the prairie is the loneliest place I ever saw. To see so far and still see nothing. I just longed for a tree." For many years Frances wrote her sister in Ashton weekly and visited the family with her children every summer. She continued to send Fred her old copies of *Century* magazine. But gradually over the years her correspondence with her brother in Texas became less frequent. Although she frequently visited with her sister in Ashland, she eventually lost contact with the family.[62]

The family continued to buy land. By 1888, Fred Foote and his family had accumulated 6,729 acres by ownership or lease. On this land they grazed 4,000 sheep and assorted other livestock. Their taxes paid to the three counties amounted to $124 annually. By 1895, the ranch covered 7,590 acres.

Transition, 1880–1910

THE RAILROADS PROFOUNDLY CHANGED THE EXISTING agricultural system. In 1882, the Gulf, Colorado, and Santa Fe Railroad came through McLennan County, giving farmers unhampered access to Galveston and national markets. Over the previous decade, any summer when yellow fever or other diseases threatened Galveston, Houston quarantined the port city and closed the railroad, supposedly to prevent the spread of epidemics. But the Houston merchants also managed to close the road just in time to capture the cotton crop and ship it from the Houston warehouses to European markets.

As a consequence, in 1878 the businessmen in Galveston decided to build their own railroad to the interior cotton belt of Texas and to bypass Houston. They chartered the Gulf, Colorado, and Santa Fe Railroad, building west to Bremond below Harris County, sending a spur to Houston, then moving north through Temple and McGregor and on to Fort Worth. At the Oklahoma border it met the Atchison, Topeka, and Santa Fe Railway lines running south, giving the new system an entrance to northern and eastern markets.

With easy access to national markets, farmers moved to northwestern McLennan County and began to fence the open Blackland Prairies. Small towns, including McGregor, five miles from the Caufield Ranch headquarters, grew along the rail line to market local crops. As free and open range for cattle grazing came to a close in McLennan County, the cotton culture became dominant.[1]

Caufield continued to invest his earnings in land, eventually accumulating more than 20,000 acres, becoming one of the largest landowners in McLennan County. But livestock continued to be an important and profitable portion of their ventures as the Caufield Ranch began to ship cattle from the new McGregor rail yards. They began to move their cattle operations west to open grazing land.[2]

During the drought of 1886, the Caufields searched for grazing land, eventually purchasing land in northern Mexico, south of Tombstone, Arizona Territory. They shipped 6,000 head by train to El Paso and then drove them overland to a new ranch near the small village of Magdalena in the Mexican state of Sonora. Henry Caufield sent his twenty-three-year-old son, Thomas, and other trusted relatives to manage the cattle on this range. The ranch was successful, and by 1889, T. B. Hood, manager of the Mexican ranch, noted that he had counted 1,133 calves in 1887 and had sold 69 steers for $1,000 so far that year. He begged for a "car load of good young horses" to handle the increase in the cattle herd.[3]

While Henry Caufield maintained his operation in Mexico, his family and the Cavitts dealt with another interfamily affair. Bud Cavitt, one of Josephus Cavitt's sons, was living with his new wife in Coryell County on the Cavitt league, raising cattle along the Leon River. He began to suspect that his wife was cheating on him with his cousin Sid Cavitt. While riding through the little hamlet of Cavitt, Bud noted Sid's white horse outside the saloon. He went in to confront his cousin and ended up shooting the man. Thinking he had killed Sid, Bud quickly rode to his cousin Henry Caufield's ranch. After hearing the story, Henry put the boy on the train to the Mexico ranch with a letter to the foreman. A few months later Bud learned he had not killed his cousin but had severely wounded the lad.

Bud continued to work in Mexico for about six months before he became involved with a girl in a cantina in the town of Magdalena. The girl was the girlfriend of the local jefe, a local deputy sheriff. The two men had it out in the cantina and the Cavitt boy killed the deputy. Bud raced for the border and returned to the McGregor area. When he arrived, he discovered that he had not killed Cousin Sid. However, feeling guilty about the shooting, Bud's wife had cared for Sid while he recuperated. She and Sid had fallen in love and run away together. Bud swore off women as "entirely too much trouble."[4]

The new rail lines resulted in heightened immigration as primarily German farmers poured into the northwestern corner of McLennan County. The population of the county grew nearly fourfold in the two decades following the Civil War, rising from 6,000 in 1860 to more than 20,000 by 1880. Increasing settlement changed the nature of cattle ranching in McLennan County. The newcomers began to fence the open prairie and forced the Caufield family to abandon open-range cattle grazing. Farms, fences, and population also pushed the Chisholm Trail westward, making cattle drives from McLennan County longer and more expensive. Soon the Blackland Prairie between the three Bosque Rivers—the three come together at Waco to form the Bosque, which runs for five miles before merging with the Brazos River—filled with farmers and fencing. The free grass was gone. Free-range cattle ranching, which was dependent on large open spaces of cheap grasslands, moved westward as well.[5]

As Henry's children married, they no longer wanted to live on and manage the Mexican cattle lands. In 1892 the family decided to sell the ranch in Mexico to T. B. Hood, the ranch manager, and invested the proceeds in banking. The family sold the land in Shackleford County in 1903 when they abandoned their range cattle operation to concentrate on growing cotton.[6]

By 1890, the decline in the cattle industry had forced Central Texas ranchers like Henry Caufield to diversify from open range grazing into specialized livestock breeding. Beef prices had fallen after the great blizzard of 1886 and remained low the rest of the decade. Because cattle overgrazed the Texas prairie, the droughts during the following years kept herd sizes low. The railroads had brought immigrant farmers to the area, and windmills and barbed wire opened the Blackland Prairies to farmers, who now were able to fence the open range. Cotton began to replace cattle ranching as the primary agricultural product of Central Texas.

The more affluent and sophisticated consumers in the eastern cities began to demand young and tender beef. Texas ranchers responded by introducing different breeds in their livestock programs. This forced Central Texas ranchers such as Henry Caufield to diversify from open range grazing into specialized livestock breeding. In 1875 the Caufields introduced Durham (shorthorns) as the first crossbreed on his ranch, followed later by polled Angus and Herefords. These breeds matured earlier and produced more marbled and tender meat than the native, grass-fed longhorns. Besides being lean and tough to eat, the semi-feral longhorns were hard on fences and carried Texas tick fever. Fat and tender new breeds soon replaced the wild Longhorns.

The Caufields tried raising other types of livestock on the remaining pastureland. By 1885 they had 1,600 Merino sheep grazing on the main ranch. Sheep mixed well with cattle because they grazed on forbs, weeds, and short grasses, which cattle did not normally ingest. The mixture of purebred cattle, sheep, horses, and mules maximized the limited resources of the remaining pasturelands.

The Caufield Ranch proved to be no exception. In response to the changing conditions, Henry Caufield began to specialize in raising Shetland ponies and mules in the tree-shaded pastures adjoining the old ranch house along the South Bosque River and to convert the open pastures into cotton fields.[7]

SHETLAND PONIES

While diversifying their livestock, Caufield and his family intro-duced Shetland ponies into Texas and became, for the next thirty years, the largest Shetland pony operation west of the Mississippi River. While attending college in Tennessee, Mart Caufield had seen the small ponies and investigated where they came from. In 1890 the Caufields purchased their first purebred stallion, Ben Harrison, and a mare, Rhonda Miller, from Eli Elliott in West Liberty, Iowa. Elliott was the first major Shetland breeder in the United States. About 1880, Elliott began to import ponies directly from the Shetland and Orkney Islands, and in 1885 he established the American Shetland Pony Club as a registry for his full-blooded stock.[8]

The Caufield herd grew until they annually offered seventy-five ponies for sale. Following the death of H. J. Caufield in 1908, his sons-in-law, Joe Clifton and Josephus F. "Joe" Cavitt, continued to raise ponies until after World War I. They sold the last ponies in 1924. Eventually, the Caufield Ranch obtained a national reputa-tion. Circuses and carnivals and their performers throughout the United States became the major sales outlet for the ranch.[9]

Families, and particularly young women and children, favored Shetlands for pets because the ponies were gentle, inexpensive, and utilitarian animals that they could easily ride and that were strong enough to pull small buggies or two-wheeled carts. These ponies were only forty-five to fifty inches high at four years of age and were small enough for a child to control alone. An advertisement the Caufields placed in the *Farm and Ranch* magazine in 1917 brought a dozen responses from parents throughout the state.[10] Most wanted a pony for their child to ride to school and asked about price, color, or sex; spotted mares were the most popular. For a full-blooded spotted stallion, which could live as long as thirty years and was registered with the American Shetland Pony Club, the Caufields charged as little as $175. Half-breeds and three-quarter-breeds were even less; geldings cost only $85 to $100.

Shetlands have a reputation for having poor dispositions and for biting and kicking, but Henry Caufield maintained that properly broken ponies were never mean. United States commissioner Joe Clifton, Caufield's son-in-law, recalled in an *El Paso Herald-Post* article that, "while we were getting ready for the parade, we'd often give those Shetlands a real mauling. We would hang onto their necks, pull their tails, and crawl in and out between their legs. They'd take anything. Best natured animals I ever saw."[11]

Although the Caufield grandchildren were the first to get their own ponies, most of the children in McGregor and the surrounding farms and ranches soon acquired Shetlands. Eventually they formed a Shetland Pony Brigade, with the Caufield Ranch as the sponsor. Those who could not afford the pets could ride one at the ranch. Initially, the brigade trained in the corral next to the ranch house; later they practiced their drills on the McGregor High School grounds. The riding club continued for years, and many local children participated in its programs.[12]

The Shetland Pony Brigade became a popular event in McGregor as the club members and their parents turned costume making into a social affair in which town members sewed fancy cowgirl/cowboy outfits with large hats and fringe. The entire community watched the practices, and the riders quickly learned to ride four abreast and to perform simple drills.

In addition to being included in most of the local parades, the brigade became a feature in the annual Cotton Palace procession. Because Waco was too far to ride from McGregor and the unpaved roads were too muddy for a stock wagon—no motorized trucks existed in those days—the parents transported the ponies into Waco in cattle cars on the Cotton Belt Railroad. The mothers packed picnic baskets and entire families rode the "dinky," the electric train, from McGregor to Waco. The fathers gathered to unload the horses and saddle and unsaddle the ponies before and after the parades. Usually the families watched the parades together and socialized. Several old photographs show the Shetland Pony Brigade in front of the old Cotton Palace Exhibition Hall and marching four abreast through downtown Waco.[13]

Despite the local visibility of the Shetland Pony Brigade, the most important buyers for the ranch stock remained circus performers. Eastern circuses such as Barnum's sent buyers each year to pick ponies for their shows. Other carnivals traveled through Texas each year, including the Bailey family, who wintered their circus northwest of Hillsboro near Blum and the Miller Brothers 101 Ranch Wild West show from the Panhandle. During the winter, freedom from daily appearances allowed performers from all over the United States the leisure to travel to the South Bosque and to choose, break, and train their ponies.[14]

Once at the ranch the circus people followed a standard training routine. Each performer chose a horse matched for size and temperament and trained all winter with that animal. Because Shetland ponies were the favorite mounts for the dwarfs and midgets, the "little people," the ranch kept a special bunkhouse with chairs and beds cut down to accommodate the small riders' size. At the ranch the horses learned a variety of tricks, including allowing small dogs to jump onto their backs as they ran around a ring. When they finished their training, the diminutive riders and their mounts paraded once more down the main street of McGregor to the train station and returned to their circuses.[15]

Small-town life slowed in the winter after the crops had been harvested and the muddy roads isolated the farms. But in December 1901 a sequence of events unfolded that sent a stir of anticipation through the cold, blustery air of McGregor. A cowboy drove Henry Caufield's buckboard down Main Street to the train station. The passenger train from Fort Worth and points east had arrived and discharged passengers, something that did not happen every day in a town as small as McGregor. This could only mean one thing: that the circus performers had arrived on the train and would be riding the buckboard down Main Street en route to the Caufield Ranch to buy Shetland ponies. Usually during the ride the carnival actors waved to the crowds that gathered along the sidewalks. In anticipation of a free show, the local merchants kept a watchful eye on Main Street through their windows.[16]

MULES

The Caufield family enlarged their mule herd to meet the demand from cotton farmers. They had started to breed mules in 1852, shortly after beginning to ranch in McLennan County when the Caufield brothers brought mules, horses, and jacks to Texas from their family home in Alabama. Receipts and trail notes document animals driven overland through Louisiana and others shipped from Mobile and New Orleans to Houston. In an early letter dated May 1860, Henry J. Caufield wrote his brother Watson that "your mare had a mule colt, ten days old, the smallest thing I ever saw." The brothers used American Standard Donkey jacks, a breed much larger than the Mexican burro common in Texas at that time. In 1866, Caufield purchased the IXL brand, which became the trademark for his horses and mules for the next seventy-five years.[17]

No other animal has had as profound an impact on American agriculture, particularly the Southern cotton culture, as the mule.

Because of their ability to endure heat and abuse as well as to sub-
sist on poor fodder while carrying heavy loads over hard roads in
hot climates, mules became the animals of choice to pull the plows
and wagons on Southern farms.[18]

As livestock moved to West Texas and the open range country, farmers poured into Central Texas, placing millions of acres
of the Blackland Prairie under production. They created such a
demand for mules that by 1889 a good mule sold for $100, more
than most horses. Responding to the opportunity, the Caufields
became a large producer of mules. Originally the Caufields used
most of the animals they raised in their own farming operation,
loaned them to their tenants, or sold them to other local farmers.
Over time, by advertising in newspapers and farm journals, the
Caufields expanded their commercial mule operation to include
farms operated by son-in-law Joe Cavitt on his family league along
the Leon River. Subsequently, the Caufield Ranch became the
largest producer of mules in Central Texas, breeding up to sixty
animals annually.[19]

Eventually, mules and Shetland ponies became the major livestock product of the ranch. Several jacks regularly won prizes at
local fairs and became much-sought mates for local mares. The
Caufields received special inquiries from around the state for
Sampson, their prize jack, for stud, and Sampson's colts became
prized as matched teams.[20]

Cotton requires good soil and a warm climate to flourish, and
the fertile Blackland Prairies of Texas, an area stretching south
from the Red River through Central Texas and ending just north
of San Antonio, offered an ideal habitat. By the last decade of
the nineteenth century, Texas had become the largest producer of
cotton in the United States, growing 1.9 million bales of fiber on
7.1 million acres (0.33 bales per acre) out of the 20 million bales
grown on 15.8 million acres nationwide. In 1900 the Blackland
Prairie region produced 44 percent of the cotton in Texas, over 1

million bales, in 1900. Any area that grew large amounts of cotton needed mules to pull the plows, and the Texas Blackland Prairie region was no exception.[21]

In the Southern cotton culture, mules also became an important social symbol. The ownership of a mule elevated the owner from sharecropper status to that of tenant farmer. A sharecropper used the landowners' equipment and livestock and was legally viewed as a hired hand. A tenant farmer, who possessed his personal animals and legally owned his crop, was an independent contractor and was not subject to the whims and caprices of the landowner. In addition, mules hauled farm wagons loaded with cotton to the local gins, and adults and children rode them to town for social events.

For over one hundred years Americans considered mules more valuable than horses and, despite the difficulty in breeding mules, their numbers increased steadily. In the West, freighters and stagecoach owners preferred mules to other beasts of burden to pull heavy wagons over the dry, rocky trails. The United States Army came to depend on mules to pull its wagons transporting military equipment, and mule pack trains helped defeat the Apache and other southwestern Indians.

Mules for the cotton farmers usually came from local breeders and a few larger commercial breeders. The military, freighters, and other large-scale buyers came to depend on regional stockyards to supply their needs. In 1808 the United States Department of Agriculture listed 855,000 mules, valued at $66 million. By 1897 the count had increased to 2.2 million mules valued at $103 million. By 1910, during the so-called Cotton Boom, the number of mules in the United States grew to 4.1 million, each worth about $120. Horses during the same period decreased in number and were valued at less than $90 apiece. By 1880 the largest cotton-growing states—South Carolina, Georgia, and Alabama—had more mules than horses. In 1897, Texas had 1.1 million horses worth about $18 each and 261,000 mules valued at $30 each. By 1910 the number of mules in Texas had increased to over 1 million animals, and by 1926, Texas, the home of cowboys and cattle drives, contained more mules than horses.[22]

The mule is a fascinating creature. It is a sterile hybrid, a cross between a male donkey (jack) and a female horse. Hybrid vigor predicates that mules have a larger body size and greater endurance than either of their parents. They survive better on poor forage and live and work longer than either donkeys or horses. In coat, height, and shape, they look like a horse. But one can always tell a mule from a horse by the tail. Horses have a short tail bone with long hair. Donkeys and mules have a long tailbone with a short-haired tassel tail. And a mule brays more like a donkey, while horses and hinnies (a stallion–female donkey hybrid) neigh.[23]

Equine hybrids—mules and hinnies—have been common since early civilization. Sumerian texts indicate that they bred hybrids as early as 2800 BC. Initially, the hinny was much more common in the Middle East because donkeys ran wild in the desert, while horses were rare and imported from the Mediterranean area. Since Roman times, however, the mule, a stronger and more robust hybrid, has been bred most frequently. Hinnies are rare today.[24]

The characteristics of a mule—the sobriety, patience, endurance, and sure-footedness of the donkey combined with the vigor, strength, and courage of a horse—make the hybrid preferable as a working animal. Mules have a thicker and less sensitive hide. Thus, they can wear a harness longer without damaging their skins. Their hooves are harder and show more resistance to disease, which is especially important in muddy clay soils. A mule eats less and needs less protein and forage than horses. Yet, a pack mule will allow itself to be fully loaded by a familiar teamster and placidly follow a bell mare all day, day after day, without balking. As for being stubborn, mules quit working and refuse to perform any task it feels will endanger its life. You can work a horse to death, but a mule will stop and refuse to go on.

The hinny, a cross between a male horse and a female donkey (a Jennet or Jenny), looks more like a horse. It has the tail and head of a horse and whinnies more like a horse but has the body and legs of a mule. Hinnies are smaller, because their donkey mothers are smaller, and thus are less desirable for farm work and pulling freight, but they are favored to pull ladies' carriages.

While horses have sixty-four chromosomes and donkeys have sixty-two chromosomes, mules and hinnies have sixty-three chromosomes. Researchers have found that it is easier to breed from a male with a smaller number of chromosomes to a female with a larger number. Thus, hinnies are more difficult to produce and are far less common than mules. The extra chromosome seems to come from the male. A mule resembles a donkey more than a horse and a hinny resembles a horse more than a donkey.[25]

Generally, hybrid animals like mules are born with all the necessary sexual equipment, except the males are sterile. Eighty percent of mules are male. Although sterile, male mules still produce testosterone; thus male mules are usually gelded to make them more manageable. An occasional female mule (called a molly) has estrus cycles. In rare instances, female mules have produced an offspring. A fertile female mule will deliver a donkey colt when bred with a jack donkey sire and a horse colt when bred with a stallion.[26]

The terms used to describe donkeys and mules have changed over time. The original Large American donkey, bred from two Catalan or Spanish jacks, was a gift to George Washington by the king of Spain. The carefully bred offspring from these large donkeys became the American Standard donkey. Over the last century, however, the present donkey strains have become so genetically mixed that they are described by size rather than by place of origin. Those strains, originally noted in breeding records as Maltese, Catalan, or Spanish donkeys, are now designated as Large Standard jacks, which stand twelve to fourteen hands high. Other new categories include the Mammoth jacks (fourteen hands and larger), the Standard donkey, previously called a burro (eight to twelve hands), and the Miniature Mediterranean donkeys (less than eight hands).[27]

Because individual farmers bred most mules for their personal use or to market in local livestock yards, only a few large commercial breeders existed. Records from these breeders are sparse. The Caufield Ranch, located in Central Texas, ran a large commercial mule business and kept careful records of their mule breeding operation.

Cotton farmers looked for big, muscular animals with good legs and feet to pull plows to withstand the sticky black clay soil of Central Texas. In addition, the farmers wanted teams of mules that could plow the initial "sod busting" on the prairie, a task that would quickly break down a team of oxen or horses. Consequently, stockmen bred mules for size and strength rather than color.

The most desirable colts came from American Standard donkey jacks, which were large, hardy, and intelligent. These jacks stood up to sixteen hands high and weighed up to twelve hundred pounds. When bred with large mares, they produced the finest mules for the American market. Their offspring were easily able to pull a plow through the difficult and muddy "black waxy" soil of Central Texas. These were exactly the kind of mules the Caufield Ranch produced.[28]

As their superior breeding stock became well known, the Caufields' jacks became much-sought-after mates for local mares. Their prize jack, Sampson, a large American Standard donkey, produced large and particularly strong mules, and his colts became prized as matched teams for the new larger, multi-row agricultural equipment. Sampson became a popular sire for the nearby farmers and stood at stud year-round. Sampson and his prodigy usually won most of the ribbons in local and regional fairs. Joe Cavitt, Caufield's son-in-law, who had taken over the management of the family livestock business about 1906, registered Sampson's pedigree with the *American Jack Stock Stud Book*, which noted that Sampson had been bred in 1904 from a cross between a Spanish jack named Jack Dewey M and an American Donkey jennet. Registration as a breeding bloodline gave the jack even more prestige.[29]

The Caufield Ranch's breeding program had three components. The standard practice for breeding mules required a farmer desiring a mule to bring his mare to the ranch for mating with one of Joe Cavitt's jack donkeys. Because horses did not like the smell of donkeys, mares were often averse to breeding with the donkey stallions. Breeders often had to blindfold the mares and pen them in stalls for mating. Once the animals had mated, the mare returned to the owner's pastures. The stud fee ranged from $5 to $50 and the horse's owners paid after the colt was born. Unfortunately, stud fees were often difficult to collect, as tenant farmers moved away, denied the colts survived, or defaulted on their debts.[30]

Because the mule is a cross between species, the miscarriage and deformity rates are much higher than with intraspecies breeding; therefore, not every mating produced a viable colt. The stud records for 1916 showed twenty-six animals bred to local mares. Eighteen of these mares produced live offspring. Of the eighteen mule colts born in 1916, Cavitt was unable to locate two farmers who seemed to have left the area, and twelve months later three had not yet paid their stud fees. He collected thirteen stud fees of $10 to $20 each, a high price for the times, for a net income of $300 from this part of his program.[31]

In addition to stud fees from local farmers, the ranch annually produced twenty to sixty of its own mule colts. These sold readily to farmers seeking large animals to pull the new multi-row plows and harrows. A quality mule sold for $100 to $200.

The third element of the ranch program included jacks and jennets sired by Sampson or other donkeys, which the Caufields sold to other breeders. The whole enterprise netted about $3,000 to $6,000 annually. By the turn of the century, the mule business had become one of the most profitable enterprises on the Caufield Ranch, not only because of their superior breeding stock but also because of the family's reputation for honesty. Local farmers came to know Cavitt as an honest trader who would sell his livestock at a fair price to anyone coming to his corrals. With a creditable reputation and good stock, he conducted a lively trade.[32]

Most farming towns sponsored a horse and mule lot where local farmers, breeders, and traders purchased and sold their animals. Cavitt kept his animals in the McGregor mule yard or on his Leon River ranch, located several miles away in Coryell County, and brought the available stock into town on the third Monday of the month, McGregor's trade day. In the mule yard, salesmen offered animals from all over Central Texas. Farmers seeking a new animal or traders looking for new stock quickly recognized Caufield Ranch mules as some of the best and crowded his barns; business was brisk.[33]

Several other traders brought animals to the mule lots. Many local entrepreneurs collected individual mules bred by nearby farmers, broke them to harness, and drove the animals to regional trade days. Most did not make much profit, considering the difficulty of breaking and caring for the hybrids. Itinerant professional mule traders, known for their sly methods of fixing up and selling old or nervous animals, also traveled around the small farming communities of the state, arriving in the towns on trade day with a remuda of horses and mules for sale or trade. These wandering traders tried to trick each other as well as any innocent buyer who fell into their web. The most experienced professional traders became famous for dyeing the gray hair of older animals to make them look younger, for pumping air under the skin of sick animals to make them look healthy and muscular, and for resorting to other tricks to obtain higher prices for worn-out mules. They even learned to disguise the age of an animal by filing its teeth. Farmers learned to avoid such roving traders.[34]

Joe Cavitt, after assuming control of the Caufield Ranch breeding program in 1906, expanded and commercialized its livestock operation to fill the Central Texas regional demand and to increase ranch revenues. In 1910, he began to advertise his mules in various regional magazines and newspapers. A favorite for local farmers was the *Texas Farm and Ranch*, and for several years, Cavitt paid $20 annually for a full-page advertisement for the Cavitt Mule and Shetland Pony Farms. He also advertised in local newspapers. An advertisement in the *Comanche Chief and Pioneer Exponent*, a weekly newspaper, cost only $1 for four notices but produced one quick sale. As his reputation grew, he eventually sold most of the animals to buyers from counties as far north as Denton and as far west as Tom Green. Unfortunately, although the demand was constant and Cavitt received letters every week looking for animals, many purchasers paid their debts slowly, sending only small partial payments and begging for more time.[35]

Many buyers continued to depend on Cavitt for advice and insight even after they had purchased their animals. One buyer, Milton Wallace, wrote a constant stream of letters about his jack studs, the progeny of Sampson, that he had recently purchased from Cavitt. In March, his two jacks, Chief and Big Bill, won first and second place at the local county fair. The next month the jubilant Wallace reported they had serviced thirty-one mares. Then the animals took two weeks off, to the consternation of the new owner. During the donkeys' vacation, the owner beseeched Cavitt for advice on improving their performance. Among other solutions, Cavitt recommended better feed and a private, quiet breeding lot. When the animals picked up the pace after several weeks, the owner gleefully reported they had serviced five mares in less than a week.[36]

The mule has never been a very romantic animal. Unlike the gallant, lively horse, the patient, plodding ox, and even the simple, humble burro, mules never received much respect—until someone needed to pull a plow through gummy black clay or carry a heavy load over difficult terrain. For over one hundred years, the mule was the primary beast of burden in the rural South and played a central role in the cotton culture. But by the 1950s agricultural mechanization, especially tractors, had replaced the mule. In the mountainous West and desert Southwest, with few developed roads, the mule continued to play an important role in pulling freight wagons and in pack trains, and mules continued to pull wagons loaded with borax in Death Valley. Nevertheless, the relentless advance of infrastructure—roads and bridges capable of serving automobiles and trucks—finally made the mule redundant. As demand decreased, existing animals were not replaced; breeders turned to more lucrative stock; mule lots closed; mule alley (in the Fort Worth Stockyards) closed; and the mule became a rarity on American farms. After dominating the livestock economy for almost a century, as the agricultural economy mechanized, mules rapidly declined in numbers and importance and now have virtually vanished from American farms. As the number of mules plummeted, they became relegated to the role of a genetic oddity and an archaic pet. The day of the mule had passed.

By 1883, the Caufields and their neighbors began to ship cattle by railroad directly to the Chicago stockyards. They gathered their stock at the new cattle pens in McGregor, where the ranchers carefully delineated the brands and earmarks on the cattle before they were shipped so they could divide the proceeds accurately. In 1885 their records indicate they sent several carloads of cattle to the Union Stock Yards, where Gregory, Cooley & Co. sold the cattle in lots over several weeks. They netted $1,324 on a $1,550 sale price for the first lot of forty head. Additional lots of Caufield cattle sold for $5,576, $3,568, and $1,212, a total ranch income from this one shipment of $10,356. Neil McLennan, Josephus Cavitt, and Noah Neff sold additional cattle in the same shipment.[37]

Neff had ridden to Chicago with the cattle shipment to ensure that they were fed, watered, and well treated. The railroad recognized the need for stockmen to care for their animals during the week-long trip and provided one free passage for every four cattle cars. The free passenger also cared for injured and fallen livestock. Neff drew $40 to cover his expenses for the trip. He must have enjoyed the job, because he rode with the shipments every year for a decade.

The ranchers continued to ship cattle on the railroad. In 1885, the Caufield Ranch netted $4,516 on six carloads. In 1886, they sent five carloads and sold them through Paxson, Shattuck & Son. McLennan netted $995 on his share. In 1887, the cattle arrived just before the market fell and Caufield sold 102 head at $3 a hundredweight for a total of $2,770 (about $27 a head). Later that summer the price of cattle fell to less than $10 a head and did not reach previous prices until World War I.[38]

Stockyards soon opened closer, including those in St. Louis, Kansas City, and Fort Worth, which made it no longer necessary for cattle owners to ship their stock long distances. The Fort Worth Stockyards opened in 1903 and the ranchers immediately began to send their cattle to the new facility. Swift and Armour opened slaughterhouses near the new stockyards and paid competitive prices for livestock. They could butcher the animals locally, ship the carcasses to Eastern markets, and still make a profit. In Chicago, the commission agents had charged high prices for freight, yardage, forage, and commissions. They charged again to send bank drafts to the ranchers back to Central Texas. When the rival stockyards opened, they charged lower prices for forage and commissions and the cost of shipping was considerably less. Fort Worth was also much closer, which decreased expenses: freight charges, commissions, and shrinkage (the weight loss of cattle from urine and feces excretion). In addition, the Texas banks also did not charge to transfer funds within the state.[39]

Changes in the banking system also made local stockyards more attractive to Texas stockmen. After 1885, Caufield and his partners used the new banking system to forward credit to their local banks rather than carrying cash on them during the long trip home. The group transferred the money through the Drovers National Bank in the Union Stock Yards to the Waco National Bank. The Chicago banks began to delay payment and to charge for transfers, making local stockyards more attractive sale sites.[40]

The Caufields responded quickly to the changes in the local economy. Cattle had overgrazed the prairie and now farmers had fenced the open range. As ranchers lost access to free open grasslands for their cattle, cotton replaced cattle ranching as the primary agricultural product of Central Texas. The Caufield Ranch proved to be no exception. Henry Caufield had begun to specialize in raising mules and Shetland ponies in the hilly, tree-shaded pastures adjoining the old ranch house along the South Bosque River. He gradually converted his remaining open pastures into cotton fields.

Mary Jane Caufield Young and her husband were farther from the new rail lines and felt their effect much less than Henry. Following the cessation of hostilities in 1865 and the return of Federal troops to the Texas frontier, William Young had moved his family back to Coryell County and resumed raising sheep. Although the size of their herds had fallen to about half the prewar level, the next ten years were ones of prosperity as the price of wool rose and their flocks expanded. Wholesale prices for wool, which had been 30 cents a pound in 1861, dropped to 20 cents a pound during the years immediately following the war, but no lower than

20 cents during the ensuing decade. Unfortunately, the price of wool followed the general downward drift of farm prices at the end of the nineteenth century, reaching lows of 8 cents a pound in 1897 before rising to 39 cents in 1900. Prices continued to be high throughout the first two decades of the twentieth century. By 1880, the family's herds had increased from 1,131 to 2,655 head. Sheep sold for $1.25 to $2.50 a head throughout this period.[41]

As prosperity returned to the Young family after the end of the Civil War, they built a large stone house on a small hill near a spring-fed creek that ran toward the nearby Middle Bosque River. The creek passed an older wooden home that was turned into a bunkhouse. Although Young hauled the lumber himself by oxcart on a ten-day trip from Marlin, the house was expensive. Built in 1871, the two-story house took two years and cost more than $2,000 to construct—quite a sum for those days, equivalent to about $200,000 today. The costs included $1,010 for materials, $115 for hauling, $115 for sand, $460 for masons, and $368 for carpenters. The resulting structure contained six rooms, two staircases, and a chimney in every room. The kitchen was a separate structure in the back of the house. A kitchen, dining room, and bathroom facilities were added over the years. Young added a barn, sheep pens, hog pens, and cattle sheds as well. An elegant driveway and garden that included the small cemetery were built. This was quite a mansion for that part of the country. There the Youngs embarked on their new life and raised a family.[42]

Young and both his first and second families lived in the structure. The second family inherited the dwelling and lived in it until 1927, when the house burned. Today, fallen stones cover the ground and only the remnants of walls remain, covered with vines.

After the Civil War, William Young's family continued to grow. Four additional children were born over the next decade. The Young children were Elizabeth (Lizzie) Caufield Young (b. 1858), William (Willie) Watson Young (b. 1860, d. 1866), Mary

Ann Young (b. 1861), Catherine (Katie) Cavitt Young (b. 1863), Josephine (Josie) Young (b. 1865), and William Thomas Young (b. 1866). Willie, who died at five, was buried on the hill next to the stone house. Mary Ann married Frederick Foote, Lizzie married D. W. Freeland, Katie married E. G. Tenney, and Josie married E. A. Brenholtz. All the husbands continued to work on the Young ranch. The three daughters lived within a few miles of their parents. They watched closely over the happenings at home and church, teaching Sunday school and discussing events extensively.

As the depression following the end of the Civil War ended, the people around Turnersville began to think of building a real church. The congregations in the area agreed to build a union church; one Sunday each month was allotted by turns for Methodists, Presbyterians, Church of Christ (Christian), and Baptists. They agreed to share the cost. William Young took the lead in negotiating and financing the church. He sent several wagon teams to Waco and the railroad at Valley Mills to pick up the needed wood and other fixtures. The wagon returning from Waco was delayed by rain and muddy roads, arriving at Turnersville midday on a Sunday. Young declared they had blasphemed the Lord's Day by working and that the wood was not fit for a church. He bought the lot and used it to build hog pens on his farms. He sent the wagons back to get another load, cautioning them not to drive on Sunday. The church stands today.[43]

The Franco-Prussian War created a shortage of wool for uniforms in the latter part of 1870. The price jumped from 18 cents a pound in 1870 to 33 cents a pound in 1871, peaking at 38 cents a pound in 1872. San Antonio handled 600,000 pounds of wool in 1871, more than 3 million pounds in 1879, and 8 million pounds in 1886.[44]

The high prices for wool started a nationwide "sheep boom" as ranchers throughout Texas and the West moved into large-scale sheep production. A Mexican export duty of 37.5 to 50 cents a head retarded the natural market to the south. Herdsmen imported most of the local sheep from Missouri and Arkansas, adding a few from Mexico. As a result, the numbers of Texas sheep increased rapidly throughout the state but primarily in South Texas: from 2 million out of 39 million nationwide in 1867 to 6 million out of 57 million in 1885.

In the Cross Timbers region of Coryell County, sheep numbers rose from 10,000 to more than 100,000 head. In the Hill Country of Texas, Captain Charles Schreiner founded a cooperative wool and mohair market and warehouse at Kerrville to handle the growth in wool production. Schreiner shipped his wool through San Antonio to Houston and Boston. Young prospered in this period and was soon joined by a young neighbor, Frederick Foote, who also began to raise sheep. As the boom continued into 1890, factories in the East processed 15 million pounds of wool, but soon the price of wool began to fall from oversupply.[45]

Young kept careful accounts of the expenses for his herdsmen and of the wages he paid all his workers. He generally kept two men busy year-round. In 1866, Young paid George Redfran $15 monthly to herd sheep for three months. A $5 cash advance, $2 for cloth for shirts, $3 for two pairs of shoes, and $2.50 for tobacco gave the herdsman a $32.50 payout at the end of the quarter. Likewise, herdsman John Jones received a $5 cash advance, $2.75 for 2 shirts, $2.50 for tobacco, $2.50 for two pairs of shoes, and $1.25 for a rope deducted from his pay of $15 per month for four months, earning a net income of $46. Other wages were similar. Shearing cost 5 cents an animal, averaging $18 a day for each worker. Two days of plowing paid $2. These seemed to be standard wages for the region and the work. The total expenses for the wool of 1879 showed shearing costing $87; sacks, $26; and of hauling twenty-three sacks (7,642 pounds) of wool to Houston, $24. The wool brought $923, for a net profit of $748. Young usually made about twice that, sending eighty sacks of wool in 1884.

The Young family continued to prosper on their nearby sheep ranch and began to look at amenities for their children. Since education was important to these Scotch-Irish Presbyterians, and since there were few settlers in the region, Young contracted with tutors for the children even though he was on the county school board. In 1874 he hired a Miss Elizabeth Hovey for $10 a month to teach his and neighboring children using the church building at Thorp Springs as a schoolhouse. He purchased five dictionaries ($3.33), two grammar books ($2.50), a music book ($1.33), and three other books ($2.55) for the school. The following year he paid Mrs. Ann Black $50 for the six-month school year. By 1880 the school in Turnersville had grown and became the center for education for the town and surrounding farms and ranches. Young, with his sons-in-law, contributed the majority of the funds to build a new schoolhouse at Turnersville in 1896. Many of the children drove or rode to school on Shetland ponies purchased from the Caufield ranches.

Unmarried women, especially teachers, were under constant surveillance by the town. Mary Young wrote about one new teacher, "I don't like her looks. She is about 15, low and fleshy. She dresses in bright colors and wears much jewelry." Perhaps this censure was because Mary was twenty-five and unmarried and allowed only "proper, Christian" clothing by her father.[46]

Every one of the children of William Young and almost all of his grandchildren attended college. Most attended Daniel Baker College, the Presbyterian school in Brownwood. For a time, Young lived in Brownwood, supervising the education of his progeny. At one time nineteen children from the Turnersville Unity Presbyterian Church were attending college. The family stated that a member of the Freeland family attended Daniel Baker College every year for thirty-five years.[47]

The Young household took religion very seriously. The family did all possible chores and cooking on Saturday so Sunday could be a day of rest. Young even considered whistling an unseemly act of frivolity and levity. Church attendance was mandatory. All the Young daughters, at one time or another, served as Sunday school teachers or pianists for the congregation. Prohibition also fit their views quite nicely.[48]

The Unity Presbyterian Church of Turnersville, established in 1871 by elder Levi Tenney, was one of the first Presbyterian churches in Coryell County. The Presbyterian church in Gatesville was not built until several decades later. The initial church building located near Thorp Springs about a mile southeast of Turnersville was a log cabin that also served as a schoolhouse for the younger children. A newer building, erected in 1877 and rebuilt in 1882, was a simple wooden frame building located in town. It also served as a school. William Young and later his sons-in-law were the major contributors to each of the new buildings. In 1906, the congregation erected the present Unity Presbyterian Church building.[49]

Levi Tenney, later a well-known figure in the Presbyterian Church of Texas, officiated as moderator and later served as minister of the newly formed church. In 1882 his son, Edward Tenney, married William Young's daughter. Levi Tenney left the area for a larger church about 1885. The church obtained another preacher, hiring Dr. Charles McHucheon and his young wife, who later became the second wife of William Young. McHucheon had first come through the area raising money for a Presbyterian church in Gatesville, obtaining $70 from the citizens of Turnersville, including $20 from William Young and $10 from Fred Foote. He returned to service the community full time until his death in 1887.[50]

Young also continued to purchase land as it became available. By 1887 he owned 2,795 acres worth $10,190 and livestock worth $6,265, including 2,200 sheep, 120 horses, as well as cattle and hogs. In 1892, after the division of his estate with the children from his first wife, Young had 1,362 acres left, along with 2,700 sheep and 30 horses. In addition, Young was agent (lessee) for

D. E. Kerney's 1,147 acres and 240 acres from Mrs. L. E. Young (his brother George's widow). He had thirty-one sheep in the herd belonging to his children, for which he paid them a prorated share of each year's wool.[51]

Entertainment was not lacking, even in the countryside. Church on Sunday was a social gathering lasting most of the day. Although the weekdays were filled with work—cleaning, washing, ironing, and cooking—the Young home was just off the highway from Crawford and visitors were frequent, often staying overnight. Likewise, Mary visited her sisters in town, spending the evenings and nights with their families. Reading and letter writing filled the evenings. Weekends often consisted of trips to town for goods, conducting business, or parties or get-togethers at other neighbors' houses. In a two-month period, Mary Young visited ten friends, received ten or more visitors, and went to eight parties and dinners. She chose not to go to several more.[52]

The center of William Young's first family was Mary Ann Young. She was a prolific correspondent, writing several dozen letters each week. Judging from her correspondence, Mary Ann Young was also quite opinionated. While she was being courted by Frederick Foote, her sister Josie was also being courted by Edward Brenholtz. Mary Ann did not like Brenholtz, who was a Quaker from Illinois. She considered him an opportunist who exploited his relationship with her sister to move into the big house and live well. She thought him lazy, never doing his share of the work about the ranch, and a hypocrite for quoting scripture to her father and "sweet talking the old folks" while cussing and lying behind Young's back. She called him a "serpent" who bad-mouthed brother William and anyone else who stood in his way to fortune. The girls' mother protected and favored Brenholtz (in Mary's opinion), while her father ignored the whole situation.

During the 1885 holiday season, Fred Foote married Mary Ann Young at her parents' home near Turnersville, Texas, after a six-month engagement. Fred had told his family of his interest in Mary as early as the spring of 1885 and announced his engagement in August. The exact date of the wedding was not decided until late November of that year. As the wedding plans developed, Mary wrote her brother William all the details. During the summer, Mary began to accumulate her trousseau, starting with a calico dress. She shopped in Turnersville, Gatesville, and Waco, picking out lace trim and brown fabric for her wedding dress, a hat, and matching shoes, all of which were shipped via Turnersville; she anxiously awaited each item. She lamented her father's parsimoniousness in not allowing her free rein to buy her clothes and accessories. She even threatened to run away and get married elsewhere several times. Fred kept her steady and on track. As the money from the wool and from her sheep came in, William Young gave his daughter amounts sufficient to purchase a wool dress, gloves, and other accessories.

At last, the couple settled on December 31 as their wedding date and Mary began to prepare for the event. For several weeks before the wedding, Mary had fussed about her personal goods and clothes and their transfer to her new home. She seems to have tried to take most of the family linen. Her mother gave her ample sheets and blankets but stopped her from taking anything else. Next she stewed over the food for the reception. She baked three cakes. The ranch hands brought her a turkey they had killed. She got a goose from her mother and her father purchased a barrel of apples. The ceremony was held at the ranch with Dr. McHucheon officiating and mainly family in attendance. The wedding went off without a hitch.[53]

Six months after Mary was married, Brenholtz married Josie Young in a ceremony at the Young home. The couple continued to live in the Young home, but their relationship with old William Young began to change. He tolerated much less from the couple, especially after his wife died. Within a year they had their first child and William moved them to a tenant house several miles from the family home. With time and after the arrival of children, Mary Ann began to soften toward her sister but never seems to have had much use for her brother-in-law. The other sisters, who were older and had their own families and homes, seem to have tolerated the situation with more equanimity.

Mary Jane Caufield Young died in April 1888 and was buried next to her child in a plot near her stone house. She had been in ill health for several years and as she faded during the last six months, the sisters took turns caring for her. Sister Lizzie Freeland seems to have carried most of the burden. After her funeral, the family carried her body from the dining room where the service had been held to her garden for burial. Forty people attended her funeral supper. They enclosed her grave in an iron fence and planted her favorite herb, garlic, about her tombstone, where it continues to grow today.[54]

Matters changed in the Young family also. Several months after his wife's death in 1888, William Young married Mrs. Sarah Ferguson McHucheon, the widow of the minister of the First Presbyterian Church of Gatesville. The family had been friends for many years. Reverend McHucheon had been the minister of Unity Presbyterian at Turnersville before being called to Gatesville. Mrs. McHucheon had moved back to Turnersville after her husband's death and renewed her close friendship with the Youngs. She helped during Mary Jane Young's final illness and comforted William Young after his wife's death. Of course, the girls were scandalized, particularly Mary Ann Foote, who had a few thoughts on the situation, making tart remarks about her elderly (sixty-one-year-old) father dressing in a "black suit, fancy cravats, and hat" while courting his new wife.[55]

Before his marriage, Young divided his wife's effects between their children. Mary Ann Foote sent her brother's share of personal effects—quilts, bedspreads, and pillows—to him at Vanderbilt

University in Nashville. William Thomas ("Willie") Young returned to Turnersville briefly at the end of the school term and the beginning of the summer but left before the household was divided. William got the family Bible and a gold nugget brought back from the gold fields by Watson Caufield and given to Wat's sister Mary Jane Young. Lizzie got the family organ. She saved a lock of their mother's hair for each child.[56]

Young then proceeded to divide his real property. First, he wrote a detailed document noting what he and his late wife had invested in their joint business affairs. He set aside the livestock and land that had been purchased by their mother from her inheritances and the gain from the sheep she had purchased. In addition, he divided approximately one-half of his own livestock and land among his five children. Each of the children—the four girls and son William—received about two hundred acres and two hundred sheep and other livestock. To avoid any future litigation that his first family might inflict on his second family after his death, Young demanded a quitclaim from each of his children on the remainder of his property. The rest—about 1,362 acres (including the big stone house and the surrounding 399 acres), 2,700 sheep, and 30 horses—he kept.

The youngest child, William Thomas Young, had attended business school at Bowling Green, Kentucky, before transferring to Vanderbilt, where he obtained a degree in engineering between 1888 and 1891. William E. Young sent his son $30 a month to cover tuition and living expenses during his school years, carefully deducting the amount from the boy's income from the ranch. Mary Ann and William remained close and corresponded throughout their lives. While his sisters remained close to home, William T. Young never returned to ranching. After designing and building bridges for the Louisville and Nashville Railroad, he worked for several years for the Youngstown Bridge Company out of Nashville. He then established and ran his own civil engineering firm, building bridges throughout the South. W. T. Young married in 1892.

Mary Ann and William Young continued an extensive correspondence for another fifteen years. Before her marriage she wrote her brother weekly. Afterward the correspondence continued with letters twice a month and never less than monthly. In fact, the Young family all wrote frequent letters. The other sisters wrote William every month or so. But Mary Young was the queen of correspondence, writing ten to fifteen letters weekly to relatives and friends and receiving seven letters and five postcards in one week. Fortunately, most of these letters have been preserved.[57]

Young and his new wife married quietly at the Turnersville Unity Church in September 1888. They went on a honeymoon, then returned and began to remodel the stone house. Once again the daughters were scandalized. Mary lamented the hardships she, her siblings, and their mother had endured because of her father's penurious ways. Now he dressed in suits and his wife wore silk. The house had been remodeled and painted only once in their lifetimes and here he was doing it all at once for this new wife—including new lace curtains! The next year Mary tartly noted the birth of her half brother, "the new prince," and that she just had not had time or "the desire to visit the old home place." W. E. Young's second marriage produced four children—Josephus Cavitt Young (b. 1891), Nancy Lee Young (b. 1893), George Thomas Young (b. 1894), and Charlotte Elizabeth Young (b. 1895), all of whom attended Daniel Baker College in Brownwood.

After their marriage, William Young undertook to educate Sarah McHucheon's two girls by her first marriage and his own children by his new wife. Eventually, Young and his wife moved to Brownwood. The family states that for many decades there was always a child or grandchild of the Youngs attending Daniel Baker College at Brownwood. William continued to supervise the sheep ranch until his death in 1898 but left the day-to-day operation to his sons-in-law Frederick Foote and Freeland. On William's death, his four new children divided the remaining half of his personal estate, which consisted of 1,362 acres, 1,200 sheep, 36 horses, 56 head of cattle, and 16 hogs.

Young was buried next to his first wife, Mary Jane Caufield, and their infant son on the ranch he loved. His second wife was buried next to her first husband. All Young's remaining property was divided between his families. The second family continued to live in the old stone house until it was devastated by a fire in 1926.

Today, on a lonely hill in northwest Coryell County along a creek near the source of the Middle Bosque River, two old pecan trees rise from a small cemetery plot surrounded by an iron fence. The plot contains the remains of William Young (1805–1898), his first wife Mary Jane Caufield Young (1825–1888), and their first child William, who died in 1866.[58] The iron fence is rusting and sagging beneath the weight of the cows that scratch their sides on the spikes. The family who cared for the plot have moved away. Cattle walk along what was once a driveway and road to the house. The land is now owned by other families. Time has faded the memory of the people who suffered the hardship, lost their children, and endured on the frontier of Central Texas.[59]

There is an interesting story behind that grave. Family lore says that "young Willie" died of "brain fever," probably meningitis. While dying, he continuously played with some pecans given to him by a neighbor. The family buried him with the pecans in each pocket of his coat. However, pecans are unlikely to sprout from six feet below ground. More likely, the family planted the pecans on each side of the grave and the trees grew from those seeds. The trees have grown together. In the grip between the trees, they encircle a tombstone and have lifted it three feet above the ground. Only the back of the top of the stone is now visible.[60]

Responding to the new market forces, after he took over the management of the Caufield estate, Joe Cavitt diversified the focus of their operations, trying, usually unsuccessfully, to find profitable investments. Cattle continued to provide a constant source of income for the Caufield Ranch, and Cavitt did well as the European wars drove American food prices ever higher. Annually, he shipped several hundred head from his ranches to the Fort Worth stockyards, where the French-Webb Live Stock Commission Company handled the selling of the animals. In 1915 he sold three carloads—105 head of cattle—through Evans-Snider-Buel Livestock Commission Agents at the Fort Worth stockyards for a net of $3,628. In 1918 he sold 118 head for $4,439 and 284 head for $15,648. In 1919, with the market prices high because of the demands to feed European armies, Cavitt sold four carloads of cattle (327 head) from his Leon River ranch and from the Caufield ranches for over $20,000. He shipped the animals to the Fort Worth stockyards from the McGregor depot, taking advantage of the free ticket given by the Santa Fe Railroad to stockmen who shipped more than four carloads to travel with their stock. Later that year he shipped an additional 247 head, which sold for $16,256. In 1920, Cavitt continued to take advantage of the war prices, selling 269 head of cattle for $18,349. By 1922, during the drought years, Cavitt sold only $934 in livestock. He continued to ship cattle to Fort Worth, sending carloads every year until the Depression.[61]

Cavitt diversified and raised other stock on the McLennan County ranch, including goats, sheep, and pigs. He was an innovator in using pedigreed animals to optimize his herds genetically. In 1905, Cavitt purchased registered sows, "Moncie" and "Myrtle," purebred Essex swine, to upgrade the animals at the Caufield Ranch. In 1915, attempting to further improve the quality of the livestock, he invested in pedigreed Duroc-Jersey pigs from the Texas A&M Department of Animal Husbandry. For several decades he annually shipped swine to the Fort Worth Stockyards, collecting $577 for eighty hogs in 1909.

Cavitt kept a mixture of livestock—sheep, goats, horses, and cattle—on the remnant of the pasture that remained after conversion to cotton. In 1906, he purchased 285 Angora goats and 36 head of sheep for $400 from his friend Henry Mitchell. Shipping the animals on the railroad from Wheelock cost $36. Cavitt placed them on the Caufield Ranch, sold their wool, and, in 1910, sold several hundred head of goats for $3.50 each, making a tidy profit.[62]

Under the title of IXL Poultry Farms, Cavitt tried raising Leghorn chickens. He formed a partnership with C. T. Pool, who was living on the ranch. Beginning in 1911, Cavitt purchased incubators from the Cyphers Incubator Company in Buffalo, New York. Finding quality eggs proved a continual problem, especially in 1916. That year Cavitt had to return several shipments that had low hatch rates. He had initially purchased 500 fertile eggs from M. Johnson, a breeder of single-comb White Leghorns in Bowie, Texas, for $35. Although Johnson sent an extra 100 eggs to cover infertile ones, more than 250 eggs of the new batches of 1,000 proved infertile, and many others failed to hatch. Cavitt tried several other egg producers. He turned to Trinity Valley Farms in Mesquite and Oak Grove Poultry Farm in San Antonio, purchasing 500 eggs from each. Oak Grove proved to have sold 250 infertile eggs. The problem with infertile eggs recurred every couple of years, to Cavitt's consternation.[63]

To boost sales, Cavitt exhibited his full-grown chickens at the Cotton Palace in Waco. Although he often sold roosters for $20 each to local farmers who wanted them to breed with their hens, he slaughtered most of the chickens and sold them locally through the Cavitt-Lee Hardware Store and local butcher shops. This enterprise never did make much money and was abandoned a decade later when Pool died.

Cavitt added corn, oats, and wheat to furnish crop income from fields in rotation with cotton. In 1918 he earned $4,381 on oats from his farms. In 1919 he collected $4,610 from the McGregor Milling and Grain Company on 200,000 pounds of oats and wheat and $2,190 from the Oglesby Rolling Mills on 64,913 pounds of wheat. Most of the attempts to diversify the products from the Caufield Ranch were only modestly successful or failed. The money was in row crops, especially cotton.[64]

As Central Texas farmers fenced the open range and cattle ranching became less profitable, Caufield moved his cattle operation to West Texas and Mexico and broke more land in Central Texas to the plow. He began to plant cotton until, by the end of the nineteenth century, he had planted most of his former ranch land in cotton.

5

Cotton, 1910–1930

THE COTTON ERA IN THE SOUTH SPANNED 150 YEARS between two important innovations. In 1793, Eli Whitney revolutionized the cotton industry by inventing the cotton gin, which mechanically separated cottonseed from the fibers. This development coincided with the increased demand for cotton lint for steam-driven looms in England, which, in turn, stimulated the economy of the South, where climatic requirements were right for the extensive cultivation of cotton.[1]

The cotton boom began when the Industrial Revolution in Britain mechanized the two primary steps of textile production, spinning yarn and weaving cloth, and spurred a burgeoning market for cotton. By raising demand and prices, it stimulated an increase in world cotton acreage. The textile industry successfully used steam and later electric power to drive spindles and looms and to mass-produce cotton clothing. Additional industrial advances in textile looms in England and the northern United

States continued to produce ever more cotton fabrics at ever more reasonable prices.[2]

Cotton became the most important commodity in the southern United States and such an economic force that the institutions that grew around cotton farming came to define the Southern way of life. Cotton production was labor-intensive and trapped a large, poverty-stricken labor force in the rural areas.

Texas was the largest producer of cotton in the United States, and the United States was the largest cotton producer in the world. For fifty years (1880–1930), cotton would dominate the agricultural market of Central Texas and serve as the focus of interest for the Caufields. The population of McLennan County increased fourfold following the Civil War. Farms and population had forced the cattle trails westward, and by 1880 cotton had begun to surpass cattle as the chief cash crop of McLennan County. From 1900 to 1910, McLennan County was the largest cotton producing area in Texas. In 1910, McLennan County produced 80,000 bales of cotton processed by 287 gins.[3]

Small interior towns in the South serviced the cotton crop as their main economic function. Cotton thrived in the soil of Central Texas. Railroads accelerated town building by facilitating the marketing of locally grown cotton and establishing gins and mills to service the processing of cotton and other agricultural products. Stimulated by the rail lines and the success of local cotton farmers, the process of town building proceeded rapidly in McGregor. With the amalgamation of neighboring hamlets and villages and also the establishment of businesses, banks, and processing mills for agriculture products, the town grew rapidly.

Raising cotton depended on a cycle of cultivation that included plowing, planting, chopping, picking, and ginning. Each of these steps required its own specialized equipment. Cotton farming was facilitated by such innovations as the metal plow, the introduction of mules, improved wagons, roads, and railroads, and, later, the advent of the tractor. Each improvement allowed more acreage to be placed in production. In addition, electricity, the gasoline engine, and irrigation made cotton production more resistant to the vagaries of the weather and drought. Nitrite fertilizers increased production on worn-out and depleted croplands. Improved transportation and related infrastructure—trucks, bridges, and paved roads—enabled the movement of cotton to the gins. Modern technology also added crop dusting, the spraying of herbicides for weed control and defoliation, to the rhythm of cotton farming. New cotton hybrids suitable for drier regions increased cotton acreage just when the boll weevil drove farmers onto the Great Plains, where the colder winters killed the cotton-destroying pest.

Because the major cost in cotton production was labor, any process that mechanized the labor of cotton production would increase the productivity of the cotton farmer and augment his income. Yet, the life of the sharecroppers, the landowners, the cotton brokers, and the textile workers changed little until the final step in mechanization—the cotton picker—at last forced the laborers off the farms and into the cities.[4]

The changes in methods of cultivation and partial mechanization increased productivity and allowed farmers to plant greater total acreage, boosting the amount of cotton each American farmer harvested. In 1791, before the invention of the cotton gin, the southern United States produced 2 million pounds of cotton lint (4,000 bales); by 1795, production tripled to 6 million pounds of lint (12,000 bales); and by 1811 cotton production reached 62 million pounds (124,000 bales)—a fortyfold increase. In 1879 the United States harvested 17 million bales of cotton, reaching a peak of 26 million bales of cotton in 1932.[5]

The income of Southern farmers increased little during the seven decades following the Civil War. Prior to the war, the average income for Southern workers equaled that of their Northern brethren: about $150 to $200 annually. In 1900, while salaries nationally averaged $310 a year, a teacher in the South could expect to earn around $159. By 1937 the average income in the South was $314, compared to $604 for the rest of the country. In 1949, when the median income of white Southerners was $1,900, that of nonwhites was about half that of their white neighbors.[6]

Ginning, the first successful mechanization of cotton production, continued to adapt to keep pace with cotton production. As farmers produced more cotton, merchants developed larger gins and substituted steam and electricity for animal power. Cotton gins found means for removing dust and debris when planters developed mechanical harvesters.

In 1933, cotton ginning cost 30 to 50 cents a hundredweight, or $1.50 to $2.50 a bale (at 500 pounds to a bale) at the large gins, but up to $7 a bale at smaller gins. Additional charges included bagging and ties ($1.50 a bale) and transportation (10 cents a bale). Total costs were 9 to 10 cents a pound, or $50 a bale.[7]

At the gin, 1,400 pounds of field cotton yielded 500 pounds (one bale) of cotton lint, 75 pounds of waste, and 875 pounds of seeds. Three bales of cotton produced 2,000 pounds of cottonseed, which when processed gave 575 pounds of hulls, 310 pounds of oil, and 925 pounds of cake. The cottonseed cake and hulls sold as cattle feed. These by-products provided an estimated $6.67 an acre additional income to farmers.[8]

Cottonseed developed as an additional source of income. This was especially important, since seeds constituted 50 to 60 percent by weight of picked cotton. The gins cut their costs by firing their steam engines with recycled debris from the cotton. The farmer paid up to 75 percent of the cottonseed to the ginner, keeping 25 percent for the next year's crop. Later, the ginners learned that cottonseeds could be pressed for oil, sold as cattle food, or sold for future plantings.[9]

The cost of labor in cotton farming has played an important role in the development of rural Southern life, whether through slavery or the debt peonage of sharecropping and tenant farming. Sharecropping tied the cotton farmer to the land. Poor health, malnutrition, ignorance, small farm size, and the tenant system lowered cotton production. This aspect of cotton cultivation has been one of the most popular topics for historians, particularly those interested in social development in the South. Many authors, such as S. D. Myres Jr. and Charles S. Johnson, dedicate their books entirely to these socioeconomic aspects of sharecropping and tenant farming.[10]

Because labor was the most expensive portion of cotton production, any factors that increased the land farmed by each worker increased productivity and profits. Initially mechanization increased the productivity of cotton farmers by simply increasing how much land each could farm, while the amount of cotton raised per acre remained the same or declined. One man with a horse and a one-row wooden plow could farm about four acres a day. One man, a mule, and a steel plow could farm about eight acres a day. One man, two mules, and a two-row plow could farm sixteen acres a day. One man, one tractor, and a four-row plow could farm forty-five acres a day. Today the most effective farmer in the newest tractor pulling a sixteen-row plow can farm 150 acres daily—a thirty-seven–fold increase in productivity.

Before the tractor, partial mechanization and animal labor allowed the American farmer to cultivate seventy-five to one hundred acres per person versus only two to four acres per person in India and other underdeveloped countries where most cultivation is still performed by hand labor. With the introduction of tractors, the cost of cotton cultivation per bale fell from $12 to $3 to $4 per bale.[11]

In 1895, Foote expanded the farming sector of his operation, building five sharecropper houses at a cost of about $250 each. More than two hundred people lived and worked on his land. He located each house adjacent to the fields the tenant rented and today the sites can be recognized by a grove of trees on the edge of a field with the remnants of a well and windmill nearby.[12]

Farm crops began to provide a major source of income for the Foote ranch. Foote finished fencing his farmland, spending $51 for 550 cedar posts and $40 for 1,279 pounds of wire. Although oats sold for only $48 and corn for $191 in 1897, these figures indicated that the ranch was now self-sufficient in livestock feed and had a surplus to sell. Serious cotton production began in 1895 with $942 income. Cotton began to play an important role in the Foote ranch economic plans. In 1901, Foote farmed 940 acres with an average production of eighty-nine pounds of lint per acre and a bale of cotton every five acres (at 15 cents a pound, $9.35 an acre income).[13]

By 1904, the Foote sheep ranch had converted 2,000 acres to cotton and row crops. Foote owned or controlled over 9,000 acres, but most of the land was unusable for row crops. He and his brothers-in-law managed all the land in a ten-mile arc around the town of Turnersville. In 1910, twenty-eight tenants and families lived on the farms, each renting from fifty to one hundred acres. Income from the farms—cotton, oats, and corn—totaled $3,860. This represented 189 pounds of lint per acre (a bale of cotton for every three acres) or $4.10 income per acre ($410 for a one-hundred-acre farm, half of which belonged to the landowner). Wheat production totaled 1,796 bushels, which sold for $840.

The cotton culture also brought with it a rigid social structure. At the top was the large landowner who rented his land to tenants or sharecroppers. Below the landowners were the tenant farmers, who might own some of the land they farmed but also rented land from the landowners. The tenants owned their homes and their equipment. They farmed on percentages; usually a quarter of the cotton or a third of the grain belonged to the owners. The tenants owned their crops and could sell to whoever paid them the best price. On the bottom of the heap was the sharecroppers. They owned nothing. Their homes, their equipment, and their crop belonged to the landowner. They furnished their labor and usually received a third of the cotton crop as their payment for a year's labor. They had to accept the price the landowner offered. Often they remained in debt to the local general store for their year's food and clothing, sometimes for years at a stretch, and received no cash in payment.

A rapid increase in the number of tenant farmers relative to owner-operators characterized the last two decades of the nineteenth century as landowners switched from livestock to cotton. The self-sufficient farmer who raised all his own food, selling little for cash, began to disappear. Fluctuation in land prices, the lack of free land, and the cost of land made mortgages necessary. Banks demanded cash as down payment for mortgages. By 1910 the Caufield Ranch supported more than twenty families.[14]

The sharecroppers tended to live in houses like the one built for the Rylander family in Turnersville, made entirely of wood with "board and batten" walls; the lumber used for the walls was one-inch-thick, eight-inch-wide boards nailed to a frame. The spaces between the boards were covered with a one-inch-thick, two-inch-wide board. The houses were one room, fifteen feet long, twenty feet wide, and eight feet high, with a garret above the beams. The single room served as a combination dining room, kitchen, living room, and bedroom. The children slept in the attic on straw pallets. The house had front and back doors with windows on each side. A stone fireplace or woodstove served for warmth and cooking. The tenants covered the walls with newspaper to keep the wind out.

In quarters like these, furniture was crude, books few, and ornaments absent. The housewives added implements for canning and spinning. Kerosene lamps furnished light at night. There was a crude privy out back, and several outbuildings, including a barn for the mules and other domestic animals and a small shed for tools and storage. Most tenants had a small garden by the house, where it could be watered with wastewater from the kitchen. A well furnished water and a nearby windmill pumped the water for humans and animals alike into an elevated storage tank. The weight of the elevated water provided pressure for the faucets inside. Some houses contained a cistern to catch rainwater from the roof.

Cooking was a grueling job. The woodstove had to be stoked to the appropriate temperature on both freezing winter days and blistering hot summer days. Since most foods that could be preserved ripened in the summer, the cook had to endure indoor temperatures from the woodstove that soared into the 100 degrees or more. Clothed in a cotton shift, which quickly became plastered to her body, the woman prepared the food for cooking and canning. But this job was necessary for her family's survival. The food the woman preserved would feed the family through the winter months.[15]

Obtaining water was not easy for the tenant farmer families, nor was washing clothes. Water had to be pumped from the well and transported into the house in buckets weighing twenty or more pounds. Laundry was generally done outdoors in large iron pots on wood fires. Water transported from wells or creeks was heated to boiling, soap added, and the dirty clothes stirred in the boiling water until clean, hauled out by hand or on wooded spatulas, placed in another kettle of clean boiling water, then rinsed in a final cold-water bath before being hung out to dry in the prairie wind. The more fortunate families had a windmill to pump the water into an elevated water tank, as well as indoor plumbing.[16]

The cycles of the cotton crop tied the lives of cotton farmers, whether landowner or sharecropper, to the land. School districts offered classes during the winter months, when children had few duties in the fields. Once the farmer harvested his cotton and sent it to market, bills could be paid, debts settled, and new purchases contemplated. In the fall, after the cotton was picked, the farmers planted other crops, such as wheat or oats, butchered hogs after the first frost, broke horses, weaned calves, and drove steers to market. Molasses could be processed on autumn days after the cotton was harvested from the fields.[17]

Schools played an important role in the lives of the cotton farmers. The middle-class farmers demanded that their children have an education. The tenant farmers yearned for education to lift their children out of poverty. Parents established local schools, which were funded by the farmers within three miles of the schoolhouse. This was considered the farthest a child could walk in bad weather. The schoolhouses were one- or two-room structures in which a single teacher taught all ages and grades simultaneously. Usually the small independent schools were run by three-person school boards who made all the decisions, hired the teachers, maintained the school house, and obtained supplies, fuel, and water. The schoolhouse often served as an education center for children and recreational outlet for their parents.

To support their tenants, the Caufields donated the land for a school about one mile from their main ranch house. About 1880, through a community effort, a typical two-room schoolhouse was erected. Receipts for the lumber indicated the total cost for the schoolhouse was $127 (about $6,500 in today's currency). The building also served as a local community center and briefly as a church. In 1923, the largest enrollment in the Caufield School was sixty pupils.

Aquilla Jones and his wife established another local school at Harris Creek. The Joneses gave twenty acres for a school, a cemetery, and a union church. A later addition to the Harris Creek School, windows and moldings, cost $809. In 1925 the Harris Creek School, the Caufield School, and the South Bosque School were consolidated into a two-storied brick building placed along the Cotton Belt Railroad tracks near the hamlet of South Bosque (population 26). An eleven-grade high school was available in McGregor and a twelve-grade high school in Waco.[18]

The school year revolved around the cotton crop. Classes began in late October, after the cotton crop had been picked and ginned. It continued until planting time in April. During breaks in the cycles, the parents sent their children to school. Therefore, school districts offered classes when children were not needed in the fields. Sometimes there were brief sessions in July and August. Because of the time consumed by farming, in rural areas the school term was 117 days, compared to 160 days in urban areas.

Young Cavitt Caufield walked daily across the fields to the Caufield School to start a fire in the stove. On weekends he cut and carried the wood needed for the week. Caufield described the school as a "two room affair" with a "potbellied stove" in the back. The teacher sat up front behind a desk and in front of a blackboard. "We had desks and benches. All ages were taught in the same class by the same teacher. I don't know how she did it." School records show Tom Caufield applying for free textbooks from the state as late as 1917.[19]

The modern incarnations of these small locally controlled schools are the Woodway Consolidated School District, with elementary, junior, and high schools in Woodway and Hewitt. The old brick South Bosque school was torn down and the bricks used to build a modern home. South Bosque withered and died when the local highway was rerouted and the Cotton Belt Railroad abandoned its lines to McGregor and Gatesville. The next year Ralph Buice closed his gin and moved his grocery and filling station to the new highway.

All the Caufield children and grandchildren attended high school and college. The girls usually were sent east to a Presbyterian finishing school in Nashville, Tennessee. The younger boys attended Presbyterian schools in Tennessee. Tom Caufield met and married his wife, the daughter of the college's chaplain, while attending school there.

Another important element in a cotton farmer's life was the annual production of molasses. Because sugarcane could be grown in most southern climates, molasses played a significant role in the diet of Southern cotton farmers. A small stand of red-ribbon cane planted in an area unsuitable for cotton produced enough molasses to feed a large family year-round. Molasses often furnished the major source of calories for a poor farmer's family. Farmers poured it over all their food, particularly corn bread, another dietary staple.

Josephus Cavitt ran the press for his farms and the surrounding areas and took control of the process. After the cane was cut in the fall, farmers transported it by wagon to Cavitt's press under the oak trees along the South Bosque. There the cane was ground between circular stones by the ranch's mules. The juice flowed through sluices into a central vat, where it was slowly heated, evaporated, and cooked into molasses. Each cook had their own recipe; some cooks added sulfur and others did not. Cavitt placed the final product in tin buckets and distributed it according to the amount of cane each farmer brought. Cavitt kept a third of each farmer's molasses as a fee for processing. He stored the tin buckets in a small wooden shed at the old ranch house, periodically taking some molasses to town to sell in his hardware store, to give as gifts, or to be consumed by his family.[20]

Cotton raised on the Brazos River bottomland was the main source of the Cavitt family income. They rented the land for $6 an acre to J. W. Woods. Every year Woods complained of the cost of levee building, weed control, and upkeep on tenant houses. One of his pet peeves was the Johnson grass that settled in the flooded fields and that was so difficult to eradicate. Yet he continued to rent the rich alluvial soil for many decades.[21]

Woods first proposed building a levee along the Little Brazos River in 1905. He planned to use convict labor and projected little cost for the six hundred yards needed to connect to the adjoining farm's levee. He never seemed to have hired the convict labor.[22]

During this time, Joe Cavitt took the responsibility for investing the income of his mother and siblings, and often thrust himself into family matters concerning land and investments. Cavitt was a rich man when he married Mollie Caufield. The Cavitt family cotton farms, situated on the fertile soil of the Brazos River bottoms at Wheelock, near Hearne, produced annual incomes of several thousand dollars for each family member. Banks at that time paid little or no interest on deposits, so Cavitt sought short- and long-term investments with high interest to increase the family's income.

The Cavitt family was quite large. Joe Cavitt was born in Wheelock in 1867, part of a family consisting of thirteen siblings. Ten reached adulthood: four sisters—Ruth (who never married), Jessie Cavitt Taliaferro, Florence (Lizzie) Cavitt Goode, and Cora Cavitt Armstrong—and six brothers—James, Bell (who was a bit slow), Sheridan (or "Bud," who became increasingly erratic and alcoholic as he aged), Sid (who also was a bit slow and had trouble with alcohol), Sam, and Joe himself. The girls married well. W. F. Taliaferro was a physician in Beaumont; Robert Armstrong was a civil lawyer in Marlin; and William Goode was a banker, cashier, and part owner of the First National Bank of Bay City.[23]

In Coryell County, Fred Foote had continued to mechanize as he increased his row crop production. In 1887 he purchased a disc harrow and cultivator from the Warrior Mower Company in New York for $75 and shipped the implement via St. Louis for $24.32. When the machine arrived at the ranch, several parts were missing, resulting in a three-month delay before it could be placed in the fields. Foote purchased Clarke's new flexible disc harrow from Higgins Corporation in Boston. Other purchases included a sulky plow, another grain drill, a reaper, and another kind of harrow. Delivery could be slow. The harrow shipped by the factory from Little Falls, New York, took four weeks to reach Gatesville.

Foote received a series of letters advertising the value of a new crop, Johnson grass. The plant grew in most soils with three cuttings a year for hay even during drought. He eventually purchased seeds and tried it on his land. The grass was invasive and almost impossible to eradicate once planted. It has since spread across the country and remains a constant pest. When the Cavitt cotton farms along the Brazos River flooded because of a lack of levees, Johnson grass was introduced into their fields. Although they fought it constantly, it persists today.[24]

Meanwhile, Mary Ann Foote raised her family and managed the house. Frederick Foote Jr. was born in January 1888, Clarence in December 1888, Ruby in 1890, Hazel in 1892, Adrian in 1895, and Nathaniel in 1901. Fred and Mary Ann gradually enlarged the house to accommodate their growing family. Mary Ann continued to be a prolific letter writer, noting in 1891 that she had fifteen more letters to write that weekend.[25]

6

Small-Town Life, 1910–1930

WHEN JOSEPHUS CAVITT MARRIED MARGARET CAUFIELD, he was a prosperous businessman. He had joined the First National Bank of McGregor as senior vice president by purchasing a considerable portion of the bank's stock. Soon he dominated the town.

By 1908 the Caufield children had moved from their parents' farms into the surrounding towns, as did most of the ambitious members of their generation. There they established businesses and banks or entered professions. All the younger Caufields had attended high school and obtained some college education, so they were well equipped for the transition. At the time the children began investing in various rural businesses, the United States was entering several decades of unprecedented prosperity, and few businesses did not make money. But only the thrifty and good managers would survive the Great Depression of the late twenties and thirties.

In the Southern cotton culture, the farmer and the small town remained a single economic unit in which they were dependent on each other. In the Old World, farmers lived in villages and walked to their fields. However, in America, because of the abundance of land and the distances between neighbors, farmers built their houses on their farms, lived near the fields they tilled, and walked to town. The small town remained dependent on agriculture, and it processed the produce from the farms in cotton gins and flour mills. These served as a marketing and distribution points for local crops. The farmer, in turn, bought his supplies and goods in the local stores. Texas communities thus did not develop into self-sufficient settlements but became the mercantile centers for the economic units that included the surrounding farms and ranches. Since American farmers lived away from the towns and had a choice of where to sell their products, they forced the towns to compete for their business. A town became a city when industry made it independent from the surrounding farms. Once a factory moved into a town, it rarely returned to its agrarian roots.[1]

Initially, natural geographical advantages—fords, springs, crossroads, approaches to mountain passes, or heads of river navigation—determined the location of most Western towns. The advent of railroads changed that. Proximity to the train tracks became the most important factor in determining the success of towns and villages. McGregor followed this pattern. Founded in 1882 at the site where the east–west Cotton Belt Railroad (Texas and St. Louis Railroad) from Waco to Gatesville crossed the north–south Gulf, Colorado, and Santa Fe Railroad tracks, McGregor grew rapidly.[2]

Initially, the isolation of the frontier determined that population centers were self-sufficient, offering a wide variety of manufactured goods and services and providing more goods as the population grew. Before the railroad system was completed, most villages remained isolated, and a semiannual shopping trip into town usually satisfied the Western appetite for the comforts of life. The small villages, located at the intersection of two roads, consisted of a mercantile store, several churches, a school, and a doctor's office, and contained fewer than one hundred residents. As the villages grew into towns, more specialized enterprises, such as butcher shops, banks, and grain and feed suppliers, began to replace the general stores. These local businesses constantly changed management, location, and names as merchants established new shops and old ones closed, were sold, or moved elsewhere. The typical urban capitalist before 1900 was often a former planter's son who had sold his land and moved to town, founded a bank, opened a cotton gin, or established a mercantile business. Other small-town businessmen remained absentee landlords. These included members of several generations of the Cavitts and Caufields.[3]

Up until the twentieth century, the country town was also the basic social institution of American life. In the nineteenth century, the majority of the population in the United States lived in towns with fewer than 3,000 residents. They contained the churches and the schools that set the moral and educational values of the area. One of the most significant changes in American culture was the growth of urban areas and the migration of rural Americans into the cities.[4]

The town of McGregor was born on the back of a flatbed railroad car on September 11, 1882. On that day the Gulf, Colorado and Santa Fe Railroad auctioned lots on 140 acres they had purchased from Dr. Gregor McGregor of Waco, who owned the land where the railroads crossed. The railroad named the town for Dr. McGregor. The nearby small towns of Comanche Springs, Banks, and Eagle Springs moved to the new location literally. Some merchants loaded their houses and business buildings onto wagons and moved them to the new locale, placing the structures on the lots they purchased. Since the tracks of the Santa Fe and the St. Louis and Southwestern (Cotton Belt) rails crossed at the site of the new city, prosperity seemed ensured for local merchants. Within months, McGregor had twenty businesses. Because of the railroad, McGregor became a center for the shipping of agricultural goods and delivery of manufactured goods, making it the second largest town in the area, and one of the most prosperous.[5]

The Santa Fe Railroad that reached McGregor in 1882 was not the Atchison, Topeka, and Santa Fe Railroad (now the BNSF Railway) but an earlier local version partially financed by the larger rail line. Periodically, Houston had cut all rail traffic between Galveston and Houston to prevent the spread of yellow fever epidemics, real or imagined. The quarantines usually started in September or October, just when the cotton harvest was moving to market. The quarantines stopped goods normally destined for the port of Galveston in Houston and allowed them to be shipped to foreign ports via the Buffalo Bayou instead. After a few years of this game, the Galveston businessmen had enough and decided that they needed a direct link to the Northern markets that did not run through Houston. William Lewis Moody, John Sealy, and a group of Galveston merchants financed the Gulf, Colorado, and Santa Fe Railroad (GC&SF) from the port city.

The railroad went through McGregor because nearby Waco decided not to pay for the rail to pass through their city. The city leaders noted the railroad's previous self-serving behavior. The railroad had recently reneged on a payment by Belton for the line to go through that town. The GC&SF took Belton's money; then, when another investor offered more valuable land, it bypassed Belton and established its own town twenty miles north at what became Temple. The railroad did not give the money back to Belton. Waco decided that the new GC&SF could not be trusted, and they declined the opportunity to have the line traverse their city. The Waco merchants had recently passed bonds to pay to have the Katy railroad come through town and had a tap or spur line constructed to connect with the Houston–Dallas line. Several other rail lines already passed through the city.

After the railroad arrived, the local agricultural economy rapidly changed from ranching and subsistence farming to fenced diversified livestock and cotton farming. The first cotton gin in McGregor was built in 1882, shortly after the railroad arrived. By 1883, McGregor had become the economic center for a large rural area in the northwestern corner of McLennan County.

By the end of the nineteenth century McGregor was a typical Texas farming community, both prosperous and provincial. It served as the rail and agricultural hub for northwestern McLennan County. The north–south Santa Fe and east–west Cotton Belt Railroads ensured that the farmers had access to national markets. Successful merchants and local landowners built spacious houses within walking distance of the brick stores that lined both sides of Main Street. Like other small towns, McGregor developed a "booster" spirit, promoting the local cotton market, wares, and real estate and competing for the local farmers' business. The town soon had the high school for that part of the county and churches representing most of the major denominations. And, as in most small towns, everyone knew everyone else's business, and everything that happened was the subject of conversation and speculation.[6]

One of the most important merchandizing events was the monthly "trade day." Each local community chose one day a month, usually attached to a weekend, as a special day when businesses opened early and stayed open late. McGregor's trade day was the third Monday, and the town bustled with business that weekend. The merchants scheduled special sales and offered entertainment such as band recitals, parades, and speeches. Politicians made the rounds on trade days to meet their constituents and garner votes. Traveling salesmen, mule traders, merchants from surrounding towns, and equipment salesmen set up booths and rented space to display their wares. Farmers and their families traveled from the surrounding homes to conduct business, enjoy the shows, and visit friends. Traveling preachers scheduled revivals to correspond with local trade days to widen their audiences and increase the chances of capturing converts.[7]

When outlying county residents came to town, the family usually planned to spend the entire day. They brought farm products to sell, the women purchased goods for their families, the families visited relatives and neighbors, and the men tended to their legal business. All the activity supported the grocers and merchants and expanded the economic basis of the entire town.

As McGregor grew in importance, farming families from outlying areas came to town on the weekends in their wagons, buggies, or cars. This trip was a thrilling event for young children. One girl related that "our excitement continued to grow as we neared the city limits of this small country town. . . . This particular morning the street was overflowing and we soon saw the reason why. They were having a revival. We drove over the bumpy railroad tracks to the end of the block, which put us right in front of the dry goods store where we were to do our trading." The girls bought hair ribbons and ice cream. The boys watched the stockyards and mule sales. The parents purchased food and clothing, visited with friends, and gossiped about the latest news. The girl quoted above and her family spent the entire day shopping, returning home tired but happy.[8]

By 1890, McGregor had eighty-three businesses, including three cotton gins, a grain elevator, an artesian water company, and several hardware and grocery stores. In 1900 the community had a population of 1,500 and had a weekly newspaper, the *McGregor Plainsman*, as well as two hotels, several physicians' offices, two cotton gins, a flour mill, and a major grain storage facility.[9]

Church was an important part of rural life. The Cavitts and Caufields were Presbyterians and actively supported their local church. They raised the money in 1911 to build a sanctuary. Each pledged $300 to $500. The elders gave George Caufield the responsibility of obtaining the furniture. The church remained small and could afford a full-time minister only intermittently.

Dr. Charles Caldwell from the First Presbyterian Church of Waco preached monthly to the small congregation. Other traveling ministers filled the pulpit most other Sundays. The church closed in the 1950s and was sold, and the remaining congregation drove to Waco for Sunday services.[10]

The sense of community in McGregor led local leaders to organize and join neighborhood clubs and national fraternal organizations. Local bands were popular with the musically inclined and gave summer concerts and marched in parades in elaborate uniforms. Local clubs put on theatrical productions to raise money for local causes. Most "respectable" men joined in the fun and staged an "all-male wedding" with one dressed as the bride and others as bridesmaids. Not to be outdone, the women staged an "all-female wedding." Large crowds attended all the productions, and the plays went into extra showings. Joe Cavitt and George Caufield became active in the local Masonic chapter and attained some state prominence in the organization. The Odd Fellows and the Elks had large chapters in McGregor.

Politics attracted many of the successful merchants and the area's "movers and shakers." Cavitt became a member of the McLennan County Democratic Party central committee. He attended district and state conventions and solicited funds for the national and state party. Cavitt represented McLennan County at the Texas Farmers' Congress in 1911. He later joined its successor, the McLennan County Farm Association, and by 1924 was on the board of directors of the organization. In the campaign of 1920, he raised $143.50 from thirty-two of McGregor's business leaders, presenting a list of the contributors to the state party convention. Both Joe Cavitt and George Caufield were elected mayor of McGregor.

As Josephus Cavitt's prosperity increased, his importance spread throughout the region. In 1913 his first cousin, John Cavitt, recommended Joe for the board of trustees of the Texas Presbyterian

School for Girls in Milford, Texas. John Cavitt had helped found the school in 1902 and the college was a small success. The school was very conveniently located for the farming families, having been built just a few blocks from the rail lines in Milford, a small town north of Hillsboro. Mart Caufield's daughters and Lizzie Caufield Clifton's daughter and other family members attended the college for various lengths of time. Mary Ann Foote's daughter Ruby attended the college for a semester. Ruby was homesick and spent most of her time in the infirmary, barraging her family with letters, until at last they relented and she came home. Ruby never went back to school.[11]

The trustees actively involved themselves in the running of the college. A serious discussion at a trustee meeting in 1915 involved putting a fire escape on the residence hall, and the trustees visited the school to determine the feasibility of placing the fire escape on the outside of the building. In 1916, John Cavitt and a committee traveled to Mississippi and Alabama, interviewing candidates for the presidency of Texas Presbyterian School for Girls. The committee decided on a Mr. Edward Summerfield from West Virginia as the new president. The trustees then worried that he was single and decided to place a Mr. and Mrs. John Pasty, the English teacher, in the rooms of the women's dormitory formerly occupied by the previous president and his wife. Mrs. Pasty took charge of the home economics department. In 1917 the board of trustees cosigned notes and pledged $100,000 for the Caribel McDaniel Memorial Endowment Fund to build a new administration building. Joe Cavitt donated $10,000 and his cousin John gave $10,000. J. K. McDaniel contributed the majority of the funds: $50,000. The fund eventually contained $110,000. After Joe Cavitt had served as a member of the board of trustees, they elected him president of the board in 1928.

During the difficult years of the Great Depression, the college suffered for income as enrollment fell. With little outside income and endowment, the college was dependent on the tuition paid by the students. The trustees rented the land around the college to a local farmer who was soon unable to pay his cash rent. Enrollment remained low during the Depression and eventually, in 1935, the remnants of the school were consolidated with Austin College in Sherman.

World War I interrupted the rhythm of life in McGregor. Many of the young men in the area were drafted. Before the United States entered the war, W. S. Amsler, son of the bank president, took a job with the YMCA running rest areas for the soldiers. In September 1917, Norman Cavitt, serving as first lieutenant, Cavalry, American Expeditionary Forces, left New York for Europe. Volney Cavitt, Joe's only son, received his draft notice in July 1918 while attending college at Sherman. He was classified 1A. John Henry Caufield left for the front in December 1918 and returned in January 1920. All the local boys would return home safely.[12]

As the war engulfed the country and raised patriotism to a fever pitch, every small town tried to surpass its neighbors in supporting the American cause. The Caufields and the Cavitts, as leading men in McGregor, became active leaders in the efforts to sell government bonds and gather donations for the American Red Cross war fund. Tom Caufield served as the chairman for the county chapter, and Mrs. J. F. Cavitt served as a member of the executive committee. Caufield gathered pledges totaling several thousand dollars, ranging in value from $25 to $200, from McGregor businesses and forwarded them to the Waco office of the American Red Cross. As the war ground on, the National Red Cross office began to insist that all funds be forwarded to the national office. When some donors did not meet their pledges, the local Red Cross chapter tried to send Caufield out to collect the promised funds and then tried to hold him personally responsible for the unpaid balances. After a series of increasingly nasty letters, Caufield quit in disgust.[13]

Not to be outdone, George Caufield, as mayor of McGregor, led local residents in gathering scrap metal for the war effort and the Masonic lodge in collecting and donating war stamps from their members. He also spearheaded the community effort to sell war bonds at a series of rallies where McGregor purchased over $150,000 in Liberty Bonds and War Savings Stamps, $65,000 over their allotment. Joe Cavitt became the district chairman of the Council of National Defense. Because of local gossip about his son, who was reclassified as 4F after he failed the visual examinational for the draft, Cavitt announced in the newspaper that he was donating all the profits of the McGregor Oil Mill to purchase Liberty Bonds. (The mill failed to make a profit that year, just like all his other businesses.)[14]

Henry Caufield had ushered the family into the banking business in the 1880s when he became an initial investor and board member of the Citizens National Bank of Waco. In the late 1890s, feeling his advancing age, he no longer wanted to travel the fifteen miles into town to attend bank meetings and sold his shares to a young cashier named Walter Lacy. Under Lacy's stewardship, the Citizens National Bank would dominate the banking business in Waco.[15]

In 1906, Joe Cavitt and his family were able to purchase a minority interest in the First National Bank of McGregor. Established in 1898, the First National Bank had thrived in the rural town. In 1907, Cavitt persuaded his brother-in-law George Caufield to purchase five shares for $800 and become assistant cashier.

In 1911, Joe encouraged George to purchase a one-fifth interest in the Bank of Oglesby, a state bank that they later merged with the First National Bank of McGregor. George paid $2,000 for his shares in the small Oglesby bank. When he suffered financial losses during the disastrous cotton crops of 1923, he sold his shares in the Oglesby bank to the First National Bank of McGregor, which manages the institution to this day.[16]

In 1906 the First National Bank of McGregor had capital and surplus of $75,000. By 1913 the First National Bank of McGregor had a capital of $50,000, deposits of $161,000, and profits of $46,000, with a board of directors that included Samuel Amsler, Dr. J. E. Brown, Charles Smith, J. F. Gulledge, and J. F. Cavitt. Cavitt became executive vice president of the bank and George Caufield joined the board in 1913 as vice president.[17]

Cavitt insisted that George Caufield purchase the trappings of a successful businessman. In 1904, while in North Carolina on vacation, George arranged to buy the home of R. L. Bewley, the chief cashier at the bank, who was moving to Austin. The two-story house was on two lots, had a servants' house, and comprised seven rooms including a bathroom and three bedrooms. Utilities included hot and cold water inside, water outside, and electricity in every room. It was quite a house for its day. Bewley had paid $6,000 for the home new and had added $19,800 in improvements. George purchased the house for $5,000, borrowing the money from the bank.[18]

Management of the bank was often difficult. One of the major directors, Dr. Brown, became ill, dying several years later, and was unable to participate in the bank's management. Amsler, although titular president because he owned the majority of the shares, was not an effective leader. Cavitt assumed leadership of the institution and served as unofficial, temporary, and interim president over the next decade. George Caufield later rose to become vice president.

Banking became a Cavitt family enterprise. Cavitt led his sisters to purchase several hundred shares of the First National Bank of McGregor, giving him a majority minority interest in the bank and a place on the board of directors. Cavitt's sister Florence (Lizzie) and her husband William Goode invested in the First National Bank of Bay City ($50,000 capital). Goode eventually rose from cashier to president. Mr. Goode became ill and died in 1920 but his widow kept her interest in the bank for many years.

In 1916, Cavitt's sister Lizzie Goode sold her twenty-seven shares in the First National Bank of McGregor for $175 each. She needed money to buy a new house. Her income was tied up in timberlands purchased by her first husband in Louisiana. Brother Sam Cavitt bought her shares for $4,725. Lizzie, evidently short of cash, complained that she did not get her stock dividend before the shares sold. She had sold the stock before the dividend was due to be paid, but after a series of letters Sam Cavitt sent her the $50 dividend anyway. Lizzie then returned the money as not really hers. Both brothers were a bit exasperated.[19]

The merchants at this time were generally divided into those who traded in hardware, those who retailed groceries, those who handled clothing, and those who sold drugs. The hardware business in McGregor involved three stores. Cavitt-Lee Hardware catered to the prosperous population of McGregor. Their store contained stoves with chrome accessories and elaborate carriage harnesses. Cunningham Hardware sold to the small rural landowners and tenant farmers. They sold plain stoves and fancy mule harnesses. The sharecroppers went to a third store that sold combination iron heating and cooking stoves and plain harnesses.

Small retailers generally advertised a wide range of goods produced by a variety of manufacturers. Jobbers, usually traveling by railroad, collected small orders from these merchants and supervised the shipping and delivery of goods. For many of the larger items, the hardware store served as a middleman, securing the order, sending it to the manufacturer, and charging a commission when the item arrived at the store, where the customer picked it up.[20]

Cavitt-Lee Hardware was originally founded as Lee Hardware in 1905 by William Lee. The store served the local community and surrounding area, providing a full range of goods: in addition to hardware, it sold furniture, windmills, and undertaking equipment. But within a year, although business was booming in

McGregor, Lee Hardware was not doing well. Cavitt purchased a majority interest in the store for $5,000 and renamed the emporium Cavitt-Lee Hardware. He built an impressive two-story building on Main Street in McGregor with stables and storerooms at the back. In support, most of the Cavitt and Caufield families purchased their goods there, and Cavitt shipped goods, including beds and mattresses, to relatives as far away as Bryan and Wheelock. In addition, he required his wife's tenant sharecroppers to purchase their goods and "furnish" through his store. The hardware store became a great success and provided the foundation of Cavitt's income.

Over the next decade, Cavitt and Lee purchased other competing stores, lumberyards, and businesses, combining them into their main store and placing smaller local outlets in the surrounding hamlets. The process was often complicated. In 1909, Joe Cavitt and G. W. Lee, with Henry Hanover as partner, purchased the Oglesby Lumber Company from a Dr. Boone. Located in the nearby town of Oglesby, the lumber yard siphoned business from their McGregor store and the Cavitt-Smith Lumber Company, next door to Cavitt-Lee Hardware. The owner of the J. H. Barton Lumber Company of Pittsburg, Texas, offered the business and remaining merchandise for sale. The owner leased the land and buildings for $20 annually and the lease was transferable. E. R. Bolton, vice president of William Cameron and Company, contacted Cavitt and his partners to purchase the business and to eliminate a pesky competitor.

Dr. J. Boone, of nearby Lime City, a local producer of white lime, had once owned the lumberyard and carried notes on the merchandise. He wanted to dispose of the business but also wanted to be able to continue to purchase merchandise wholesale. The buildings and land were valued at $600, the inventory at $6,750, and the fixtures at $150. The current owners rented the top floor of the building to the Masons for $10 a year and the Masons wanted to continue to rent. Another complication, as so often occurred when Cavitt purchased land, involved clearing the title in the Coryell County district court from claims by the heirs of a William Beatty. This necessitated a lawsuit at an additional cost of $100.

Having eliminated unwanted competition, cleared the title, and overcome all obstacles, the partners operated the store as a branch of Cavitt-Lee Hardware, managed locally by their partner Henry Hanover. While Hanover served as manager and secretary-treasurer of the company, J. Q. King was the local operator. G. W. Lee served as president and Cavitt as vice president. The new partnership paid a 25 percent dividend of $775 for Cavitt's thirty-one shares the first year after they purchased the operation. At the end of 1909, Cavitt borrowed $16,000 for new merchandise for both stores. The next year Cavitt earned a $3,100 dividend. Soon, however, business decreased and the company was absorbed into Cavitt-Lee Hardware with a loss.[21]

The hardware store prospered as the local economy thrived on cotton sales. By 1918, the Cavitt-Lee partnership stock was worth $20,000 and the stores in McGregor and Oglesby had $37,000 in undivided property. The McGregor store contained $36,000 in merchandise and the Oglesby store contained $8,000 in unsold goods. The entire operation was now worth $73,000. Ominously, $20,000 in accounts receivable remained unpaid. In 1921 the McGregor store had an inventory of $41,000 and a net worth of $86,000. The stock was valued at $60,000, but accounts receivable had risen to $32,000. Cavitt was president, George Caufield was vice president, and the Lee brothers were on the board of directors of the McGregor store. The Oglesby store remained small, containing $6,000 in unsold merchandise and worth $38,000. The joint operation was now valued at $112,000.

The partners engaged in other businesses as well. Initially they rented the second floor of the storerooms in McGregor to an establishment that made tinned goods, bending sheet tin into buckets and other tinware that was sold downstairs in the emporium. Later, G. W. Lee, who had attended mortician school, opened a funeral and embalming service above the store. Lee raised the bodies through the freight elevator and carried them into the mortuary in the second floor of the storehouse, where he embalmed them for burial. He widened the opening for the elevator on the second floor to allow the caskets to be moved upstairs to the "showing room," where he laid out the bodies for viewing in a small glass-enclosed room on the second floor of the main building. Eventually, Lee separated his funeral home business from the hardware store and moved into a separate facility. He and his son continued to operate the funeral home for the next fifty years.

Thanks to the automobile, a farmer living in rural McLennan County was in weekly touch with Main Street. The county resident might go to town for his groceries or hardware weekly. Rows of shiny black Model Ts lined Main Street as the more prosperous farmers came to market and brought their families. And Cavitt-Lee Hardware was one of the first places they went to make those purchases.[22]

The prosperity from cotton allowed the Cavitts and Caufields to indulge in one of their enduring fascinations: automobiles. Tom Caufield bought a Hudson Super Six. George Caufield purchased a Pierce Arrow. Wat Caufield bought a Ford. Everyone felt prosperous and began to take trips: the Cavitts to Colorado, the George Caufields to North Carolina. The local farmers, also feeling flush with the high cotton prices, purchased tractors and Model T Fords.[23]

In 1910, Joe Cavitt purchased a Jackson touring car through an agreement with M. A. Holmes of Fort Worth, the state agent for the Jackson Automobile Company. The Jackson was a vehicle made by the John Deere Plow Company and distributed throughout the Southwest. Cavitt began to sell automobiles from a garage behind the hardware store. Each car sold for $1,800. (A Ford

Model T sold for $300 to $500.) At that price he had few buyers. The car had serious mechanical problems, and after a few years he dropped the dealership and John Deere stopped making cars.[24]

PROHIBITION

The Caufield, Cavitt, Young, and Foote families became involved in the social movements that swept American society, particularly the rural population. In the latter decades of the nineteenth century, the American countryside underwent dramatic changes. As farm income decreased, young people moved into the cities and an industrialized urban society replaced the dominance of the rural population on the American political scene. The city became a symbol of vice, full of vulgar immigrants who squandered their meager wages on drunken revelry in the saloons and starved their poor wives and children. In reaction, a movement to prohibit the selling of alcoholic beverages—the temperance or prohibition movement—gained momentum. Prohibition became part of a rural evangelical movement pitting the good, moral values of small towns against the wickedness and dissipation of industrialized urban centers.[25]

But prohibition was, first and foremost, a movement to abolish the saloon, associated with lawlessness and loose morals. Urban reformers also worried that in saloons the lower-class white people and African Americans drank too much, draining economic productivity. As the frontier approached final settlement, stable rural communities emerged dominated by a conservative, white Protestant middle class who supported prohibition. Some came to interpret the movement as an assault on the urban poor and working class by middle-class zealots, others as a proving ground for nascent feminists attempting to influence the new industrial world. Regardless of its source, prohibition became a major force in the political arena of Texas in the mid-1880s.[26]

The prohibition of the sale of alcoholic beverages and closing saloons once again became a major political issue during the turn of the nineteenth century. The cause pitted middle-class women and religious institutions against new immigrants and the "rougher element," especially African Americans and Mexicans. Backed by preachers and church people, the prohibitionists assumed the moral high ground and campaigned to legally outlaw the sale of alcoholic beverages.

In Texas, the fight became one among local, county, and state parties. The "dry" element evoked memories of small towns and time-honored Protestant folkways and rejected the corruption of the cities. Earlier, in 1885, a savage campaign to outlaw drinking in McLennan County had been led by Dr. J. B. Cranfill from Crawford and B. H. Carroll, pastor of the First Baptist Church of Waco. The Youngs, Cavitt's cousins from Turnersville, had been a part of this campaign. The strategy at that time had been to pit the moral, "dry" rural areas against the corrupt, "wet" urban precincts. The campaign failed, losing in both the rural and urban precincts. The issue lay quiet for a time, but the prohibitionists made an attempt in 1911 to vote a statewide prohibition of alcoholic beverages. It failed in a much closer vote.[27]

Central Texas, particularly in McLennan County, experienced an unprecedented surge in temperance activity, and Waco became the center of white evangelical culture in Texas and headquarters of the state's prohibition movement. Led by an intensely religious segment of the rural population, the Baptists and other denominations made a major attempt in the election of 1885 to make McLennan County dry. With activity centered on Waco University, the predecessor of Baylor University, Waco became a hotbed of temperance activity. The plan was to use votes in the rural areas, which they felt were strongly for the dry cause, to overpower the "wet" vote from the cities.

Dr. James Cranfill, a physician, teacher, and Baptist minister from Turnersville and Crawford, became a leader of the local prohibition movement, and the members of the Coryell County protestant churches avidly joined the movement. From 1881 to 1882, Cranfill had published a newspaper, the *Turnersville Effort*, so he was quite familiar to local residents and recruited them to his cause. The members of the Young family were strict Calvinists and actively embraced the prohibition movement. Mary Ann regularly attended the evening meetings of the Temperance Council led by Dr. Cranfill.[28]

In several letters Mary Ann Young documented the fervor of the local prohibitionist meeting held in Turnersville when they expelled several young men for drinking and/or dancing. The council reinstated one young man when he confessed his "sin" and begged forgiveness. This was entertainment and high drama in the small village on the Texas plains. Through the prohibition movement and Baptist connections, Cranfill would later move to Waco and eventually to Dallas, where he became the founding editor of the *Baptist Standard*.[29]

Unfortunately for the Prohibitionists, politicians from the Democratic Party viewed the movement as an attempt to diminish their control of the political process and denounced the election as an un-American attack on personal liberty. They deplored the involvement of religious leaders in the political process as "boding no good to either church, or state, or religion, or society." After a vigorous and often nasty campaign, the Prohibitionists lost the election of 1885. McLennan County voted to stay "wet," and the Prohibitionists lost even the rural areas they thought were in their pocket. Turnersville voted "dry." After the election, the movement receded, reemerging from time to time as individual church leaders championed the movement to increase church membership.[30]

Like many small communities, McGregor with its heavily Baptist population attempted to pass local option dry ordinances repeatedly during the early years of the twentieth century. However, the population was divided between Lutheran German settlers—who liked their beer—and more fundamental Protestants. The precinct changed from wet to dry five times over fifteen years. The drys succeeded, only to be outvoted by the wets two years hence. One local saloon owner remarked that the wet/dry controversy only determined whether he "could sell booze out the front or the back door." Fortunately, state law precluded referendums on local option prohibition within a year of an election on a similar subject, or the town would have voted every year.

Prohibition became a burning issue in Texas politics again during the 1917–1918 election. To the despair of his family, Joe Cavitt became an ardent prohibitionist. He led the local political forces in election after election and became involved in the state Prohibition Party. Joe Cavitt had actively supported prohibition since 1905, when he first led the campaign to vote McGregor dry. This year, as part of a statewide referendum, Cavitt eagerly embraced the prohibitionists' cause, raising hundreds of dollars in the McGregor area, which he used to print circulars supporting the dry cause. He served as the local banker for prohibition movement funds and sent telegrams of support to local religious and political leaders. Arthur James Barton, the new and activist president of the Anti-Saloon League, wrote praising Cavitt for his efforts. Once again prohibition lost the election, both locally and statewide.[31]

Other members of Cavitt's family did not embrace his cause. His in-laws, the Caufields, thought he was "a bit nutty on the subject." Wat Caufield liked his toddy and kept his whiskey jug hanging in the well. His wife, Kate McLennan Caufield, a staunch Presbyterian, did not approve and refused to have liquor in her house. If you wanted to have a drink with Mr. Caufield, you asked if you could have a "drink of well water." Caufield was more than happy to oblige. The other Cavitts were known as "hard drinking men."[32]

In 1919, after women had obtained the vote and while male soldiers were away fighting in World War I, Texas voted for state-wide prohibition just in advance of the adoption of the Eighteenth Amendment. In this case, the triumph of progressivism, the attack on the liquor trust, and the xenophobia of the World War succeeded in achieving what had eluded the prohibitionists for over thirty years. Eventually, the Eighteenth Amendment settled the issue for more than a decade.[33]

After the repeal of national prohibition in the 1930s, McGregor remained wet during the Second World War and became one of the few places the soldiers stationed at Fort Hood or a worker at the local ordnance factory could buy a drink between Brownwood and Waco. After repeated efforts during the 1950s, the dry element finally succeeded in passing a prohibition ordinance that remains in force today. In 2005, McGregor did allow the sale of beer at stores. Cranfill would be happy to know that his home ground—Turnersville and Crawford—have remained dry for over a century.[34]

Cotton prices fell between 1910 and 1916. Cavitt and the McGregor bank had invested heavily in a number of local businesses, most of which experienced difficulty. Other local cotton-based businesses suffered during this period as well. Joe Cavitt and the First National Bank of McGregor intervened when necessary. The Grantham Brothers Gin suffered insolvency in 1912, but, as Joe Cavitt wrote to Charles Smith, "they shut their eyes, gritted their teeth, and went day and night. They will reduce their indebtedness with us to about $1,000 by next year." George Gulledge and his McGregor Dry Goods Company did not do as well. In 1913 the bank was more conservative and would not make a loan to a failing business; Cavitt lent his personal funds to secure an $11,000 note. In 1915 the company went bankrupt. Cavitt tried to salvage or sell the business but had to put it through liquidation in 1917. It was a total loss.[35]

The largest money loser was the McGregor Cotton Seed Oil Mill. The mill extracted oil from cottonseed and cottonseed hulls, which sold at a premium for livestock supplements. In addition, the mill had bins for storage of grain and other agricultural commodities. These could provide a tidy profit if managed correctly.

At this time cottonseed oil was an important by-product of the cotton business. After 1880 the manufacturing of cottonseed oil became feasible with the perfection of mechanical crushers capable of separating the seeds from hulls and lint and extracting oil from the seeds. Railroads provided the means to ship the oil, which became the major ingredient of margarine and other food products.

Unfortunately, the McGregor oil mill had a troubled past, and its problems continued. The original owners had retired their debt but, during the depths of the agricultural depression of 1912, had again borrowed from the First National Bank of McGregor against the plant. Like all good bankers, Cavitt patronized the businesses that owed him money and in 1912 processed 70,000 pounds of his own cottonseed hulls through the facility.

Because of concerns about poor management, the bank kept a close eye on the owners and required that they provide a personal endorsement of the stock to the bank to secure their notes. Eventually the mill could not pay its notes and Cavitt and other bank officers attempted to retrieve the bank's investment. At the end of 1914, Dr. J. E. Brown, Sam Amsler, and Joe Cavitt, the bank officers, took over the operation of the oil mill. Cavitt, confident he could turn the business around, invested heavily in the mill. That year the mill issued 500 shares, 100 owned by George Caufield, 119 owned by S. Amsler, 142 owned by Joe Cavitt, and 122 owned by Bud Cavitt. Cavitt secured loans from John and Norman Cavitt for $10,000 to finance his part ownership.[36]

The cotton mill continued in financial difficulties. In 1916, in order to finance the operation of the McGregor Cotton Seed Oil Mill, Cavitt and the bank secured a loan of $25,000 from J. D. Sugg in San Angelo. Initially, under Cavitt's leadership, the mill broke even or made a little money. But it remained heavily indebted and during turndowns in the economy had no reserves upon which to draw. The oil mill even lost money during the prosperous war years of 1917 and 1918. Eventually, financial records indicate that during the poor cotton markets of 1921 to 1925 the business began to lose $25,000 annually.[37]

Several reasons led to the eventual failure of the business. Waco had established itself as the premier cotton processing center for Central Texas and contained a rival cottonseed oil mill. To succeed, a cotton oil mill needed volume, which meant most of the cottonseed from farms up to ten miles away. Cavitt never overcame the competition. He needed to contract with local cotton gins and farmers for their seed. The gins were interested because they purchased the seed from farmers at one price, then resold the seeds to the mill at a higher price. Cavitt cut his own profits by offering premium prices to local farmers who would haul their seed to his mill. However, the other gins undermined his attempts and shipped their seed to Waco, which paid an even higher price. Although he eventually purchased several cotton gins in South Bosque, Oglesby, and McGregor, which supplied seed to the mill, Cavitt was unable to make the business profitable. In 1919 he briefly closed the plant after trying several times to revive the business under different managers. He never attracted enough cottonseed and finally sold the mill in 1923 after losing over $50,000.[38]

In addition to the McGregor Cotton Seed Oil Mill, Cavitt purchased and ran the McGregor Milling and Grain Company with Sam Amsler as president and brother S. A. "Bud" Cavitt as vice president. Joe Cavitt served as secretary-treasurer. A. J. Hickerson had established the grain mill at the turn of the century but, during the recession of 1910, fell on hard times. Cavitt and his friends in the bank purchased the mill's stock to save the bank from foreclosing. Its holdings consisted of the mill itself, with storage capacity for 10,000 bulk bushels and 10,000 milled bushels; two other storage facilities with a capacity for both 25,000 stacked and 25,000 bulk bushels; an adjacent small building that could hold 20,000 bushels; and a barn that could shelter twelve carloads of hay. In 1910, Cavitt processed 26,000 pounds of his own oats through the mill for a profit of $421.65. That year the mill made $3,100; in 1912 it made $7,800; in 1913, $9,200; and in 1914, $9,600. The business grossed $39,000 in 1915 for a net profit of $2,605. The dividends accumulated, reaching $21,000 in 1915. But the profits did not cover the debt service.

At the end of 1915, Cavitt sent a check for $100,000 to the American Exchange National Bank of Dallas to settle his accounts and notes for his failed agricultural businesses. This one payment wiped out all the profits in all his businesses over the previous decade, and he still owed money. Cousin John carried personal notes of $20,000 and a note for $7,000 on the grain mill.[39]

In 1912, Cavitt with his brother-in-law George Caufield made an ill-fated attempt to develop and sell a new agricultural implement, the cotton chopper. McGregor and most other farming communities had a local person who tinkered with farm equipment and frequently obtained patents. Some entrepreneurs even began production of their inventions. A local inventor, June Schrieb, invented and patented a horse-drawn mechanical device to thin the weeds in the rows between the cotton plants. The machine contained several curved blades that, when placed between the rows of plants, undercut the weeds and other plants growing there. In 1906, Schrieb exhibited the cotton chopper and a mechanical washing machine at the State Fair of Texas and won several awards. Schrieb started production of both machines in McGregor but soon failed because of poor management and slow sales. The

McGregor National Bank held the notes on the business. Cavitt became interested in producing the implement locally and took over the indebtedness. If the labor-intensive chopping of weeds between cotton rows could be mechanized, the potential savings for cotton farmers would be immense.

Cavitt began to build and market the implement from his factory in McGregor. He incorporated the Texas Cotton Chopper Company in 1912, later changing the name to the Texas Implement Manufacturing Company, with $200,000 capital in 1916. Production began in a local blacksmith's shop. Northern steel mills made the iron parts on order and shipped them to McGregor for assembly. By advertising in several trade journals, Joe Cavitt lined up a number of North Texas hardware stores to serve as dealers. Cavitt sold the implement to the dealers for $65 wholesale and they, in turn, sold it to farmers for $85 retail. By 1921 he had sold more than 1,000 cotton choppers.

Unfortunately, while the cotton chopper did well in level alluvial soils, it did not function as well in hilly or broken fields. As his initial success turned sour and dissatisfied customers complained to his dealers and to the company, Joe tried to make both the farmers and the dealers happy by replacing defective parts. He sent a salesman, M. A. Jones, around the local area to satisfy customers and sell the cotton chopper to local retail outlets. But bad weather, poor roads, poor credit, unscrupulous retailers, poor cotton prices, and a bad product hampered Jones. He gave up after six months.

Cavitt continued to produce and market his cotton chopper intermittently for a decade before finally, in 1925, liquidating the company at a deficit. He lost $50,000 on this venture, including $6,000 in Liberty Bonds he had used to secure his debt. Joe had failed once again to turn a company around.[40]

In 1919, Cavitt had been well on his way to being a millionaire. He had accumulated over 2,700 acres of McLennan County cotton land. He owned eight to twenty lots in McGregor. His net worth was over $100,000 in land in McLennan County alone and he paid over $1,000 in property taxes, making him one of the largest landowners in the county. In addition, from his family, he had inherited all or part of 3,000 acres in Coryell County along the Leon River and several thousand acres of Brazos River bottom land in Robertson County. He owned interests in a cotton gin, a cottonseed oil plant, a mule barn, a hardware store, and a drug-store. He had 1,000 head of cattle and 2,000 head of sheep, as well as pigs, mules, and Shetland ponies.

In 1920, Josephus Cavitt had reached the height of his influ-ence. He was vice president of the McGregor National Bank, secretary-treasurer of McGregor Milling and Grain, vice president of the McGregor Cotton Seed Oil Mill, president of Cavitt-Lee Hardware, and secretary-treasurer of the Oglesby Lumber Company. He was secretary-treasurer of the local Masonic lodge; he was a member of the Democratic Party Central Committee; he was on the board of directors of Texas Presbyterian College; and he was prominent in the state prohibitionist party. His wife was on the board of directors of the local Red Cross. He would soon be a member of the board of directors of the McLennan County Famers Association. He was a big man. Yet, despite his apparent assets and influence, Cavitt lost money that year.

Beginning in 1919, various groups drilled for oil or leased land in the area. However, the newfound oil wealth eluded the Cavitt and Caufield families. Despite the large amount of land they owned, oil was never found on their land. Attempting to cash in on the oil boom, Cavitt and George Caufield formed the McGregor Oil and Milling company, selling $50,000 in stock at $100 a share. Cavitt purchased twenty-three shares. Later they formed the Ranger Quarry Company to furnish gravel and fill to the oil fields. The businesses were handled by D. A. Kelley, a prominent Waco attorney. Neither company made money. The families' prosperity remained rooted in the old economies of livestock and cotton.

The Second Generation, 1920–1940

THE CAUFIELD FAMILY BEGAN THE TRANSITION TO urban life before the turn of the century as Henry Caufield's children moved from their parents' farms into the surrounding towns. Henry Caufield initiated this process as he attained wealth and aged. He entered politics and was elected McLennan County commissioner from 1872 to 1876. He helped settle a local financial crisis by reestablishing the value of county bonds and building a new courthouse. At the turn of the century, he established and funded a local school district in the form of the Caufield School, until it was consolidated with a neighboring district. Caufield invested in several of his sons' businesses, including the McGregor National Bank, and in cotton gins and hardware stores in McGregor and the surrounding communities. Henry Caufield invested in the

Citizens National Bank of Waco about 1896 and was on the initial board of directors.[1]

In 1908, Henry decided to divide his property between his children. Brother Watson Caufield had died on the ranch in 1904 and was buried in the family cemetery plot at Harris Creek. Martha Jones Caufield had died in 1906. Henry was alone now. Each child received about 2,000 acres as their inheritance.

Even before the death of patriarch Henry Caufield, the economic engine of the Caufield family began to change. Cotton became the major crop as the family converted ranchland to cotton fields and the livestock was moved to the wooded areas prone to flooding along the branches of the South Bosque River.

A new way of life opened up for the children as the next generation moved further from their agricultural roots. The children reached adulthood, married, and moved to town, most to nearby McGregor, but several to Waco. There they became absentee farmers and began to engage in business in their new, more urban environment. The farms and ranches, although the primary source of their income, became secondary to their business enterprises.

Several of the children died before their father. One daughter, Deedie Caufield, died as a young adult from rheumatic heart disease. Mart Caufield died in 1905 from tuberculosis he contracted at college in Clarksville. He left a widow and two small children. Henry Caufield had purchased a ranch near Albany from Butler Dunn for Mart to manage in the drier West Texas air. Mart and his family lived on the ranch for seven years. Afterward, as he became weaker, he lived in Miles, Texas, near San Angelo, until his death. After Mart's passing, Tom served as trustee for his brother's portion of the Caufield Ranch. He managed Mart's widow's and daughters' affairs. In 1919, after Tom's death, Mart's wife sold her share of the farms to George Caufield and Joe Cavitt so the girls could attend Texas Presbyterian College and obtain teaching certificates.[2]

Initially, only one of Henry Caufield's children decided to remain on the original ranch. Martha Elizabeth Caufield, who had married Joe Clifton, continued to live in the old ranch head-quarters, caring for Henry and his ailing wife, Martha. After Martha's death in 1906, Henry fell and broke his hip. He spent his last years in town living with his other daughter, Mollie Cavitt. The Clifton family inherited the old homestead and continued to farm the river bottom lands. After his wife's untimely death in 1910, Clifton and his children sold their share of the ranch to George Caufield and Joe Cavitt. The Clifton children carried the notes on their mother's farms until just prior to Joe Cavitt's bank-ruptcy, when John Cavitt assumed the notes.[3]

One son, Tom Caufield, moved to Waco and was elected McLennan County tax collector in 1896, a position he held for twenty years. Cautious and thoughtful, Tom Caufield served as a counterbalance to his ambitious, reckless brother George and domineering brother-in-law Joe Cavitt. Tom had been sent to run the ranch in Shackleford County, then to Mexico to oversee the operation there. He had attended Southwestern Presbyterian College in Clarksville, Tennessee, where he became close friends with Joe Cavitt's brother John and Charles Caldwell, later pastor at the First Presbyterian Church in Waco. At Clarksville he met and married a local Presbyterian pastor's daughter, Lillie Hendricks. These close friends of Tom's and his wife and her family advised him to be conservative in financial and moral matters, and he fol-lowed their advice.

In September 1919, Thomas Caufield took his son George to St. Joseph's Hospital in Chicago to repair a cleft palate. A Dr. Brophy charged $1,200 for the repair and a tonsillectomy performed beforehand. The total cost for the operation, hospital, and trip was $2,250, an incredible sum for the day, equivalent to four times an average worker's annual earnings. Caufield paid cash. While in Chicago, Tom developed acute appendicitis. He had come in early the night before, thirsty and suffering from indigestion. Having had a difficult night and still not well in the morning, he called a doctor, who medicated him, never thinking he was seriously ill. By noon he was worse and went to the hospital. They took him to the operating room and removed a gangrenous appendix. After an initial rally, Caufield developed peritonitis and died the following day.[4]

Thomas Caufield's steady leadership was lost due to his untimely death. Without their brother's stabilizing influence, George Caufield and Joe Cavitt became increasingly reckless in their investments. As George and Joe expanded their farming operations, Joe Cavitt purchased Tom Caufield's portion of the ranch, 918 acres, in 1920 from Tom's widow.[5]

In 1894, Caufield had acquired a new son-in-law when his twenty-five-year-old daughter, Martha (Mollie), married twenty-seven-year-old Josephus F. Cavitt, the son of Volney Cavitt and nephew of his best friend, partner, and mentor Josephus S. Cavitt. In 1885, Cavitt had moved to McGregor and engaged in local businesses. Joe was the rich son of a rich father. His family owned thousands of acres of cotton land along the Brazos River near Wheelock. Joe was tall, over six feet, and weighed over two hundred pounds. He was loud and very sure of himself. He was somewhat of a bully and disliked by many of the people of McGregor. Joe Cavitt was to dominate the family in the next generation.

Son-in-law Josephus Cavitt and son George were the most ambitious of the family, establishing, owning, and managing assorted businesses and rental properties in McGregor. By 1920, George Caufield and Joe Cavitt had purchased the farms of all their siblings except Watson Caufield's.

George was a weak personality. The youngest of the Caufield children, twenty years younger than his oldest brother, George had never been subjected to the hardships of the frontier. He hated working with his hands. He enjoyed being rich and, while seeking his family's respect, eagerly joined Joe Cavitt in all his speculations. George Caufield became a banker with money from his father and later established an auto supply business in Waco. His businesses became closely allied with those of Joe Cavitt. Meanwhile, he spent lavishly on his family, traveling to North Carolina for protracted vacations and sending his car ahead by special rail.

Joe Cavitt and George Caufield did not fit the description of "thrifty." Joe Cavitt owned a mule lot, a cotton gin, Cavitt-Lee Hardware, Cavitt lumberyards, and his wife's farms. He established the Texas Implement and Manufacturing Company, which made the cotton chopper. Unfortunately, the machine had faults and few were ever sold.

When the agricultural crisis hit in 1925, George Caufield found himself overextended and was forced into bankruptcy, losing his home and farms. Joe Cavitt had spread himself too widely in his numerous small businesses, and as the agricultural depression continued into 1928, he, too, was forced into bankruptcy.[6]

In 1882, Henry Caufield's oldest son, Watson, married Katharine "Kate" McLennan, the daughter of Henry Caufield's friend, Neil McLennan Jr. The wedding cemented the friendship that the three young men had developed on the Texas frontier. Henry Caufield had married his friend Wiley Jones's sister, Martha, and now Henry's oldest son had married the daughter of their friend Neil McLennan. The three men remained the best of friends until their deaths.

In 1884, as a wedding present, Henry and his brother Watson built a house for Wat and Kate on their section of the ranch. The house sat on a knoll along a creek in a grove of huge live oaks about a quarter mile from the South Bosque. Watson served as the head carpenter. They shipped the wood by oxcart and railroad from Houston. The house was a standard four-by-four: four rooms downstairs shared the same walls with four rooms upstairs. The living room and dining room were paneled with mahogany.

Sliding doors separated the large area. A wide porch encircled the building, with a screened porch on the back for summer sleeping.[7]

It was the first two-story house in that part of McLennan County and had all the embellishments available at the time. The trim was in mahogany, the walls in oak, the floors and shutters in cypress. The kitchen was in back, as was the privy. Water came from a well dug across the creek in front and pumped by a windmill into a large storage facility that provided running water indoors.

They shipped furniture in over the new rail lines from the East, consisting mainly of heavy Victorian Eastlake pieces, and added other furniture, as needed and as affordable, over the years. The family, over time, added a central kitchen, indoor plumbing, electricity, central heating, and air-conditioning. The house, finished in 1888, is still the ranch and family headquarters today.[8]

While the house was being built, Wat and Kate lived in a four-room cottage half a mile up the creek. There they had their first child, Eula. Eula managed to survive an unfortunate accident that occurred while she was an infant. The baby was being held and fed by her Black nurse on the front porch of the house when the nurse's husband returned from hunting along the river. He laid his gun against the wall and picked up the child. The gun slid to the floor, discharged, and killed his wife. Kate Caufield hated that house from that time on.

Kate McLennan Caufield was the dominant personality in this family and she carefully managed their ranch and supervised the tenants, making and saving money wherever possible. Wat was quiet and studious. He had a large library of well-read books. He kept extensive account books and assiduously worked his land.[9]

Kate managed their farms very carefully as well. The tenants knew that although the negotiations would be done by Watson Caufield, the final decision on their renting land would be made by "Mrs. Kate." After talking with Wat, they always visited the kitchen to give their "howdy" to Kate Caufield. Most also knew that if they asked Wat if he had a "cup of cool water," he would lead them out of the house to the well on the other side of the creek where a jug of whiskey hung in the cool well water. He would offer them a drink and, of course, take a neighborly drink himself.

Desiring to enter the high society of Texas ranching families, in 1910 Kate Caufield moved her family to Alamo Heights in San Antonio. The largest town in Texas at the time, San Antonio offered good schools, cultural events, and domestic conveniences that attracted the children of prosperous Texas ranchers and cotton plantation owners. The Watson Caufields rented the large house on their portion of the ranch to their overseer and lived in San Antonio until the Depression brought them home.[10]

Kate Caufield refused to borrow money. After losing half their land to pay the debts of one of Wat's brothers, she refused to lend even to family members. When the Depression hit and the price of cotton fell, they received an overdraft notice from the First National Bank of McGregor. Wat Caufield traveled to McGregor and discovered their McGregor cotton factor had not sold any of their cotton for two years, "waiting for the price to go up." Wat found the cotton stacked in bales around the house. Instead of going up, cotton had fallen from 15 cents a pound to less than 10 cents a pound. He immediately sold the cotton for what they could get. They were broke.

Kate sold their house in San Antonio and moved back to their old home near McGregor with their recently divorced daughter Elizabeth Caufield Arnold and her son Watson Caufield Arnold. Watson "Sonny" Arnold was a senior at Alamo Heights High School the year they moved. Because McGregor had a high school going up to only the eleventh grade and the family planned for him to go to Baylor University, which required twelve years of school, Sonny attended Waco High School, riding a bus every morning to town. He earned a scholarship to attend Baylor the next year, working during the summer building barns and raising sheep. During the school year he waited tables in the girls' dormitory and eventually graduated from Baylor Law School. His grandparents remained on the ranch until their deaths. Arnold and his four sons still own and manage their land to this day.

Eula, Wat's and Kate's eldest daughter, had married a young man from Tyler who owned a buggy sales establishment. He died during the flu epidemic of 1918 and Eula remarried a wealthy rancher, W. T. "Monty" Montgomery. He had purchased a cattle ranch on the Medina River east of San Antonio that had been part of the old Juan Seguín family holdings. Montgomery made his money as a road contractor and met the recently widowed Eula Caufield Connelly when he rented a room in the Caufield home while constructing the state highway from McGregor to Waco. He was a Hereford rancher and raised several Grand National Champion Hereford bulls. He was also a board member of the Texas and Southwestern Cattle Raisers Association and president of the Texas Hereford Association. They continued to live in San Antonio and on their ranch. When they retired, they sold the ranch on the Medina and moved to a home in Olmos Park in San Antonio.

When they learned of their financial distress, Wat and Kate Caufield quickly sold the family's Alamo Heights home in San Antonio and moved back to the ranch in 1935. On the land, they lived frugally until cotton prices rose once again. At the beginning and at the end of the Depression they owed no money. Because of Kate's influence, the Watson Caufields were the only members of the family to retain ownership of their lands.[11]

By 1935, only the Watson Caufield family still owned their portion of Henry Caufield's vast ranch. On their remaining 1,000 acres they continued to raise cotton until the 1950s, when the farms began a transition to grains, primarily corn in rotation with maize and wheat. Today the ranch is in a corporation owned by the four sons.

Joe Cavitt managed most of his family's investments. When the cotton crop was sold, Cavitt's sisters, Ruth and Cora, and their mother sent their crop income to Joe to invest or loan out. In 1911, Ruth received $583.84 as her share of the income from the Brazos bottomlands. The loans were usually small, $50 to $500, carried high interest at 8 to 10 percent, and came due in sixty to ninety days. Joe Cavitt personally handled most of these notes rather than processing them through the First National Bank of McGregor. Because expenses were low in the small towns of Texas, the Cavitt family could live very cheaply and still have large amounts of money to invest each year. They purchased most of their goods at the Mitchell Brothers Mercantile Store near Wheelock. In this store, eight pounds of coffee cost seventeen cents; twenty-four pounds of flour, 72 cents; and ten pound of sugar, 53 cents. The Mitchells were cousins by marriage and longtime friends and partners of the Cavitt family. In addition, the sisters received a portion of the income from the store. Thus, a little money went a long way.

Another source of long-term income was investments in real estate, which needed constant supervision. In 1904, Cavitt purchased the Corner Drug Store building in McGregor for his sisters. He supervised the site, collected the rents and sent them to his sisters, and maintained the property. One of the local physicians, a Dr. Connally, rented space in the building for $25 a month. Druggist Frank Smith paid $50 a month for the front half. An awning placed over the store front in 1905 provided a sheltered sidewalk across the neighboring eight stores.

Expenses remained high. Because the building was built on the ground, the wooden floor rotted, warped, and sank in 1910, just as Smith was putting in a $3,000 cold drink stand. Repairs cost only $75 but, combined with the $300 in repairs paid the previous year, insurance, and annual taxes of $20, the family did not make a lot of money on the building. In 1916 the roof needed repairs. Cavitt attended to the problem through Cavitt-Lee Hardware. In 1918 a replacement for the awning cost $500. They sold the store in 1920 for $5,000, a small profit.

The sisters freely traded their partial ownership in the store, as they did all their properties and investments. Those needing ready cash sold their portion of the real estate to whoever had excess income for investing. Cora Armstrong bought sister Ruth's interest in the store in 1908, for which she was paid $1,000, because Ruth wanted to go to Colorado Springs. Ruth later bought Lizzie Goode's portion of one of the farms when the Goodes needed cash for investing in their sawmill and timberlands in Louisiana.[12]

Joe Cavitt kept accounts for his family in the McGregor bank and distributed their funds according to their wishes. The Goodes were the most frugal. For example, they purchased an acetylene gas generator for their home. The generator powered eleven lights. They felt the acetylene gas lighting was much better than electricity, "mellower" and much less expensive. They also lived quietly and well. Robert was a respected attorney in the community of Bryan.

Unfortunately, the sisters and their mother spent much of their time in a constant round of visits—to Wheelock, Bay City, Bryan, Hearne, Austin, San Antonio, San Marcos, McGregor, New York, and Colorado—and they were at home less than six months a year. And when they were at home, they entertained a continuous list of guests and family with hired help. The girls hated to be alone at the old homestead and felt entitled to whatever luxuries their inherited wealth could buy. Money trickled and flowed through their hands. Even then, they could not spend all their inheritance over the next twenty years, but they managed to put a significant dent in their wealth.[13]

In 1906, after selling the 659-acre "Arkansas Place" for $4,200 cash, the girls felt particularly flush. The land was on Cedar Creek in Coryell County and had been part of their inheritance from their father, Volney Cavitt. With their new income, Cora went to New York City and West Virginia for the summer. Ruth and her mother went to Colorado Springs. Joe and his family met them later with sister Lizzie and her husband in Saratoga, Texas, to take the waters for a month.

The money from the sale was soon gone, and Ruth wrote Joe to complain about her low bank balance. After he admonished her for spending too much money, Ruth wrote back: "I'll be economical if I can go to New York so I can stay all winter. It is a fine place to wear any old thing you happen to have."[14]

Joe Cavitt also managed the business affairs of several of his brothers and served as trustee for his brother Albert Sidney "Sid" Cavitt. Sid was a heavy drinker, did not manage his money well, and could be difficult to deal with. In 1904, Joe Cavitt purchased 6,400 acres (ten square miles) near San Angelo for his mother, Clara Cavitt, from the estate of Harold Westcott for $11,000, or about $2 an acre. The sale included 607 head of cattle ($6,070), eleven horses ($600), and wagons, harnesses, and nine sacks of salt ($130), for an additional value of $6,730.

Clara Cavitt placed this ranch in trust for her son Sid, to be managed by his brothers Joe and James Volney "Jim" Cavitt as trustees. Whenever they negotiated with Sid, Jim and Joe Cavitt took their other brother, Sheridan ("Bud"), along. Bud seemed to be able to handle Sid better.

The brothers tried to be careful stewards. The San Angelo National Bank served as the local overseer of the lands and accounts. A portion of the leased ranchland was state school land on which principal and interest was paid annually, and another portion was railroad land that was clear of debt. Initially, they leased about half a section to a "Pat" Patterson for $17 an acre. Sid primarily raised sheep and some cattle on the remaining land. But taxes and payments to the Texas Permanent School Fund were a constant source of concern, as Sid often ignored taxes and debts. In 1909, even though the ranch had produced a good income, Joe Cavitt had to pay the taxes because Sid had already spent his money. The bank was not very helpful, making payments to the wrong entities, resulting in a constant flow of letters from Joe Cavitt to keep matters straight. Because of Joe Cavitt's careful management, the land sold for $150,000 ($30 an acre), and each sibling received a share.[15]

Sid Cavitt never could decide if he wanted to stay on his ranch or live in town. He moved back and forth constantly, neglecting his cattle and sheep. When he did work on the place, he had some success. In 1909, he sold thirty-three bags of wool for a net income of $1,400. But Sid did not like to winter on the ranch and would move to town, leaving his brothers to find someone else to care for the livestock. He would spend his cash income and leave the taxes and land payments to the state for Joe or his brothers to handle. Cousin Norman Cavitt, Joe Cavitt's cousin John's son, often spent the winter on the ranch caring for the livestock and visiting with his uncle Sid.

Titles always caused problems. In 1916, the trustees litigated several suits over the title to several hundred acres. R. R. Wade owned two small tracts of land, seventy-three acres in all, in the middle of one of the large Cavitt-owned pastures. Since 1911 he had received rent of 20 cents an acre but in 1916 he offered to sell the land for $12.50 an acre, an exorbitant price for that time. When the owner threatened to sell to another buyer who would need access through the Cavitts' larger tract, the trustees bought the land. Later the county decided to build a road through another pasture. Settling the dispute with the county over price took several more years.[16]

Sid married in 1916 and his wife, Maude, proved to be a great help in keeping him steady. Joe Cavitt and his sisters sent presents to the wedding but did not attend because they thought the new wife a bit "low class." But her life was tough on an isolated ranch in West Texas, and she had to deal with her Cavitt relatives. She cooked and cleaned for the workers. Amenities such as flowers were difficult to raise. Even a garden was problematic. "The hogs came through the barbed wire fence and rooted out the garden," she wrote. Their mother, Clara Cavitt, visited Sid frequently and her attempts to keep peace seem to have caused more problems than they solved.[17]

By 1917, Sid decided once again to run the West Texas ranch, and when the lease expired, he moved back on the land. The spring wool that year brought 23.2 cents a pound for thirty-two bags of wool—7,500 pounds, or $1,500 in net income on the San Angelo market.[18]

In 1919, Sid sued for control of his land in the San Angelo courts. The local firm of Wright and Harris represented the Cavitt brothers. The court reset the trial date several times, resulting in confusion, inconvenience, and expenses. Joe Cavitt had to pay the expenses of his witness and, with the constantly changing trial date, the cost mounted. The case continued intermittently until 1926. That year Sid also wanted to lease his mineral rights for oil. The brother trustees decided to let him do as he wished on the oil leases and to spend the money as he wished. The trustees, however, never dissolved the trust: Sid never gained control of the land, and when he died in 1948, the remaining siblings and their heirs sold the land.

Another troublesome relative was first cousin Mary Cavitt Washington. Joe Cavitt became involved in her divorce settlement. Mary had married a man from West Virginia. Initially they lived on her portion of the family league on the Leon River, but the climate and work were too hard for her husband and they moved back to his home in West Virginia. On the death of her father in 1886, Mary received $6,650 from the estate and 573 acres from the family league in Coryell County, which she sold to cousin Bud Cavitt for $10,000. In 1910 she left her husband and later divorced him. She sued for her inheritance. Her husband had used her money as though it had been his own, purchasing an orchard and home near Romney, West Virginia. Mary returned to live with her father, the elder Josephus Cavitt, near Wheelock. Joe and his cousin John worked several years to recover her money. They hired a West Virginia attorney, recorded depositions, and made trips to court, eventually winning the case on appeal. Mary eventually received $3,236 cash and the orchard, which she later sold for $2,800. Later the purchaser of the orchard was constantly late paying his notes, another chore placed on the cousins' shoulders.[19]

Some of Joe Cavitt's relatives did quite well without his supervision. First cousin John B. Cavitt and his adopted nephew, Norman, kept careful watch over their land near Wheelock and often invested with Joe. Brother Sam lived nearby and also farmed his own land. Their share of the Cavitt inheritance had been several thousand acres of Brazos River bottomland, including the J. Dunn league.

John personally and carefully supervised his farms and tenants, and the cost for tenants could be quite high. In 1910, he built seven two-room houses, cribs, and wells for new tenants costing $1,900. He paid the cost by letting the builder lease three hundred acres for three years. In addition, John operated several mercantile companies, including Skinner Mercantile in Rogers and the McWhinney Mercantile Company in Holland. The Cavitt family in Wheelock traded with Mitchell Brothers Mercantile, of which John also owned a portion.[20]

But life was not always smooth. In 1913, John and Sam Cavitt suffered from a series of barn burnings by a disgruntled tenant. The man fled and the brothers were never able to prosecute the perpetrator. Other tenants sometimes left suddenly, taking the Cavitt livestock with them. And there were always disputes over boundary lines.

John, however, carefully managed his money while living a bachelor's life with his nephew, Norman. John became a moneylender and banker. By 1919 he held notes for $125,216 and expected an annual income from interest alone of $8,784. In 1922 he personally had notes out for $165,245, most at 7 to 10 percent interest, and received an income of $13,341 on his money. He also made money on his cotton, cattle, and mercantile businesses. He listed his only annual expense as $100 for lawyers.

Because of their thrift, Sam, John, and Norman often had extra cash, which Joe Cavitt frequently borrowed for his speculations. In 1906, when the brothers purchased a major portion of the First National Bank of McGregor, Sam wrote: "If his ideas are correct, we will surely get rich, in fact will make that barrel of money we have talked of so long." The brothers later loaned Joe Cavitt $7,000 to purchase the McGregor grain mills. The duo also loaned cash to Cavitt on his land. When Joe went bankrupt, they eventually lost money in most of his investments.

By 1922, Joe Cavitt's major debtor was his first cousin John, and Joe was already a year behind on his interest. By 1925 he owed John $18,654 in first and second liens secured by his wife's farms and owed Norman $10,000 also secured by the farms. The cousins had carefully tied each note to a piece of property. John Cavitt always expected to get his money back. When the agricultural depression came, neither brother nor their cousins had borrowed money, and although they lost on some of their investments with Joe, they kept their own land and ended up owning most of Joe's land as well.[21]

Other family members were also careful with their money. Will and Lizzie Goode, Joe Cavitt's sister and brother-in-law, were the most frugal. In 1907, Will and Lizzie moved to Sparks, Louisiana, to run the Old River Lumber Company, which made cypress shingles. They were willing to live rather primitively until they could sell their investment. Another sister, Cora, had married Robert Armstrong, a prosperous and respected attorney in the community of Bryan. The Armstrongs also lived quietly and well. Both families survived the Depression with their fortunes intact.[22]

The Cavitt family gradually began to sell their land holdings to cover their living expenses. They were offered $75 an acre for their "Brazos Bottoms" in 1906 but refused to sell. In 1906, they did sell the Arkansas Place on Cedar Creek in Coryell County for $6 an acre. Cora and Ruth purchased Florence's portion. Ruth received a total of $4,200 for the sale.

The sale proved to be more difficult than anticipated when a defect in the title delayed closing. During a switch in land in 1886, the wife of one of the owners had failed to sign the deed. This and a poor description of the land boundaries allowed her daughter by another marriage, a Mrs. William Ashe, to claim part of the land. This defect resulted in litigation lasting for three years before the title could be cleared through a default judgment. Mrs. Ashe offered to settle for $500 but Joe pushed the litigation through, paying only $87 in expenses.[23]

The old Cavitt league on the Leon River was another enterprise Joe Cavitt managed. The land lay in Coryell County between the small hamlets of Cavitt and Leon Junction. In 1862, Joe's father, Volney Cavitt, and his uncle Josephus Cavitt had purchased 12,000 acres along the South Bosque and Leon Rivers next to their own league for $10,600 from the heirs of J. L. L. McLean and Sophia St. John. The owners were Northerners and had to sell to avoid confiscation by the Confederacy. Joe Cavitt had purchased his siblings' and cousins' shares in the league and accumulated 1,986 acres of his own in the Andrew Cavitt survey. He also purchased 177 acres from his cousin Clara Cavitt, 348 acres from his brother B. B. Cavitt, and 611 acres from his cousin Mary Washington. His brother Bud had another 2,500 acres on one side of his land, and his cousin John had 2,500 acres on the other side.

The Cotton Belt Railroad ran through this property and served as a constant source of irritation. Animals wandered onto the tracks and were frequently injured. In 1907 the railroad paid $215 for a Hereford bull killed by an engine. However, in 1917, when Cavitt complained that several jacks and Shetlands had been lamed by a cattle guard along the right of way, the railroad blamed the horses and mules for walking the cattle guards and refused to be responsible for their injuries. When taken to court, the railroad relented and paid for the animals.[24]

The taxes were a mess. The land had been passed down undivided, and many cousins and others had failed to pay their share of the taxes on different fields in different years. Joe Cavitt tried to straighten it all out. Even then, in 1916, Cavitt received a notice from C. E. Stockburger, tax collector for Coryell County, that the taxes on the jointly owned 1,982 acres had been only partly paid and that receipts for several other years were missing. Cavitt paid all the taxes and expenses, clearing the indebtedness on the entirety. Brothers Bud and Joe worked in concert to improve the land, building levees along the Leon River and fences along the railroad.[25]

Joe tried various methods to make money on the property. He harvested pecans, selling 1,700 pounds at 8 cents a pound in Fort Worth. He contracted to sell cedar posts from the Leon River farms and offered to sell railroad ties to the Cotton Belt Railroad. He tried to raise cotton along the river. A flood in 1907 to 1908 was particularly disastrous, breaking the levee along the river and devastating the cotton crop. Cavitt suffered heavy losses.

Although cotton was now the major crop on the ranch lands, livestock remained an important source of income. Joe Cavitt bred cattle, Shetlands, and mules on the place. The farm produced forty-four heifers, which sold for $2,204 in 1917; between twenty-five to fifty head went to the stockyards most other years. Later, in 1909, mother Clara Cavitt and her children sold their part of the Andrew Cavitt league in Coryell County for $3 an acre. Eventually, Joe Cavitt sold the land to his brother Bud and cousin John.[26]

When Clara died in 1920, the family let Joe Cavitt handle both the funeral and the estate and to split the land among the siblings. The estate included $38,000 in notes and cash, plus the old homestead with house and 333 acres of land. Each child received in cash or in land the equivalent of $4,461. The four girls took an undivided interest in the home place. They calculated that brother Sam Cavitt owed the estate $16,000 and he paid the balance over several years. Joe personally covered several bad notes he had underwritten for his mother and lost more money than he received from the settlement.[27]

8

Fall of the Cotton Kingdom, 1930–1950

RAISING COTTON IS A GAMBLER'S TRADE. WHEN COTTON prices rose during World War I, Texas farmers cleared ever more land and planted it in cotton. Indeed, cotton was the only crop most farmers planted and by 1924, 56.7 percent of Texas cropland had been planted in cotton. However, in the mid- to late 1920s, the luck ran out for Texas cotton farmers. Low prices, poor weather, the boll weevil, and drought struck Central Texas farmers for four straight years.

The farm crisis, which began in 1925, was nationwide and affected all agricultural crops. The Great Depression settled on the country's farmers long before the stock market fell in 1929. The Cavitt and Caufield farms suffered just as much as the other farmers.

Over a forty-year period, from 1880 to 1920, mechanization became an important force in American agriculture. Between 1860 and 1890 the United States Patent Office issued more than 10,000 patents for agricultural implements—over 5,000 on milk separators alone. The annual value of American manufactures of agricultural implements rose from $21 million to over $100 million. As a result, the amount of labor and the number of persons needed to plant and harvest commodities fell every decade—by 50 percent in the latter part of the nineteenth century.[1]

Mechanization lowered the cost of production, increased the number of commodities farmers could raise, and raised the standard of living. It had the earliest and greatest effect on the grain crops. The use of disc plows, broadcast seeders, harrows, and combines ("combining" reapers and thrashers) in the wheat fields made the work of one man eighteen times as effective in 1896 as in 1830. Thus, mechanization dramatically reduced the number of people needed to feed and clothe the population of the United States. The wealth and leisure time produced by these advances allowed farmers more time to attend church, educational, and cultural events, a luxury missing in prior generations. This made the fall in prices during the last decades of the nineteenth century somewhat more bearable.[2]

Farm mechanization also led steadily to fewer and larger farms. The increased cost of land and the expense of machinery reduced the number of farmers who owned their own land and increased the number of tenant and hired workers. By the 1870s, the number of farms had dropped even as the number of acres in cotton production increased.[3]

Anticipating good crop prices and hoping to mechanize and increase their yields, farmers—both tenants and landowners—borrowed heavily to pay for tractors and cars. Unfortunately, after World War I ended, the disbanded armies no longer needed uniforms, and the devastated economies of Europe were unable to afford new clothing. Although the price of cotton had stabilized around 20 cents a pound during the war and rose to 35 cents, in 1920 it began falling, reaching 5 cents in 1926. The value of cotton fell to the lowest levels in thirty years and prices remained depressed.[4]

In order to buy the new labor-saving equipment, farmers had to borrow money. And few farmers could resist a new car or tractor when times were good and bountiful crops sold for good prices. Unfortunately, farmers entered the Depression with large debts that would cost them their farms when prices fell and drought cut production. Throughout the farming districts nationwide, the value of land decreased as the country moved deeper into the Great Depression. The cotton-growing areas suffered more than others.[5]

The Caufield and Foote families embraced mechanization, beginning with barbed wire, wells, and windmills. Their expenses for various farm implements were formidable. In Coryell County the Foote family kept careful records of their expenses as they mechanized. One of the first purchases the ranch made was a Fort Scott drill to plant wheat. The implement cost $450 plus $50 shipping from the W. A. Hoffman Company of Fort Worth to Gatesville—a fabulous sum for those days. At this point Foote was raising grain—including 9,600 bushels of corn and 3,000 bushels of oats—and thirty tons of hay, primarily as feed for his animals.

In 1925–1926 a severe drought struck Central and East Texas, causing crop failures. Farmers were unable to meet their debts and borrowed more in anticipation of a better crop the next year. Landowners who purchased seed, housing, and mules for their tenants were unable to meet their expenses. Those who allowed their sharecroppers to charge at their stores carried even heavier financial burdens. Deeply in debt, sharecroppers abandoned their farms and moved west, leaving the owners with no hope of recovering their outlays.

When cotton prices fell, so did the income of the merchants and bankers in the small towns. McGregor and Joe Cavitt were no exceptions. The fall in prices, as well as the decrease in the amount of cotton produced, combined to give the farmers a knockout blow. Merchants followed shortly thereafter.

Nineteen twenty-one had been a good year. Cavitt produced 128 bales of cotton, which sold for 22 cents a pound ($15,500). In 1924 the family farms produced three-quarters of a bale to one bale an acre, selling at 25 cents a pound, netting $12,000 to$15,000. In 1925, after the drought hit Central Texas hard, Cavitt earned just $12 on 120 acres of cotton that the previous year had earned $300.

George Caufield made no crop at all in 1924 and actually lost money. George needed every penny of income to cover his debts, having borrowed heavily, up to $125 an acre at 8 to 10 percent interest, to cover previous expenses and losses on an auto parts business in Waco.[6]

George was a poor businessman and made a series of bad investments that led to his downfall when cotton prices fell. George even lost money on his investments during the 1920s, the greatest period of prosperity in our country's history. In 1909, George had purchased a portion of the land of his sister, Martha Caufield Clifton. Bart Moore, a cousin and trustee for Martha's children, had taken a note for the $10,250 balance on land valued at $26,850. By 1917, George was behind on the notes to the Clifton children and Joe Cavitt took over 250 acres, plus part of the debt. In 1920, Moore foreclosed on the note and sold the land to Joe Schleper, Albert Jus, and George Buchanan, former tenants.

George had borrowed money to finance his lifestyle and his investments, depending on income from his farms to pay the debts. As long as the cotton income flowed, he was safe. As early as 1914, he borrowed $9,000 from the First National Bank of McGregor. He often made small unsecured loans to local farmers. But when the agricultural depression began, tenant farmers and other landowners were unable to pay their loans and he began to slip further behind on his own payments. When cotton prices fell, George found himself in financial trouble.

In 1914, George purchased a 320-acre farm in Hale County from C. O. Surratt, hoping to refinance at a higher price. The banks refused to lend money even on the price he paid. He was unsuccessful in leasing the land for oil and obtained land leases only for cattle. In 1921 he tried to sell his Hale County farm for what he had invested. By the end of 1922, George sold the land at a $5,000 loss.[7]

In 1916 he speculated in real estate in Hamilton County, purchasing 130 acres from H. N. Porterfield by assuming $4,000 ($22 an acre) in indebtedness. George obtained an $11,000 note from Joe Cavitt, which he covered with $5,000 equity for the note on the farm, leaving a $6,500 note balance. He tried to borrow $6,000, but the bank would loan only $4,000 on the land. He had invested $2,000 in lots in El Paso, which he placed in escrow for the note. When he was late with payments, the bank went to court and foreclosed on the land and the lots. Another loss.

In 1919, George purchased a building at Fifth and Ellis in Waco from O. J. Miller for $6,500. Establishing the Caufield Company, he moved his family to Waco and began to run an automobile repair and parts store. He purchased a new home for $7,500 with a $300 note. By the end of the year the Caufield Company had assets of $57,549 on sales of $45,455 and a loss of $26,630. He soon accumulated $11,000 in bad debts, making only $8,040 net income, a net loss of $2,115.

George Caufield and J. C. Kilgore often made investments together. From 1917 to 1919 they sold supplies to Camp MacArthur, an Army training camp outside of Waco. Because they failed to document their sales properly, the Quartermaster Corps delayed payment for several years and never paid the entire bill. The partnership lost $7,500 when Kilgore defaulted on their note.

George's auto parts business did not prosper, and by the end of 1921 he was in financial trouble once again. When he had purchased the Nelson-Bell Battery Company in 1919, he paid $100 a share. Now he sold 412 shares in the company at $75 to J. F. Miller. He then had to sell one-third of the business and mortgage the inventory. T. A. Clifton purchased 432 out of 1,000 shares for $90 each. By 1920 the total loss on the company was $26,630, a large sum for those days.

The partners had started the Ranger Quarry Company in 1918, selling sand and gravel to wildcatters. The first year they had $17,347 in costs and $19,000 income, for a profit of $2,070. When J. C. Kilgore defaulted on his notes in 1918, Caufield loaned the company $8,600. They also established the Waco Oil and Refining Company and the Waco Oil and Development Company, with George holding fifty shares in the refining company and four shares in the development company. The purpose was to acquire oil leases. This company went into default in 1921. George covered part of his losses from his farm income, $865 in income from his thirty-five shares in the First National Bank of McGregor, and $240 from his shares in Cavitt-Lee Hardware.

George Caufield had only $2,130 income from his farms in 1920 as drought settled on the county. The bank stock paid $700 and Cavitt-Lee Hardware stock paid $210. At the end of the year he owed an additional $15,000 to the First National Bank of Brenham. He had two hundred acres in cultivation and owed $8,600 cash balance with seven notes for $564 each. His income in 1922 was $9,500, including $333 from his bank stock. He had to sell 639 acres of his cotton farmland to Joe Cavitt for $85,382, or $133 an acre. However, this covered only the outstanding notes on the land. In 1924 he sold his last 430 acres in McLennan County for $67,625, or 157 an acre, which after paying his mortgage left a net personal debt of $11,462.[8]

The process following the deterioration of George Caufield's investments was painful and convoluted. George began frantic rounds trying to collect what he could on his outstanding notes. Most were a total loss. Joe Cavitt tried to help his brother-in-law, but without success. Joe purchased several pieces of land from George for himself through various entities, including ten acres in McGregor for the cottonseed oil mill. At the end of 1924 he was broke and trying desperately to save what he could.

In 1925, George Caufield filed for bankruptcy, moving from his fine McGregor home to a small cottage made from part of the original homestead. George lost his bank shares, his big cars, his land, and his fine home and furnishings. He became a tenant on his own land. His wife and three sons, Ambrose, George, and twelve-year-old Cavitt, shared his fate. Cavitt Caufield, for whom the family had shipped their car to North Carolina so he could be nursed from asthma by drives in the hills, now walked across the muddy fields to start the fires at Caufield School to pay his tuition. He had to live with friends in McGregor and work evenings at the drugstore to go to high school.

Caufield never recovered from the shock and never attempted to engage in commerce again. He never really farmed the land; his sons did most of the farming until they could escape to other jobs. His wife accompanied him and never uttered a word of complaint. After her passing he eventually went to live with a son in West Texas until his death. His son Cavitt said his father was a poor businessman who "liked to be a big shot but not the working part of it."[9]

Slowly, Joe Cavitt's prosperity also began to unravel. In 1922, Joe borrowed money on his wife's land from C. K. Durham and Son for a total of $39,000 and another set of notes for $43,900. He was able to refinance $35,000 of the notes from Gum Brothers, Dallas Trust and Savings, and the Dallas Joint Stock and Land Bank. But that year the boll weevil hit hard, the crops were scanty, and Joe's income decreased again. In 1926, cotton sold for 10 cents a pound, which was about the cost of raising the crop. In 1927 it sold for 6 cents a pound. The delinquency notices began to arrive from the loan companies.

At this point, however, Joe Cavitt still owned 2,846 acres of cotton land, a house, and fourteen lots in McGregor. But debts on the land came due as insurance companies withdrew from farm mortgages and called in their notes. Bankers would not refinance the notes. In 1924, Joe's troubles increased. He was behind on his notes. He owed the Dallas Trust Company a total of $107,000. Gum Brothers Company wrote Cavitt in 1925 to remind him that the taxes had not been paid. Cavitt was behind on two of his notes to the Farm Credit Company of Dallas for $8,000 each. They held four other $8,000 notes for a total of $48,000.

By 1926, the failure of the cotton crops for two years in a row and a series of bad investments began to press Joe Cavitt financially. His days were numbered as he sold his assets one by one to pay his debts. The cotton chopper factory closed with losses. Then he sold the cottonseed oil mill at a loss. The grain mill was also sold at a loss.

Cavitt had been left with a large outstanding balance at Cavitt-Lee Hardware from the unpaid "furnish" or advances to his sharecroppers. In 1926, G. W. Lee pounced on a bargain. He forced Cavitt to sell seventy-six shares of the store's stock for $200 a share by assuming the unpaid balance of $4,800 at the store and a note Cavitt owed for $10,000. Lee changed the name of the store the next day to Lee Hardware. Cavitt was out and began to trade with Lee's rival, Amsler Hardware.

By 1928, Josephus F. Cavitt had been forced into bankruptcy, owing $50 to $100 an acre on land that now sold for $25 an acre. Although he tried desperately to find lending institutions to carry his debt, he was unsuccessful. The Farm Credit Company sold 315 acres of his land for $37,000, leaving a balance of $13,000 due. His other farms sold for $18,000 and $22,000. German tenant farmers working the Wat Caufield farms purchased both farms. And both sold for less than the bank had invested in the loans.

In 1928, Cavitt outlined his prospects in a letter to his son Volney:

In '24, I had about 1000 acres of cotton worked out when the hail struck it, which made the year unprofitable. Then in '25, I had to borrow money to pay the last years expenses. '26 made a very good crop but half the cotton died and the rest brought a very poor price, 6cts, which caused me to fall behind even more. In '27 I planted about 650 acres of small grain when the cotton died and harvested a light crop which did not return the cost of making and harvesting. All the while living expenses, taxes, and interest were accumulating and the loan companies wanted their money. . . . From this you can see I have nothing left. I am now farming the place for John and Norman [Cavitt] on the halves. The Baileys have bought our home [in McGregor] and we have until March 1st to get out. We are going to the ranch. The home place was exempt.

Joe's nephew Cavitt Caufield stated, "Uncle Joe got into too many things and was never able to keep them all going."[10]

Joe Cavitt went to work for the Texas Highway Department as an inspector. No one seemed to really like him and many thought him a bully. Years later, when he was teasing George Caufield about losing a fortune, George responded, "Well, Joe, that may be, but remember you lost two fortunes." Cavitt just walked away.[11]

Before the cotton prices fell, Frederick Foote converted a large portion of the ranch to cattle and began a program raising pure-bred Herefords. In 1918 he installed dipping vats for both the cattle and sheep. His neighbors resisted at first, but they soon joined him in the tick eradication program, and the Foote dipping vats became widely used by the local livestock raisers.[12]

As his prosperity increased, Fred Foote began to invest in ventures outside his ranch. In 1895 he purchased the land for the Turnersville schoolhouse for $110 and donated it to the town. Besides his involvement in the Presbyterian church, Foote organized and expanded the adjoining cemetery and served on both the school and cemetery boards for decades.

Although the population of Turnersville never rose higher than 250, in 1907 a group of investors chartered the First State Bank of Turnersville with an initial stock valuation of $10,000. G. F. Boone was president and Fred Foote and E. S. "Lige" Wallace were on the board of directors. When the bank consolidated with the National Bank of Gatesville in 1928, it had grown to a capitalization of $50,000. Foote believed that he was too old to continue on the new board and resigned his position.

The same three men owned several buildings in town, including a cooperative gin and a hardware store. Finally, Foote and his neighbor E. Humes built and promoted the Turnersville telephone exchange, connecting Turnersville, Jonesville, Coryell City, and Cranfill Gap. At one time it contained 250 boxes. All of Foote's investments proved profitable.[13]

In 1928, after serving as a school trustee for thirty years, Foote led a movement to consolidate the surrounding small one-room schools into a school district centered at Turnersville. The consolidated schools could support a high school and prepare the children for college. It was a bitter fight. Some communities did not want to lose their schools; others did not want their children to ride buses to school; and some saw no need for the expense of a high school. Grade school education was quite good enough, in their opinion. Foote and his allies won the consolidation fight, but afterward Fred resigned from the school board.

The return of the land to livestock continued during the 1930s as drought forced a retreat from cotton. This ended tenant farming on the Foote ranches. Fred Foote continued to raise sheep on his marginal land and hired four herders for at least six months. Sheep farming remains the foundation of the ranch today.

Back in Massachusetts, Adrian Foote established a trust in 1904 for Henry and his wife, Cora, placing title to Henry's inheritance from his father, about 409 acres, into the trust. He appointed his sister Jessie as trustee, a duty that she exercised until Henry's death in 1931. Initially the trust provided $200 in annual income to the family. Henry's children assumed control of the land after their father's death, but Fred continued to manage the land. In the depths of the Depression, Henry's children received little income. There were no purchasers for the isolated properties. During the 1940s they finally sold their interests to Fred Foote.[14]

After his retirement, Adrian Foote was restless but continued to manage his rental properties in the mill town. Later, his brother Andrew retired from his Illinois bank and moved into the Ashland house, living there until his death in 1899. After her siblings left, Jessie became a piano teacher, stayed in Ashland, and cared for their aged father. Adrian died in 1910 at eighty-eight years of age. Jessie never married and served as Henry's guardian until his death. She died in the family home in 1953.[15]

After World War II, cotton production continued to decline in Central Texas. Two problems pertaining to cotton production remained: weed control and harvesting. Repeated attempts to develop and patent mechanical cotton choppers and cotton pickers began as early as the 1850s. But in the Southern states cotton picked by hand remained less expensive on a per-bale basis until after 1945, when wages rose high enough to make mechanization competitive. In 1890, cotton picked by hand cost $1.65 a bale. By 1947 this cost had increased to $2 to $6 per bale. Nonetheless, hand picking remained more economical unless farmers used machines to pick more than 120 acres.

Weed control continued to be a major expense. Cotton and weeds were chopped by hand several times during a growing cycle. In 1947, of the thirty-nine man-hours required to bring an acre of cotton to harvest, chopping and hoeing consumed thirty-two hours. Local inventors developed mechanical devices to facilitate weed control. Most of these devices had rotary blades and/or rotary plows that thinned the cotton and turned under the weeds but also tended to damage the cotton plants. Using cotton choppers, farmers could clear eighty acres a day versus three-fourths of an acre by hand hoe chopping.[16]

Most of these inventions proved unsatisfactory, and from the 1930s into the 1950s many farmers turned to thermal weed control. These devices burned the weeds close to the ground. Treatment was repeated every four to five days. But thermal burning had serious drawbacks.

Beginning in the 1950s, chemical agents, including herbicides for weed control, insecticides, and defoliants, provided the greatest advances in cotton farming. Cotton farmers first used chemical agents for insect control. Originally, the only check to boll weevil infestations was the topical application of arsenical poisons, often applied at night by hand in a molasses solution to help the poison stick to the plants. DDT and organophosphates successfully controlled the boll weevil. Cotton root rot remained a persistent problem.

The addition of herbicides solved many problems of weed control, and chemicals for weed control became less costly than cotton chopping by day laborers. Depending on the local weed infestations, farmers now use both pre-emergence and post-emergence agents. These were applied by airplane or by tractors that pulled sprayers that rapidly covered several hundred acres a day.

In 1947, the advent of the mechanical cotton picker signaled the end of the last labor-intensive phase of cotton production and began the exodus of farmworkers from the Southern countryside. However, cheap part-time labor remained available in small Southern towns until 1967, when Senator Robert Kennedy successfully sponsored legislation to apply the minimum wage to agricultural workers. Until that point chemical agents had been more expensive for weed control than cotton chopping by field laborers. Between these two landmarks the essential character of cotton farming had remained unchanged despite war, pestilence, poverty, and depression.[17] This signaled the beginning of the end of 150 years of labor-intensive cotton cultivation. Semirural workers who depended on seasonal employment in the cotton fields to supplement their wages migrated to Northern cities.[18]

The harvesting of the cotton crop was one of the last steps in cotton production to lend itself to mechanization. Before mechanization, the cotton farmer spent more energy in harvesting than in any other aspect of production. Six devices had been developed to harvest cotton: pneumatic machines designed to suck the cotton from the boll; thrashers modeled after grain reapers; chemical agents that would allow the cotton to fall freely into scoops; electric devices designed to loosen the cotton from the boll and used with pneumatic devices; strippers, which were basically sleds that pulled the bolls into a harvester; and spindles, which picked the cotton from the open bolls. The stripper and the spindle harvesters are in use today. Both cost about $2.78 a bale to harvest a cotton crop.[19]

The development of the cotton stripper derived from emergency measures taken during World War II by farmers on large, flat expanses when they were unable to hire field workers to pick the cotton crop. They used sleds and picket fences to strip the entire plant—bolls, burs, stalks, and leaves—which they hauled to the gin to be cleaned. Later improvements, including defoliant chemicals, decreased the debris pulled into the harvester, preventing clogging and improving the grades of cotton. The use of the mechanical stripper reduced harvest labor requirements on dry-land cotton farms from 17 hours to 1.5 hours per acre. By 1979, farmers harvested more than 40 percent of the cotton crop on the High Plains by cotton stripping. The mechanical cotton stripper kept many modern farmers in cotton production when the high cost of hand labor forced them to mechanize.[20]

The spindle cotton picker has a more romantic history. Before World War II, John Daniel Rust and his brother developed and patented the wet spindle method of cotton picking. Their machine could pick four hundred pounds of cotton an hour, or forty to fifty times the rate of hand pickers. The brothers delayed the commercial development of their invention until they developed a cotton picker that was affordable to small farmers. After the war, the Hobson Plantation outside Clarksdale, Mississippi, using the Rust machines, produced the first cotton crop entirely harvested by machine.[21]

When cotton pickers went on the market, farmers chose the machines for their farms according to the type of soil (sandy versus black gumbo clay), climate (dry versus wet), plants (bushy versus short), and terrain (hilly versus flat). Strippers worked best on dry, flat land with short plants, while spindle pickers were used on hilly and brushy land.[22]

Plant breeding proceeded in governmental experimental stations, initially to develop cotton varieties that fit different climates and soils and that had the longest fiber length (staple). With the mechanized cotton picker, the preferred variety of cotton raised has changed from the open boll, easily shed, longer staple cotton to tight, storm-resistant varieties better adapted to machine harvesting.[23]

In Central Texas, ranchers who became cotton farmers now turned to corn and other grains for a living. Mechanization allowed them to farm hundreds of acres without day labor. Corn, maize, and wheat became the new rotation of crops on most of these lands. McLennan County, which had 287 cotton gins in 1910, now has only one cotton gin in the entire county.

Today, vast areas of the South no longer raise cotton. In 1950, farmers harvested only 5 percent of the cotton crop mechanically. By 1960, they harvested over 50 percent mechanically. The average worker picked about two hundred pounds of cotton a day. The mechanical picker harvested 15,000 pounds of cotton a day.[24]

The fate of small towns like McGregor has been mixed. Most of the inhabitants of the small villages with populations of less than two hundred had moved to larger communities by the beginnings of the 1950s. Turnersville contains only a few empty brick buildings, and the old schoolhouse is used as living quarters for a commune. South Bosque, which existed for over one hundred years, is gone. The railroad stopped running there and the site is underwater from a new dam.

Laborers also moved away. African American farmworkers and sharecroppers relocated to larger cities where year-round work at good wages was available. For many this was a move to the Northern industrial cities. Others had moved to small towns like McGregor after World War I, working as domestic servants and part-time laborers. They served as the primary workforce for cotton chopping and picking, using the income to supplement their salaries. When mechanization began to pick the cotton crop, these workers, primarily Black, moved into the larger urban areas for better-paying jobs. Small towns lost their Black populations and shrank in size.

Just as the railroads served as a stimulus for the development of rural communities along their tracks, the interstate highways replaced the rail lines and became the stimulus for community development. In a repeat of the coming of the railroads, towns moved their business centers along the new highways. McGregor and similar agricultural communities not positioned on an interstate have stagnated for the last half century.

In West Texas, enormous farms containing thousands of irrigated acres use only a few workers, machines, and chemicals to cultivate cotton. The Southern countryside, where in previous generations thousands of workers labored in poverty to scratch out a living, has become depopulated since farmworkers migrated to Northern cities. Prosperity has superseded poverty as corporate agribusinesses plow the land and reap government subsidies. The promise of the South has been fulfilled, a unique way of life has been replaced, and cotton no longer reigns as king.

The largest element in the South was the indeterminate middle class. Mainly ignored by historians, novelists, and essayists, it contained the great bulk of white society: the non-slaveholding farmers, the business- and professional men, and the artisans. But by far the largest group was the yeoman farmers. While Northerners such as Frederick Law Olmsted pictured them as rude and unprogressive, in actuality they were hard workers who had never learned that white men could not stand the heat of the sun or that manual labor wore a stigma. They owned few or no slaves. The Northern visitors who were used to urban life and amenities were often unable to distinguish between educated rural Southern landowning farmers and uneducated tenant farmers. The planters had only recently risen from the same stock and differed only in the number of acres and slaves they owned. As the cotton culture progressed after the Civil War, many of these small farmers lost their land and dropped back into the sharecropper class, actually falling below their much-despised Black neighbors economically.

Gradually, the mechanization of agriculture, which had decreased the need for farm laborers, pushed young people away from the small towns into the larger urban areas. At the turn of the nineteenth century, urban manufacturing centers overtook the rural towns as the centers of American prosperity, and the discontented, unemployed youth of the countryside moved into the cities for better jobs. Of the small-town youth who went to college, few returned. But for many more decades the small town remained the flower of rural America.[25]

The middle class can be classified by income or by status but most properly should be classified by a particular set of values: education, hard work, and morality. Thus, middle-class persons can rise to riches or fall into poverty but still retain their core values.

Corn—
Conclusion

THIS BOOK TRACES IN DETAIL THE LIVES, INVEST-
ments, expenses, and debts of two generations of related
families that prospered and faltered as agriculture and land
ownership transitioned from the basis of American wealth.
These data offer the details of how middle-class farmers lived,
adapted, and provided an important and necessary framework
upon which the more general conclusions of macroeconomic
trends depend.

Mechanization of agriculture began in earnest in the United
States about 1880 and continued over the next forty years until it
stalled in the 1920s during the agricultural depression that pre-
ceded the Great Depression. The collapse of the Cotton Kingdom
began a decade prior to the Great Depression. The boll weevil,
cotton root rot, and drought decreased cotton production, which,
combined with low prices and foreign competition, pushed the
price of cotton below the cost of growing and harvesting the crop.
Sustained low prices forced cotton growers into collapse, and cotton left the Blackland Prairie, never to return.

In the Texas Panhandle, cotton production flourished. Irrigation counteracted drought and kept yields high. The fluctuation in cotton prices due to intermittent droughts was no longer a problem. The boll weevil did not thrive in the colder winters, and cotton root rot did not exist in those soils. Crop production rose to new highs. Profits became stable and predictable.

Mechanization had a tremendous and often devastating effect on the rural population. But life changed slowly in the rural South. When the sons of cotton tenants and Black sharecroppers returned from World War I, they did not want to return to the poverty they had experienced growing up in the rural South. The first migration of rural workers to Northern cities began in the 1920s; they found good-paying jobs waiting for them. Other farm laborers moved into rural towns seeking jobs as day laborers, working part-time in the fields chopping weeds and picking cotton at harvest. Later, millions of farmers who lost their farms during the Great Depression migrated to the cities looking for industrial work.

The increased agricultural productivity from improved mechanization caused the prices for agricultural products to drop, marking a fundamental change in the American economy. Previously, prosperity had been linked to land ownership. The United States Department of Agriculture noted that "the rapid shift from animal power to mechanical power for farm production in the interwar period constituted one of the most important changes that has ever taken place in American agriculture. It was a cornerstone in the foundation for increased production."[1] Individual farmers felt the effects of mechanization and of lower farm prices. Some adapted to the changes and survived with their farms intact, while others did not adapt and lost everything. After World War II, veterans used the GI Bill to escape the farm.

By the early 1950s, cotton production had been completely revolutionized. Herbicides killed the weeds and mechanical pickers harvested the cotton crop. Livestock and grain production advanced more rapidly than consumer demand and glutted the markets. Farm surpluses became a standard feature of American markets. The problem continues today, compounded by the ability of underdeveloped countries to produce commodities more cheaply than American farmers can.

The exodus of African Americans from the cotton fields of the South was particularly dramatic. The Great Migration of rural workers to Northern cities began in the 1960s. Millions of Black farmworkers moved into the larger Northern metropolitan areas, where they found good jobs and no segregation.

The accounts in this work can be classified as an economic story played out on the Blackland Prairie of Central Texas. In 1849, a brother and sister migrated to Texas. Through hard work, thrifty lifestyles, and the steady accumulation of land and assets, they became some of the largest landowners and taxpayers in their respective counties. Each had a daughter who married an earnest young man with significant wealth of his own. One couple, Frederick and Mary Ann Foote, continued to live modestly and work on their ranch throughout their lives. They successfully weathered the agricultural depression of 1920–1930 with their land and wealth intact. Farming sheep never had the romantic attractions of cattle, cowboys, and trail drives, but satisfaction came from economic gain and from the pride of raising animals that depended on constant human care.

Another couple, Josephus and Mollie Cavitt, moved to the neighboring town, where Joe engaged in a number of enterprises, borrowing money to finance their lifestyle of big houses, fancy trips, and small-town "boosterism." When the price of cotton—the commodity on which his debt payments were based—fell, Joe Cavitt went bankrupt and lost not only his own land and wealth but also his wife's inheritance. The moral for Americans that is still potent today is the danger of borrowing money to live a lifestyle beyond your means.

They neglected their cotton farms, using them as equity to borrow money to finance their new endeavors, and made poor business decisions. Eventually, they lost their businesses as well as their land. But both families recognized that agriculture as a road to prosperity was now limited and encouraged their children and grandchildren to go to college, obtain an education, and enter the urban professional class. Frederick Foote continued to manage the ranches until his death in 1940 at eighty-nine years of age.

Two sons, Nathaniel and Adrian Foote, stayed on the ranch and continued to raise sheep and cattle. Their siblings received a share of the land on an equal basis in value—that is, the worth of the cotton land, which was more valuable than sheep land. The boys took the less valuable pastureland and more acreage. Ironically, as the value of cotton fell, the once valuable cotton land became worth the same as the pastureland. Later generations had some hard feelings because their parents did not receive more acreage. The two sheepmen carefully tended their herds and managed the family's business. They gradually purchased their cousins' land and each owns about a thousand acres at present, on which they primarily raise sheep.

All the Caufields either lost their land or sold it except the Wat Caufield branch of the family, which hunkered down, refused to borrow money, and lived a more limited lifestyle. They weathered the Depression and they still own their land three generations later.

Today, very little cotton is grown on the Blackland Prairie, once the greatest cotton-growing area in the world. The fields have been converted into pasture. Corn and wheat are now the cash crops of Blackland farmers. Clumps of trees on the edges of fields surrounding decaying cabins mark the locations where sharecroppers lived and worked. An occasional windmill or well in the middle of a field marks the site of other homes. Just as cotton grew where cattle once grazed, now corn grows in the old cotton fields.

Appendices

[NOTE: Portions of tables below are incomplete.]

APPENDIX A

William E. Young Ranch
Sheep and Wool Production
1857–1898
c = cotton

	1857	1858	1859	1860	1861	1862	1863	1864	1865	1866
Sheep	469	740	1,057	1,100	709	794	895	1,131	1,179	1,437
Lambs	270		319	120	211		209	187	257	377
Wool (lbs.)					Sold 67	Weth- ers sold for $187				
Profit ($)		None	1,250	1,218	749					

	1867	1868	1869	1870	1872	1874	1876	1877	1878
Sheep	1,842		1,014	1,027				1,690	1,869
Lambs	188		204	177				547	534
Wool (lbs.)			9,156 (47 bags)						4,452
Profit ($)			911		1,005	642		1,347	632

	1879	1880	1881	1882	1883	1884	1885	1886	1886	1887
Sheep	1,946	2,050	1,737	2,320	1,880	1,746				2,200
Lambs	550	612		870						
Wool (lbs.)	7,642	7,643	2,274	9,476	8,696	4,218 (80 bags)				2,313 +
Profit ($)	923	1,788	2,099	1,647	2,153		2,551	4,604	2,127	3,257
Other Income ($)	c-180						Total 3,617		1,925 (577 sheep)	Total 4,475

	1888	1889	1890	1891	1892	1893	1894	1895	1896
Sheep	2,200	2,235	1,867	2,655	2,700	2,501	2,655	1,847	Sold out
Lambs	659	302			800		302		Rented
Wool (lbs.)			8,150	4,635	13,790	12,245 (55 bags)			
Profit ($)	2,406				1,441				
Other Income ($)			416 sheep						Stock $1,817

APPENDIX B

Foote Ranch
Sheep and Wool Production
w = wheat; o = oats; c = cotton

	1876	1877	1878	1879	1880	1881	1882	1883	1884
Sheep						583	600	1,088	1,856
Lambs									793
Wool (lbs.)									66 bags
Wool Profit ($)									
Herding for Morse	$300	$300	$300	$480					
Mutton Sold									Ewes: 1,000 (no. of head)
Other Livestock Sold ($)									
Land Rent ($)									
Expenses ($)						343	123		
Improvements ($)						1,496			

	1885	1886	1887	1888	1889	1890	1891	1892
Sheep	2,790	2,694	2,450	3,038	3,596	3,433	4,391	3,824
Lambs	496	874	700		1,034	625	1,025	1,002
Wool (lbs.)	20,000	15,338	26,664			90 bags 20,321 @21¢/lb.	2,055 @21.5¢/ lb. (77 bags)	30,970
Wool Profit ($)			4,916			4,289	4,626	4,444
Mutton Sold (no. of animals)	1,000 (no. of head)	1,050 (no. of head)	550 ($990)		1,161 ($2,243)	$534	1,284 ($3,456)	1,500 ($3,284)
Other Livestock Sold ($)			990	500		2,243	534	1,100
Land Rent ($)			671		1,350	320	193	307
Expenses ($)		3,402	3,402		1,331	824	814	1,276
Improve- ments ($)		1,179	1,179					

Profit: $999

	1893	1894	1895	1896	1897	1898	1899	1900
Sheep	3,563	3,412	2,807	3,295	1,698		2,598	
Lambs	616		986	674	607		750	
Wool (lbs.)	19,525	24,494	29,305 (108 bags)	25,530 @8¢/lb.		1,2141 @13.75¢/ lb.	1,4197 @15¢/ lb.	1,7122 @16¢/ lb.
Profit ($)	2,005	1,896	1,863	1,914		1,669	2,074	2,739
Mutton Sold	$620	620 ($550)	59	1,522 ($1,440)	151 ($378)	409 @$2.25/ lb. $912	100	1,190 head
Other Live- stock Sold ($)	1,269	2,027	1,023	2,458	1620	1812	258	1860
Land Rent ($)	316 c-196	64	corn 498	856	o-81	o-214 c-113		w-840 c-3,860
Expenses ($)	1,298	1,997	770	1,657	2,345	2,566	2,585	570
Improve- ments ($)	391	585	844	1,520	1,047	791	1,027	278

APPENDIX C

Foote Ranch, 1886–1887

Expenses			Income	
Herding	700.75		**Increase in Stock**	
Maids	91.86		Ewes (300 head)	525.00
Farm help	285.69		Lambs (120 head)	180.00
	1,078.30		Wethers (130 head)	130.00
				835.00
Hauling wool	178.50			
Shearing	68.91		**Wool Clip**: 26,640 lbs.	
Wool sacks	42.80		(net 23,280 lbs.)	4,916.70
	290.21			
			Mutton Sold	
			(550 head)	990.00
Feed			**Total income**	**6,741.70**
1,052 bu. seed	178.50			
1,250 bu. oats	322.50			
374 bu. corn	183.75			
15,000 bu.	452.00			
	1,136.75			
Taxes	126.94			
Equipment	46.37			
General supplies,				
doctor bills	717.88			
	891.19			
Expenses to raise sheep:	**3,396.45**			

Sheep-raising expenses	3,396.45
Improvements	1,178.70
Loans, interest	586.00
Total Expenses	**5,161.15**
Total Income	**6,741.70**
Net Cash Income	**1,580.55**

Notes

A NOTE ON ABBREVIATIONS

A LARGE FILE OF THE CORRESPONDENCE OF HENRY Caufield and his son George Caufield is held by Cavitt Caufield and is located at the Caufield Ranch, McGregor, Texas. These are cited as the Caufield Papers, CP. These have been copied and amalgamated with copies of correspondence to other family members, transcripts of interviews, and various ledgers, trail logs, receipts, and wills, and have been stored at the Caufield Ranch.

An additional seven wooden file boxes containing the correspondence of Henry Caufield's son-in-law Josephus Cavitt and his family, including ledgers, tax records, and wills, have been gathered by Cavitt Caufield and are kept at his home in McGregor, Texas. These are cited as the Cavitt papers, CvP.

The Foote family had two archives. One was letters and ledgers from William Ewing Young, designated as Young Papers (YP). The other archive was hundreds of letters in army ammunition boxes and annual ledgers of the costs and income from sheep farming, designated as the Foote Papers (FP).

INTRODUCTION

1. A discussion of the value of a unit of money in current dollars is difficult, in part, because it is a moving target. David Hackett Fisher analyzed the inflation rate for money from the Middle Ages to the present in his book *The Great Wave: Price Revolutions and the Rhythm of History* (Oxford University Press, rpt. 1999). For my argument, he finds that the US dollar has been flat from 1820 to 1940. The current inflation rate has changed the value drastically (1940–2022). The best place to review the current exchange rate is the "CPI Inflation Calculator," found online at https://www.officialdata.org/us/inflation.

CHAPTER 1

1. James G. Leyburn, *The Scotch-Irish: A Social History* (Chapel Hill: University of North Carolina Press, 1962), 173, 77.
2. Mary Katherine Thompson Galloway, Mary Kathryn Spiller Briggs, Marjorie de Maret Hicks, *The Irish of Staggers Point* (Waco: n.p., 1973), 6–12ff; Leyburn, *Scotch-Irish*, 175.
3. Leyburn, *The Scotch-Irish*, 173.
4. Leyburn, *The Scotch-Irish*, 173; Galloway, Briggs, and Hicks, *Staggers Point*, 12.
5. Leyburn, *Scotch-Irish*, 200–216ff.
6. List of Sunday school students, Bethlehem Presbyterian Church, Boligee, AL, 1840, CP.
7. Leyburn, *Scotch-Irish*, 117–20, 127, 181.
8. A "league" or "sitio" was approximately 4,400 acres and a "labor" was approximately 155 acres. A "headright" varied in size but was commonly 160 acres during this period in the region. These were the Spanish terms used in Robertson's Colony. English terms were used after the Texas Revolution. "Stagger" in Irish vernacular means a striver or one who wishes to succeed. Ellen Burnett Cavitt, *Some Tracings of Cavett-Cavitt Family*

History (Waco: n.p., 1965), 33–40ff. Joseph William Schmitz, *Texas Culture in the Days of the Republic* (San Antonio: Naylor, 1960), 94.

9. William E. Young (WEY) to Henry J. Caufield (HJC), March 4, 1848, CP.
10. Ellen Cavitt, *Cavett-Cavitt Family History*, 33–40ff.
11. The Cavitt brothers, seven of them, used the same names every generation, and keeping track of them is difficult. But generally a Josephus Cavitt would name his oldest son Volney and a Volney Cavitt would name his oldest son Josephus. There were Sid and John and James Cavitts in every generation in every branch of the family.
12. Cavitt, *Cavett-Cavitt Family History*, 97; Schmitz, *Texas Culture*, 94.
13. Galloway, Briggs, and Hicks, *Staggers Point*, 15–20ff; Cavitt, *Some Tracings*, 33–40ff. The cabin Henry built still exists and is now on the Wat Caufield ranch.
14. Most of these letters were written to and published by newspapers, particularly the *New York Herald* and the *Panama Examiner*, that sent correspondents across the isthmus to California; another chronicler includes John M. Letts, "Across the Isthmus, and Adventures in the Mines," in *The Course of Empire*, 175–98ff. An interesting journal includes that of Joseph G. Bruff who traveled the other way—from California and across the isthmus; see Joseph G. Bruff, *Gold Rush* (New York: Columbia University Press, 1944), 976–91ff.
15. Watson Caufield (hereafter cited as WC), Panama City, Panama, to Thomas Caufield (hereafter cited as TC), Greene County, AL, May 4, 1849, CP.
16. John W. Caughey, *The California Gold Rush* (Berkeley: University of California Press, 1948), 60–78ff; John H. Kemble, *The Panama Route, 1848–1869* (New York: Da Capo Press, 1972), 122–56ff.

17. Subscription renewal, Handel Co., Mobile, AL, to TC, 1850, CP.
18. WC to TC, May 4, 1849, CP.
19. Caughey, *Gold Rush*, 18, 39–41ff; Owen Cochran Coy, *Gold Days* (Los Angeles: Powell Publishing Co., 1929), 49–87ff; John M. Letts, "Across the Isthmus, and Adventures in the Mines," in *The Course of Empire*, ed. Valeska Bari (New York: Coward-McCann, 1931), 183.
20. Ibid.
21. Ibid.; Kemble, *Panama Route*, 178.
22. WC to TC, May 4, 1849, CP; Kemble, *Panama Route*, 182; Letts, "Across the Isthmus," 186.
23. WC to TC, May 4, 1849, CP; Caughey, *Gold Rush*, 76.
24. WC to TC, May 4, 1849, CP; Kemble, *Panama Route*, 166–70ff.
25. WC to TC, May 4, 1849, CP.
26. WC to Elizabeth Caufield (hereafter cited as EC), September 10, 1854, CP; Kemble, *Panama Route*, 45–56ff.
27. WC to EC, September 10, 1854, CP.
28. Coy, *Gold Days*, 157; WC to EC, October 22, 1854, CP; WC to EC, September 10, 1854, CP; John E. Baur, "The Health Factor in the Gold Rush Era," in *Rushing for Gold*, ed. John W. Caughey (Berkeley: University of California Press, 1949), 97–108ff.
29. EC to Mary Jane Caufield (MJC), May 25, 1850; July 7, 1850; December 24, 1852; February 19, 1854; October 31, 1854.
30. WC to EC, October 22, 1854, CP.
31. WC to EC, April 9, 1854.
32. WC, San Francisco, CA, to TC, Greene County, AL, April 16, 1855; Wells Fargo receipt, April 12, 1855; steamship ticket, cabin passage, San Francisco to New York; Mary Jane Caufield, Robertson County, TX, to WC, Boligee, AL, July 17, 1855; Henry Caufield, South Bosque, TX, to WC, Greene County,

AL, July 22, 1855, CP.

33. EC to MJC, November 24, 1852; February 19, 1853; February 8, 1954.

34. Caughey, *Gold Rush*, 18, 39–41ff; Coy, *Gold Days*, 49–87ff; Letts, "Across the Isthmus," 175–98ff.

35. EC to WC, April 9, 1854; TC to WC, December 10, 1854, CP.

36. WC to TC, June 29, 1857; WC to MJC, CP.

37. WC to TC, June 29, 1857, CP; HJC to WC, October 1, 1858; brand registration, receipt for purchase from McClelland Company, 1866; recorded marks and brand record, McLennan Company, TX, book 232, no. 13, June 13, 1885; cattle shipping records, 1889, CP; W. R. Poage, *McLennan County—Before 1980* (Waco: Texian Press, 1961), 64.

38. TC to WC, HJC, and MJC, December 13, 1854.

39. Cavitt Caufield, interviews by the author, CP.

40. Thad Sitton and Dan Utley, *From Can See to Can't* (Austin: University of Texas Press, 1997), 90–92; HJC to George Caufield (GC), January 22, 1856; HJC to WC, January 30, May 30, 1858; July 15, 1859; GC, interview by author, December 9, 1995, Amarillo, TX, CP.

41. HJC to WC, June 25, 1858; Cavitt Caufield, interview by author, 1995.

42. WC, leather daybook, CP; Joe Black/Patience Crain letters, Texas Collection, Baylor University, Waco, Texas.

43. Terry Jordan, *Trails to Texas: Southern Roots of Cattle Raising* (Lincoln: University of Nebraska Press, 1981), 125–57ff: Edward E. Dale, *The Range Cattle Industry* (Norman: University of Oklahoma Press, 1960), 101.

44. Mary Jane Caufield Young (MJCY) to WC, July 29, 1859.

45. MJCY to WC, July 29, 1859; bill of sale for 17 bales of cotton, Thomas Caufield, Mobile, AL, February 16, 1859, CP. The average income in the United States in 1860 was about $150 a year. Midwestern farmers made an average of $96 and

Southern farmers an average of $151 that year. This compares roughly to an average income of $15,000 today. Thus, each member of these families earned the equivalent of about $75,000 annually. (The conversion factor is about 50 to 100 times the prices of 1860.)

46. MJCY to WC, Spring(?) 1857; WEY to WC, May 16, 1858, CP; R. J. H. De Loach and H. A. Phillips, *Progressive Sheep Raising* (Chicago: Armour's Bureau of Agricultural Research and Economics, 1918), 10–12ff; Paul H. Carlson, *Texas Woollybacks: The Range Sheep and Goat Industry* (College Station: Texas A&M University Press, 1982), 76.

47. Carlson, *Texas Woollybacks*, 23; William H. Dusenberry, *The Mexican Mesta: The Administration of Ranching in Colonial Mexico* (Urbana: University of Illinois Press, 1963), 47, 200; Harris, *A Mexican Family Empire*, 134; De Loach and Phillips, *Progressive Sheep Raising*, 12; Alexander Campbell McGregor, *Counting Sheep* (Seattle: University of Washington Press, 1982), 29–31ff.

48. Carlson, *Texas Woollybacks*, 76; V. W. Lehman, *Forgotten Legions: Sheep in the Rio Grande Plain of Texas* (El Paso: Texas Western Press, 1969), 62; WEY to WC, May 16, 1858, May 15, 1859; HJC to WC, April 8, 1858, CP; Josephus Cavitt (JC) to WC, April 5, 1858, FP. Here, Cavitt discusses his trip to Arkansas and Indian Territory with his brother; JC to WC, July 3, 1859, CP. Cavitt mentions that he had purchased two Merino rams that cost "two hundred dollars apiece." De Loach and Phillips, *Progressive Sheep Raising*, 9–24ff.

49. JC to WC, April 5, 1858; WEY to WC, May 15, 1859, FP; Young ledgers, book #1, 1856, 1857, 1859, YP (1,000 head x 5 lbs./head x $0.25/lb. = $1,250 gross income, or about $125,000 today). One dollar in 1860 was roughly equivalent to $100 dollars today. The ledgers contain expenses and income to the penny. Since the exact amounts were so important to the recorders, those amounts are included as written in this work.

50. WEY to WC, April 16, May 10, 1860, FP; MJCY to WC, October 5, 1860, CP; Young ledgers, 1859, 1860, YP; Carlson, *Texas Woollybacks*, 62; MJCY to WC, October 5, 1860, CP. Although he kept detailed records of wool income and carefully recorded the increases in the flocks, Young made no accounts of the money made from selling sheep. At a cost of $6 a head and twenty-pound fleeces selling for 25 cents a pound, Young calculated the new sheep paid their expenses in two years.

51. WEY to WC, May 26, 1858; MJCY to HJC, October 5, 1860, CP; Fred Foote Jr. to Zelma Scott, family history, May 1946, FP.

52. Frank E. Simmons, *History of Coryell County* (Gatesville: Coryell County News, 1936), 18, 27; *History of Bell and Coryell Counties* (Chicago: Smith Publishing Company, 1890), 859–60.

53. HJC to WC, December 9, 1860, CP; WEY to WC, April 16, May 10, 1860, FP; Young ranch ledgers, vol. III, YP; HJC to WC, Boligee, AL, April, 8, 1858, CP; MJCY to WC, May 16, October 17, 1858, July 29, 1859, October 5, 1860, CP. A table of precipitation for Austin, TX, shows 1858 and 1860–1863 as dry years, with 1863 having the lowest rainfall in several decades; in D. W. C. Baker, *A Texas Scrapbook—1875* (Austin: Texas State Historical Association, 1991), 358; Young family ledgers, book #1, 1860–1872; vol. 2, 1873–1880; vol. 3, 1881–1892, YP. Bluetongue is an infectious viral disease of sheep now effectively controlled by a vaccine; see Robert L. Haney, *Milestones Marking Ten Decades of Research* (College Station: Texas Agricultural Experimental Station, 1989), 69; Carlson, *Texas Woollybacks*, 32; *History of Bell and Coryell Counties*, 859–60.

CHAPTER 2

1. HJC to WC, December 9, 1860, May 21, 1861, CP.
2. HJC to WC, December 9, 1860, CP.
3. Estate bills, for WC, TC, in leather packet, CP.

4. HJC to WC, December 9, 1860.

5. HJC to WC, May 13, 1861.

6. HJC to WC, April 11, 1861, CP; Certificate of Exemption for Watson Caufield, CP; Special Order #78, for Neil McLennan and another for Watson Caufield; draft list, CP; Henry Caufield is listed as joining Company E, First Regiment, Second Battalion (Cook's Battalion), Texas State Troops, and later reenlisted in Company C, Cook's Heavy Artillery, Texas State Troops, CP. HJC to Martha Caufield, December 23, 1863, CP.

7. Goff, *Supply*, 121, 153; J. Marvin Hunter (ed.), *The Trail Drivers of Texas* (Austin: University of Texas Press, 1985), 123, 267, 567, 723, 741; Allan C. Ashcraft, "Confederate Beef Packing at Jefferson, Texas," *Southwestern Historical Quarterly* 68 (October 1964): 259–70ff.

8. James Duke to WC, October 20, 1863; March 5, 1864; December 14; April 12, 1864, CP.

9. David Paul Smith, *Frontier Defense in the Civil War* (College Station: Texas A&M University Press, 1992), 49, 92–94; Mrs. E. Digby to the Secretary of War, letter, March 21, 1922, File 27, "Brigade: Bell, Burnet, Lampasas, Milam, and Williamson"; Florida Commissary Cavalry Battalion, report of persons employed in Madison, FL, May, 1863, file "Beef Drovers," Civil War Research Center, Hillsboro Junior College, Hillsboro, Texas, hereafter cited as CRC; Goff, *Supply*, 153; George W. Tyler and Charles Ramsdell, *The History of Bell County* (Waco: Texian Press, 1936), 150; Jackson, File 27, CRC; official correspondence Northrup to White, orders, June 1862, File 27, CRC.

10. WC to HJC, July 23, 1863, CP.

11. William Caufield to WC, March 5, 1861, December 24, 1864.

12. Goff, *Supply*, 153; Florida Commissary Cavalry Battalion, report of persons employed in Madison, Florida, May, 1863,

file "Beef Drovers," CRC.

13. Goff, *Supply*, 121, 153; Hunter, *The Trail Drivers of Texas*, 123, 267, 567, 723, 741; Ashcraft, "Confederate Beef Packing at Jefferson, Texas," 259–70ff.

14. HJC to WC, letter, May 21, 1861; HJC to WC, letter, April 11, 1861; Certificate of Exemption for Watson Caufield; Special Order #78, for Neil McLennan and another for Watson Caufield, CP.

15. Smith, *Frontier Defense*, 49, 92–94; Sallie Reynolds Matthews, *Interwoven: A Pioneer Chronicle* (College Station: Texas A&M University Press, 1982), 7–23; Mrs. E. Digby to the Secretary of War, letter, March 21, 1922, File 27, "Brigade: Bell, Burnet, Lampasas, Milam, and Williamson"; Florida Commissary Cavalry Battalion, report of persons employed in Madison, FL, May, 1863, file "Beef Drovers," CRC; Goff, *Supply*, 153; Tyler and Ramsdell, *The History of Bell County*, 150; Jackson, File 27, CRC; official correspondence Northrup to White, orders, June 1862, File 27, CRC.

16. Mrs. E. Digby to the Secretary of War, letter, March 21, 1922, File 27, "Brigade: Bell, Burnet, Lampasas, Milam, and Williamson," CRC; Florida Commissary Cavalry Battalion, report of persons employed in Madison, FL, May, 1863, file "Beef Drovers," CRC; Goff, *Supply*, 153; Tyler and Ramsdell, *History of Bell County*, 150; Jackson, File 27, CRC; official correspondence Northrup to White, orders, June 1862, file 27, CRC.

17. Diary kept in ledger books by W. E. Young, account book #1, 1859–1872, YP; Smith, *Frontier Defense*, 124, 147.

18. George Bernard Erath and Lucy A. Erath (eds.), *Memoirs of Major George Bernard Erath* (Waco: n.p., 1885), 106–8; diary, WEY, YP; Fred Foote Jr. to Zelma Scott, family history, May 1946, FP.

19. Young ledgers, book #1, 36, 70–93, YP.

20. HJC to WC, April 8, 1858, October 1, 1858, CP.

CHAPTER 3

1. HJC to WC, April 8, 1858, October 1, 1858, CP; Cavitt Caufield (CC), interview by author, 1995; trail logs in small leather book, Watson Caufield, 1856–1870; HJC to WC, August, 1868; power of attorney from HJC to WEY, November 10, 1874, CP.

2. Poage, *McLennan County—Before 1980*, 151; Roger N. Conger, "Fencing in McLennan County," in *Waco's Champion: Selections from the Papers of Roger Norman Conger*, ed. Marion Travis (Waco: Waco Historical Foundation, 1990), 129–37ff.

3. Walter Prescott Webb, *The Great Plains* (New York: Grosset and Dunlap, 1985), 247.

4. HJC to WC, 1857.

5. Steve Kelton, *Renderbrook: A Century Under the Spade Brand* (Fort Worth: Texas Christian University Press, 1989), viii, 45; Edward E. Dale, *The Range Cattle Industry: Ranching in the Great Plains from 1865 to 1925* (Norman: University of Oklahoma Press, 1960), 101; W. Eugene Hollon, *The Southwest: Old and New* (Lincoln: University of Nebraska Press, 1961), 254–55.

6. GC, interview by author, CP; Poage, *McLennan County*, 151; Cavitt Caufield, interview by author, McGregor, Texas, May 1995; "Local Pioneer Dies," *Waco Times Herald*, June 10, 1908, CP; Conger, "Fencing," 129–37ff; Webb, *Great Plains*, 247.

7. WC to MJCY, 1857. WC to TC, 1855; MJCY to WC, 1857; HJC to WC, 1857, 1860.

8. GC, interview by author, CP; Hollon, *The Southwest*, 242–67ff; Dayton Kelly (ed.), *The Handbook of Waco and McLennan County, Texas* (Waco: Texian Press, 1972), 52; HJC to WC, May 15, 1860, CP.

9. Poage, *McLennan County*, 82–84; Conger, "Fencing," 127–29.

10. Shackleford County records, deeds, grantor book, vol. 26,

340–41; Aldon Socrates Lang, "Financial History of the Public Lands in Texas," *Baylor Bulletin* 35, no. 3 (July 1932).

11. Andrew Foote to Frederick Foote (FF), September 23, 1885, FP.

12. M. Caroline Foote (MCF) to Henry Foote (HF), August 4, 1882; Adrian Foote (AF) to FF, September 19, 1885, FP.

13. MCF to FF, December 19, 1880, FP.

14. Interview with Nathaniel (Sonny) Foote Jr. by author, April 30, 2005, CP.

15. *Second Annual Report of the Texas Agricultural Bureau, 1888–1889* (Austin: State Printing Office, 1890), 55.

16. *Second Annual Report of the Texas Agricultural Bureau*, 306; Robert Maudsley, *Texas Sheepman: The Reminiscences of Robert Maudsley*, edited by Winifred Kupper (Austin: University of Texas Press, 1951), 69.

17. John Foote (JF) to FF, 1882, FP.

18. Frances Foote to FF, FP.

19. Carlson, *Texas Woollybacks*, 43. This newspaper was probably the *Galveston News*, which featured frequent articles by William Kendall, a Texas sheepman and former editor of the New Orleans *Times-Picayune*. AF to FF, December 20, 22, 24, 1886; January 6, 13, 24, February 8, 15, 1887, FP.

20. J. R. Franklin to FF, May, 1880; MCF to FF, November 8, December 19, 1880, FP.

21. AF to HF, November 20, 1881; Frank Randlett to FF, FP.

22. AF to HF, December 7, 22, 26, 1881; AF to FF, January 10, 1882, FP.

23. MCF to HF, May 18, 1882, FP; interview of Sonny Foote by author, May 2003.

24. MCF to FF, April 22, 1883; February 27, 1885, FP. The stories of these two brothers are quite similar to those told to Winifred Kupper by her uncle, Robert Maudsley, in *Texas Sheepman*, and in Winifred Kupper, *The Golden Hoof: The Story of the Sheep of the Southwest* (New York: Alfred A. Knopf, 1945).

25. CM, Ashland, Mass. to FF, Coryell Co., TX, April 9, 1882; MCF to HF, May 23, 1882, FP.

26. MCF to HF, March 28, 1882; MCF to FF, May 23, 1882, FP.

27. AF to FF, January 10, 1882; receipt from T. S. Standford to AF, April 20, 1882; AF to FF, January 31, 1882, FP; *Yearbook of the United States Department of Agriculture*, 1903, 496–503ff; Carlson, *Texas Woollybacks*, 45; Maudsley, *Texas Sheepman*, 121; McGregor, *Counting Sheep*, 35.

28. MCF to HF, March, 28, 1882; MCF to FF, April 9, 1882; AHF to HF, May 21, 1882; JF to FF, February 12, 1888, FP.

29. Jessie Foote to HF, November 27, 1881; John Foote to FF, December 12, 20, 1881; AF to HF, January 31, 1882, FP.

30. MCF to FF, November 29, 1883; Frances Foote to FF, March 29, 1883, FP.

31. MCF to FF, October 12, 1884; HF to FF, September 14, 1884; Frances Foote to FF, August 17, 1885, FP.

32. AF to FF, April, 29, 1883, FP.

33. Fred A. Shannon, *The Farmer's Last Frontier: Agriculture, 1860–1897* (New York: Farrar & Rinehart, 1945), 206. A rod is about 5.5 yards; there are 467 rods to a mile. Most cattle fences are three- or four-wire fences. The extra six-wire sheep fences kept the smaller lambs from climbing through. The cost of the Footes' initial six-wire fence was $247 a mile. Simmons, *Coryell County*, 68–69; Laura A. Thorp, *Facts and Anecdotes of Turnersville, Texas* (Waco: Texian Press, 1973), 180.

34. Haney, Milestones, 123 ; Shannon, *The Farmer's Last Frontier*, 140; AF to FF, February 1, 1887; Warrior Mower Company to FF, April 28, 1887, AF to FF, March 8, 1887, FP.

35. MCF to HF, May 18, 1882; J. H. Shepard to AF, June 18, 1883, FP.

36. AF to FF, September 25, 1886, FP.

37. Odie B. Faulk, *Fort Hood: The First Fifty Years* (Temple, TX: Frank W. Mayborn Foundation, 1990), 8–9; AF to FF, May

4, 1885, FP.

38. Lang, "Financial History of the Public Lands in Texas."

39. Mary Ann Young Foote (MYF) to William Thomas Young (WTY), December 11, 1886.

40. E. A. Blount, San Augustine, TX, to AF, Ashland, MA, June 7, 1882; JF to FF, October 15, 1882; AF to FF, October 3, 1884; AF to FF, October 11, 1886; AF to FF, February 10, 1887, FP. Bounty warrants, given by the Republic of Texas in lieu of pay to soldiers who fought at San Jacinto or elsewhere, were purchased on the speculators' market. They could be placed anywhere allowed by what was now the State of Texas and preempted any unfilled and unpaid titles (for example, homestead squatters working through their first year before paying for title). See Lang, "Financial History of the Public Lands," for many examples of the difficulty determining who had first and primary title on the Texas frontier. E. A. Blount, San Augustine, Texas to AF, Ashland, MA, June 7, 1882; J. H. Shepard, land agent, Columbia, Brazos County to AF, May 30, 1883, FP.

41. MYF to WTY, September 12, December 4, 1885, FP.

42. MYF to WTY, March 17, April 28, 1886, FP.

43. Ledger books from Turnersville Mercantile, June 1888 to December 1889; entries October 1888; November 1889.

44. Faulk, *Fort Hood*, 10–12ff. 8; Simmons, *History of Coryell County*, 24.

45. Carlson, *Texas Woollybacks*, 116; AF to FF, February 4, 1887, FP.

46. AF to FF, January 25, 1885, FP.

47. MYF to WTY, November 11, 16, December 30, 1886, FP.

48. AF to FF, February 10, 1887; AF to FF, April 13, 1887, FP.

49. Thorp, *Facts and Anecdotes of Turnersville, Texas*, 2.

50. AF to FF, April 13, 1887, FP.

51. J. R. Franklin to FF, May 24, 1884, FP.

52. Insurance certificate, WEY, from Phoenix Insurance

Company, September 7, 1884, YP; J. R. Franklin to FF, May 24, 1884, FP.

53. AF to FF July 28, August 15, August 22, 1886; HF to FF, September 1, 1886, FP.

54. J. R. Franklin to FF, May 24, 1884; HF to FF, May 4, 1885; AF to FF, May 27, 1885; Cyril Johnson to AF, April 3, 1886, FP. Each fleece weighed about fifteen pounds and was worth about $30. The Footes calculated that was a lot of free samples ($180, or about $9,000 in 2021 dollars).

55. The *Weekly Wool Report* from Fenno Brothers, commission merchants, Boston, noted that the "market was uneven and unsettled," quoting prices for Texas wools "at 20 to 23c," while Ohio wool brought "33 to 35c.," broadsheet, FP; *Yearbook of the United States Department of Agriculture, 1900,* 830–35. AF to FF, July 28, August 15, 1886; MYF to WTY, March 17, 1886, FP.

56. Cyril Johnson, Stafford, CT, to FF, April 3, 1886; H. Norton, Menger Hotel, San Antonio, to FF, April 24, 1886, FP.

57. AF to FF, January 28, 1887, FP.

58. Frances Foote to FF, June 17, 1885; AF to FF, September 19, 1885, FP.

59. JF to FF, October 12, 1885, FP.

60. HF to FF, n.d., 1886, FP.

61. Will, AF, 1906; Raymond Foote to FF, FP.

62. AF to FF, November 30, 1886; Andrew Foote to FF, December 12, 1886, Frances Foote to FF, December 5, 1887, FP.

CHAPTER 4

1. James Marshall, *Santa Fe: The Railroad That Built an Empire* (New York: Random House, 1945), 224–33ff; L. L. Waters, *Steel Trails to Santa Fe* (Lawrence: University Press of Kansas, 1950), 76–83ff.

2. Ernest Staples Osgood, *The Day of the Cattleman* (Chicago:

University of Chicago Press, 1929), 216–57ff; Don Worcester, *The Chisholm Trail: High Road of the Cattle Kingdom* (Lincoln: University of Nebraska Press, 1985), 153–75ff; Henry John Caufield (HJC) to Watson Caufield (WC), November 23, 1878, CP.

3. Mexican ranch letters, TC to his mother Martha Caufield, September 11, 1886; L. B. Hood, Tombstone, AZ, to HJC, February 9, 1889, CP.

4. CC, interview, 1995, CP.

5. Poage, *McLennan County*, 69–72ff, 75–85ff; National Fibers Information Center, *The History of Cotton in Texas* (Austin: Bureau of Business Research, 1989), 5–12ff; Charles S. Johnson, Edwin R. Embree, and W. W. Alexander, *The Collapse of Cotton Tenancy* (Chapel Hill: University of North Carolina Press, 1935), 20–43ff; John Stickling Spratt, *The Road to Spindletop* (Austin: University of Texas Press, 1955), 66; Sitton and Utley, *From Can See to Can't*, 20–54ff.

6. Tom Caufield (TC), Tombstone, Arizona Territory, to H. C. Clifton, November 28, 1886; TC to WEY, August 10, 1883, FP; TC, Ochoaville, Arizona Territory, to Martha Caufield, September 11, 1886, CP. The letter relates a trip for supplies into Tombstone, where "the Earp brothers have things quiet now." Caufield was grateful that "Arizona and Sonora once more breathe freely from terror. . . . Geronimo has at last surrendered." L. B. Hood, Tombstone, to HJC, February 9, 1889, CP.

7. Ernest Staples Osgood, *The Day of the Cattleman* (Chicago: University of Chicago Press, 1929), 216–57ff; Worcester, *The Chisholm Trail*, 1985, 153–75ff; Henry Caufield to Watson Caufield, November 23, 1878.

8. Registration certificates, 1890, CP; bill of sale, 1890, CP; Margaret Cabell Self, *Horses of Today* (New York: Duell, Sloan and Pierce, 1964), 74; Jim Roberts, "A Shetland—The Most

Remarkable of All," *Pony Journal* (January–February 1995), 5.

9. Patricia Ward Wallace, *Our Land, Our Lives: A Pictorial History of McLennan County* (Norfolk, VA: Donning Company, 1986), 102; newspaper photograph, *Waco Tribune*, 1910(?), CP; CC, interview, CP.

10. The magazine *Farm and Ranch* referred to in several letters at that time may have actually been titled *Farm and Home*.

11. G. G. Sturtevant, "Old Circus Days in Texas," *Frontier Times* 9 (August 1932), 481–88; William Edward Syers, "Molly Bailey and the Circus," *Off the Beaten Path* (Waco: Texian Press, 1971), 207–10; Kathleen Caufield to Watson Caufield Arnold, [1955?], CP; CC, interview, CP; photographs, CP.

12. Thayer Waldo, "Back in the Quiet Days Ponies Were Not Mean Like One That Nipped Judge's Granddaughter," *El Paso Herald-Post*, May 2, 1957, 3; CC, interview, CP.

13. Roger Conger, *A Pictorial History of Waco* (Waco: Texian Press, 1968), 82; photographs, CP; CC, interview, CP.

14. CC, interview, CP; Robert West Howard, *The Horse in America* (Chicago: Follett Publishing Company, 1965), 93–102ff; Ben K. Green, *Horse Trading* (New York: Alfred A. Knopf, 1977), v–xi; HJC to WC, June 24, 1855; C. W. Tyson to J. F. Cavitt, January 29, 1917; Milton Wallace to Cavitt, April 19, 1917, CP.

15. Copy of advertisement in *Farm and Ranch Magazine*, CP; J. G. Rowe to J. F. Cavitt, February 27, 1917; S. McManus to Cavitt, February 26, 1917; O. R. Perkman to Cavitt, February 18, 1917, CP.

16. Interview with Cavitt Caufield and Watson Caufield Arnold by Watson C. Arnold Jr., McGregor, TX, March, 1995.

17. Howard, *The Horse in America*, 93–102ff; HJC to WC, June 24, 1855; HJC to WC, May, 1860, CP; bill of sale for brand, registration for brand, 1866. IXL stood for "I eXceL," a hopeful advertisement of quality. Leather trail book, CP; Alma McKethan McBride, *The "Filosofer" of "Kukel-bur" Flat* (Waco:

Texian Press, 1975), 64–65.

18. Poage, *McLennan County*, 69–72, 75–85ff; National Fibers Information Center, *The History of Cotton in Texas*, 5–12ff; Johnson, Embree, and Alexander, *The Collapse of Cotton Tenancy*, 20–43ff; Spratt, *The Road to Spindletop*, 66; Sitton and Utley, *From Can See to Can't*, 20–54.

19. Howard, *The Horse in America*, 93–102ff; HJC to WC, June 24, 1855; bill of sale for brand, registration for brand, 1866; leather trail book, CP; McBride, *The "Filosofer,"* 64–65; Green, *Horse Trading*, v–vii; Howard, *The Horse in America*, 93–102ff.

20. GC, interview, CP; trail notes in leather notebook, CP; Howard, *The Horse in America*, 93–102ff; Green, *Horse Trading*, v–xi; HJC to WC, June 24, 1855; C. W. Tyson to J. F. Cavitt, January 29, 1917; Milton Wallace to Cavitt, April 19, 1917, CP; Spratt, *The Road to Spindletop*, 95.

21. Neil Foley, *The White Scourge: Mexicans, Blacks, and Poor Whites in the Texas Cotton Culture* (Berkeley: University of California Press, 1997), 33; Rebecca Sharpless, *Fertile Ground, Narrow Choices: Women on Texas Cotton Farms, 1900–1940* (Chapel Hill: University of North Carolina Press, 1999), 8–12; Poage, *McLennan County*, 148; Gavin Wright, *Old South, New South: Revolutions in the Southern Economy Since the Civil War* (New York: Basic Books, 1986); James Oscar Morgan, *Field Crops for the Cotton-Belt* (New York: The Macmillan Company, 1918), 30; *Yearbook of the United States Department of Agriculture 1896*, 509. The closest relative to cotton is okra, also in the Mallow family. See E. N. Fergus, Carsie Hammonds, and Hayden Rogers, *Southern Field Crop Management* (Chicago: J. B. Lippincott Company, 1944), 583–604ff.

22. Howard, *The Horse in America*, 93–102ff; *Yearbook of the United States Department of Agriculture, 1896, 1909* (Washington, DC: Government Printing Office, 1897, 1910); *Second Annual Report of the Agricultural Bureau, 1888–1889* (Austin, TX: State

Printing Office, 1890), 88, 91: Wright, *Old South, New South*; Emmitt Essin, *Shavetails and Bell Sharps: The History of the U.S. Army Mule* (Lincoln: University of Nebraska Press, 1997).

23. Maurice Telleen, *Draft Horse Primer* (Emmaus, PA: Rodale Press, 1977), 38–41ff; Paul W. Chapman and Wayne Dinsmore, *Livestock Farming* (Atlanta: Turner E. Smith and Co., 1947), 483–84.

24. Juliet Clutton-Brock, *Horse Power* (Cambridge: Harvard University Press, 1992), 54–66ff. Other mammalian species, particularly the large cats, also can produce hybrid offspring. The tigon is the offspring of a male tiger and a female lion, and a liger is the result of a cross between a male lion and female liger, just as a hinny is a cross between a male horse and a jenny, or female donkey.

25. Clutton-Brock, *Horse Power*, 43–51ff.

26. Clutton-Brock, *Horse Power*, 41–51ff. Essin, *Shavetails and Bell Sharps*, 8.

27. Note: One hand equals four inches. Telleen, *Draft Horse Primer*, 38–41ff.

28. McBride, *The "Filosofer,"* 53; GC, interview, CP; trail notes in leather notebook, CP.

29. Howard, *The Horse in America*, 93–102ff; Green, *Horse Trading*, v–xi; HJC to WC, June 24, 1855, CP; HJC to WC, January 29, 1917, CP; Milton Wallace to Cavitt, April 19, 1917, CP; Sitton and Utley, *From Can See to Can't*, 108; bill, F. R. Wingrove to J. F. Cavitt (JFC), July, 1, 1911, CvP. Cavitt followed the trend of the time and carefully registered all his animals. He also entered all the local fairs and livestock shows to market his animals and exhibited his ribbons in his stockyard office. Ribbons from the Texas State Fair and Waco Cotton Palace Fair, 1914–1920, CvP; Certificates of Pedigree, *American Jack Stock Stud Book*, 1915, CP.

30. J. J. Blackwell to JFC, June 26, 1911; JFC to J. W. Jones,

January 4, 1911, CvP.

31. Stock book, 1910–1925, CvP.

32. McBride, *"Filosofer,"* 63; Henry William Herbert, *Horses, Mules, and Ponies and How to Keep Them* (New York: Lyons Press, 2000), 81–93ff; Sitton and Utley, *From Can See to Can't*, 108; stock book, 1910–1925, CvP.

33. McBride, *"Filosofer,"* 63; Sitton and Utley, *From Can See to Can't*, 107–10.

34. Green, *Horse Trading*, v–vii. Green has written several books on anecdotes about horse and mule traders. The literature is full of other collections of anecdotes about horses and mules and professional livestock traders. For a collection of anecdotes, see William G. Long, *Donkeys of the West* (New York: Ballantine Books, 1974). Mule traders seemed to enjoy tricking each other and then bragging about their exploits. When animals were traded for each other, "boot" was the extra cash payment the trader received above the animal itself. The ages of horses and mules are estimated by the wear on certain groves in the teeth. Filing the teeth replaced those worn-down groves. For information on telling the ages of horses by their teeth, see Telleen, *Draft Horse Primer*, 69–73; McBride, *"Filosofer,"* 53.

35. Invoice from Texas Farm and Ranch Publishing Company to JFC, January 21, 1917, January 24, 1918; Karl F. Tate to JFC, January 20, 1917; C. W. Tyson to JFC, January 29, 1917; W. T. Black, Athens, Texas to JFC, January 15, 1916, CvP.

36. R. E. Bryant, Moody, Texas to JFC, February 19, 1908; J. N. Davis to JFC, January 29, 1913; Norman Cavitt to JFC, January 2, February 25, 1916; Milton Wallace to JFC, March 20, April 14, May 15, 1916, CvP.

37. Noah Neff was the father of Pat Neff, who became governor of Texas and president of Baylor University. Their ranch was along the Leon River about ten miles from the Caufield Ranch.

38. Receipt for cattle from Chicago Stockyard, 1885, CP.

39. John Sleeper and J. C. Hutchins, *Waco and McLennan County, Texas* (Waco: J. W. Gulledge, 1876), 108–9; *McLennan, Falls, Bell, and Coryell Counties, Texas* (Chicago: Lewis Publishing Company, 1893), 831–32; CC, interview; shipping receipts and payment vouchers, 1885, 1886, CP; Glenn Porter and Harold Livesay, *Merchants and Manufacturers: Studies in the Changing Structure of Nineteenth-Century Marketing* (Baltimore: The Johns Hopkins Press, 1971), 172–75ff. The rail lines allowed ranchers a free round-trip ticket for each three to four cattle cars. The men sent made certain the cattle were watered and fed during the trip and that cattle that had fallen in the rail cars got back to their feet, else they would be trampled by the other animals. Neff particularly liked to make the trip and accompanied most of the shipments.

40. Receipts, H. J. Caufield, July 28, August 3, 1885, August 31, 1886; receipts, Neil McLennan, August 17, December 17, 1887; bank transfer notes, August 18, 1887, CP; receipt, J. F. Cavitt, November 19, 1904, CvP.

41. *Yearbook of the Department of Agriculture, 1895* (Washington DC: Government Printing Office), 533, 548; *1898*, 702–4; *1900*, 830–34; *1901*, 116–17, and *1903*, 548–51, 702–4, 831–34, 776–82; Carlson, *Texas Woollybacks*, 46.

42. Article cut from the *Gatesville Mirror*, n.d., YP; Fred Foote Jr. to Zelma Scott, family history, May 1946, FP.

43. N. Foote to FF, letter, 1928, FP.

44. Neal Barrett Jr., *Long Days and Short Nights: A Century of Texas Ranching on the YO, 1880–1980* (Mountain Home, TX: Y-O Press, 1980).

45. Carlson, *Texas Woollybacks*, 69.

46. Young ledgers, book #2, 27, YP; MYF to WTY, October 15, 1885; Fred Foote Jr. to Zelma Scott, family history, May 1946, FP.

47. Fred Foote Jr. to Zelma Scott, family history, May 1946, FP.

48. Thorp, *Turnersville*, 40–46ff; Roberta Blair Powell, *A History of the Unity Presbyterian Church* (Turnersville, TX: n.p., 1972), 10–20ff; MYF to WTY, September 12, 1885; Fred Foote Jr. to Zelma Scott, family history, May 1946, FP.
49. Fred Foote Jr. to Zelma Scott, family history, May 1946, FP.
50. Thorp, *Turnersville*, 40–46ff; Powell, *Unity Presbyterian Church*, 10–16ff.
51. Young ledgers, book #2, 72–78ff, YP.
52. MYF to WTY, September 12, December 4, 1885, FP.
53. Frances Foote to FF, May 10, August 17, 1885; MYF to WTY, November 4, November 18, December 30, 1885, FP.
54. Lizzie Freeland to WTY, April 8, 1888; MYF to WTY, April 5, 1888, YP.
55. MYF to WTY, August 26, 1888, FP.
56. MYF to WTY, July 31, 1888; Lizzie Freeland to WTY, March 23, 1888, FP.
57. MYF to WTY, October 15, 1885, FP.
58. MYF to WTY, November 11, 1888; MYF to WTY, November 11, 1891, FP.
59. Cavitt Caufield, interview by Watson Arnold, CP.
60. Handwritten document by W. E. Young, Spring 1888; MYF to WTY, September 31, 1888, FP. From the tone of this letter and others, Young was wise to prevent his children from suing each other.
61. Receipt and registration papers, October 19, 1905; Henry Mitchell to JFC, April 30, 1906; receipt, Great Northern Railroad, June 15, 1906; receipt, Evans-Snider Commission Agents to JFC, February 10, 1915; receipts, J. D. Mitchell, Commission Agent, Fort Worth Stockyards, to JFC, December 13, 1918, February 3, 1919, December 21, 1919, CvP.
62. J. Mitchell to JFC, May 29, June 15, June 17, 1906; French Webb Commission Company, Fort Worth Stockyards, to JFC, April 14, 1910; J. Burns, Professor, Agricultural and

Mechanical College of Texas, to JFC, January 29, 1912, CvP.

63. Cyphers Incubator Company to JFC, September 25, 1912; invoice, M. Johnson to JFC, April 1916; Cyphers Incubator Company to JFC, April 11, 1916; Trinity Valley Farms to JFC, April 15, 1916; Oak Grove Farms to JFC, April 11, 1916; R. Guy Davis to JFC, March, 1917; A. T. Ezell to JFC, February 13, 1917, CvP.

64. Webb, *Great Plains*, 229, 317; John Sleeper and J. C. Hutchins, *Waco and McLennan County, Texas* (Waco: J. W. Golledge, 1876), 108–9.

CHAPTER 5

1. D. Clayton Brown, *King Cotton in Modern America: A Cultural, Political and Economic History Since 1945* (Jackson: University Press of Mississippi, 2001), 22–23.

2. Bertha S. Dodge, *Cotton: The Plant That Would Be King* (Austin: University of Texas Press, 1984), 26–45ff; M. D. C. Crawford, *The Heritage of Cotton: The Fiber of Two Worlds and Many Ages* (New York: G. P. Putnam's Sons, 1924), 1–50ff.

3. *Texas Almanac*, 1910–1911, 87–103 ff.

4. Gilbert Fite, *Cotton Fields No More* (Lexington: University Press of Kentucky, 1984); James H. Street, *The New Revolution in the Cotton Economy: Mechanization and Its Consequences* (Chapel Hill: University of North Carolina Press, 1957), 120ff.

5. Crawford, *Heritage of Cotton*, 132.

6. John Samuel Ezell, *The South Since 1865* (New York: Macmillan, 1963), 252, 454, 465.

7. MYF to WTY, July 31, 1888, FP. Interview, "Sonny" Foote, May 2003.

8. A. B. Cox, *Cottonseed Crushing Industry of Texas in Its Natural Setting* (Austin: University of Texas Press, 1949), 2, 8, 15, 34; William G. DeLoach , *Plains Farmer: The Diary of William G. DeLoach, 1914–1964*, edited by Janet N. Neugebauer (College

Station: Texas A&M University Press, 1991), 128. In 1931, DeLoach picked 1,790 pounds of cotton; the bale of lint weighed 515 pounds and the seed 880 pounds. His cottonseed sold for $10 a ton. The gin charged $2.83 to process the bale. The lint sold for 4.7 cents a pound.

9. Karen Britton, *Bale O'Cotton* (College Station: Texas A&M University Press, 1995); W. T. Block, *Cotton Bales, Keelboats, and Sternwheelers* (Woodville, TX: Dogwood Press, 1995); Wallace, *Our Land, Our Lives*; James Watkins, *King Cotton* (New York: Negro Universities Press, 1908); Crawford, *Heritage of Cotton*, 141.

10. Sitton and Utley, *From Can See to Can't*, 57.

11. Institute of Public Affairs, *The Cotton Crisis, Proceedings of the Second Conference*, edited by S. D. Myres (Dallas: Southern Methodist University, 1935), 156. Street, *New Revolution*, 49–62ff.

12. Sitton and Utley, *From Can See to Can't*, 66–69. Robert A. Caro, *The Years of Lyndon Johnson: The Path to Power* (New York: Alfred A. Knopf, 1982), 505–9ff; Fred Foote Jr. to Zelma Scott, family history, May 1946, FP.

13. Fred Foote Jr. to Zelma Scott, family history, May 1946, FP; McGregor, *Counting Sheep*, 155.

14. Spratt, *The Road to Spindletop*, 56–57.

15. Sharpless, *Fertile Ground, Narrow Choices*.

16. Caro, *The Years of Lyndon Johnson*, 505–8.

17. Elizabeth Silverthorne, *Plantation Life in Texas* (College Station: Texas A&M University Press, 1986), 109, 133; Sitton and Utley, *From Can See to Can't*, 91, 102.

18. Twelve grades were required for acceptance at a university. Otherwise the student had to pass a comprehensive test to be matriculated.

19. State of Texas, textbook commission to Tom Caufield, CP.

20. Sitton and Utley, *From Can See to Can't*, 91, 102.

21. Robert Armstrong (RA) to JFC, January 28, 1907; RA to JFC, January 27, 1916, CvP; Fred Wood to RA, January 25, 1916, CvP.
22. RA to JFC, August 7, 1905; Edwin Wulkson to JFC, September 25, 1905.
23. Cavitt, *Cavett-Cavitt*, 33–40ff; H. J. Caufield, *Caufield Heritage* (Waco: n.p., 1976), 57, 98, 125. The Cavitt first names can be hard to follow. Each descendant had many children and reused the family names through many generations. Unique were brothers Volney and Josephus Cavitt. They alternated first names each generation. Josephus Cavitt I (who was married to Henry Caufield's first cousin and for whom Henry worked when he first came to Texas) named his firstborn son Volney, and Volney Cavitt I named his firstborn son Josephus (who married Henry Caufield's daughter).
24. Letter to Fred Foote, FP.
25. MYF to WTY, February 29, 1891; Fred Foote Jr. to Zelma Scott, family history, May 1946, FP.

CHAPTER 6

1. John D. Hicks, "The Significance of the Small Town in American History," in *Reflections of Western Historians*, edited by Alexander Carroll (Tucson: University of Arizona Press, 1969), 155–67.
2. Spratt, *The Road to Spindletop*, 66; Poage, *McLennan County*, 69–72.
3. Gilbert C. Fite, *Cotton Fields No More: Southern Agriculture, 1865–1980* (Lexington: University Press of Kentucky, 1984).
4. Poage, *McLennan County*, 69–72; Dayton Kelley, ed., *Handbook of Waco and McLennan County* (Waco: Texian Press, 1972), 171–72.
5. Spratt, *The Road to Spindletop*, 66; Poage, *McLennan County*, 69–72. The building of these railroads is discussed in Joseph

A. Strapac, *Cotton Belt Locomotives* (Huntington Beach, CA: Shade Tree Books, 1977), 2; L. L. Waters, *Steel Trails to Santa Fe* (Lawrence: University Press of Kansas, 1950).

6. Poage, *McLennan County*, 69–72; Kelley, *Handbook of Waco and McLennan County*, 171–72; Monyene Stearns, *McGregor, Texas: The Jewel of the Prairie* (McGregor: Monyene Stearns, 2000), 6–12ff.

7. Donald Worster, *Dust Bowl: The Southern Plains in the 1930s* (New York: Oxford University, 1979), 168; Stearns, *McGregor*, 6–12ff.

8. McBride, *The "Filosofer,"* 156–63ff; Worster, *Dust Bowl*, 168.

9. Spratt, *The Road to Spindletop*, 246–48; Jim W. Corder, *Chronicle of a Small Town* (College Station: Texas A&M University Press, 1989); *Texas State Gazetteer*, 1884, 1890, 1893; Wright, *Old South, New South*, 39–43ff; Thomas Clark, *Pills, Petticoats, and Plows: The Southern Country Store* (New York: The Bobbs-Merrill Company, 1944).

10. Receipt, GC to HJ Caufield, January 17, 1911, CvP.

11. CC interview, CP; Clark, *Pills, Petticoats, and Plows*, 19–34.

12. S. S. Amsler to Tom Caufield, January 3, 1917; Norman Cavitt to JFC, September 20, 1917; draft notice, Volney Cavitt, July 17, 1918; J. H. Caufield to JFC, December 1918, CvP.

13. McLennan County Chapter, American Red Cross, to Tom Caufield, October 2, 16, November 6, 20, 1918, August 5, 1919, CP. *McGregor Mirror*, Friday, May 10, 1918 (vol. 30, no. 23), 1 and 2, CvP.

14. Robert Hill to JFC, November 25, 1913; JBC to JFC, February 14, 1916.

15. Agreement letter, January 2, 1911.

16. Ibid.

17. Agreement letter, January 2, 1911; list of expenses for G. Caufield, 1905–1908; entry, December 22, 1906, CP; Charles Smith to JFC, February 4, 1915, CvP; Harry Provence,

The Citizens National Bank of Waco (Waco: Republic Bank, 1982), 35.

18. R. L. Bewley to G. Caufield, October 25, 1904; G. Caufield to JFC, October 30, November 16, 25, 1904, CP.

19. Lizzie Cavitt (LC) to JFC, March 10, April 3, 5, May 24, June 24, 1909; JFC to LC, April 1, June 9, June 22, 1909; JFC to Jim Cavitt (JC), June 24, July 22, 1909; JC to LC, July 2, 1909; MC Cavitt to JFC, April 6, 1920, CvP.

20. Porter and Livesay, *Merchants and Manufactures*, 215–20ff; Clark, *Pills, Petticoats, and Plows*, 173–222.

21. James Cavitt to JFC, October 21, 1912; E. R. Barton to JFC, February 15, 1910; District Court, Coryell County to JFC, September 14, 1914; Henry Hanover to JFC, March 9, 1908, June 25, 1912; JFC to J. V. Cavitt, September 16, 1914, CvP.

22. Clara Cavitt to JFC, January 1, 1916, CvP; Mollie Caufield Cavitt to Mary Ann Foote, January 4, 1906, FP; Porter and Livesay, *Merchants and Manufactures*, 224–26; Worster, *Dust Bowl*, 168.

23. Agreement letter, January 2, 1911, CvP.

24. J. Frank Cavitt to JFC, June 1, 1910; JFC to John Deere Company, June 13, September 23, November 16, 1910, CvP.

25. For a discussion of prohibition, see James D. Ivy, *No Saloon in the Valley: The Southern Strategy of the Texas Prohibitionists in the 1880s* (Waco: Baylor University Press, 2003). The role of the local church is discussed in Thorp, *Turnersville*, and Powell, *A History of the Unity Presbyterian Church*.

26. Ivy, *No Saloon in the Valley*, 25–43ff; AF to FF, March 6, 1887, FP.

27. Ivy, *No Saloon in the Valley*, 112–20ff; Poage, *McLennan County*, 181; Lewis L. Gould, *Progressives and Prohibitionists* (Austin: Texas State Historical Society, 1992), 289.

28. Ibid.

29. Ivy, *No Saloon in the Valley*, 25–43ff; Frank E. Simmons,

History of Coryell County (Belton: Coryell County News, 1936), 69–71ff.

30. Ivy, *No Saloon in the Valley*, 25–43ff.

31. TC to JFC, January 14, 1910; bank statement, First National Bank of McGregor, 1918; telegraph bill, Gulf State Telegraph, October 1917; Mirror Printing Company, October 1, 1917, CvP; Gould, *Progressives and Prohibitionists*, 166–67; A. J. Barton to JFC, May 9, 1918, CvP.

32. CC, interview, CP.

33. Ivy, *No Saloon in the Valley*, 119–20; Gould, *Progressives and Prohibitionists*, 289.

34. Ivy, *No Saloon in the Valley*, 119–20.

35. JFC to Charles F. Smith, May 5, 1913; receipt, Gulledge Dry Goods to JFC, January, 1910, CvP.

36. JFC to GC, May 18, 1914, CvP.

37. JFC to Bud Cavitt, February 13, 1915, CvP.

38. Jack Lichtenstein, *Field to Fabric: The Story of American Cotton Growers* (Lubbock: Texas Tech University Press, 1990), 32. That amount of cottonseed came from 120,000 pounds of cotton, or 224 bales, and represented about $50,000 in cotton sales and about $5,000 in income from cottonseed by-products. Roger N. Conger, "Waco: Cotton and Culture on the Brazos," *Southwestern Historical Quarterly* 75, no. 1, (July 1971): 54–76; JFC to S. A. (Bud) Cavitt, February 13, 1917; Sam Amsler to Internal Revenue Service, March 5, 1919, CvP.

39. Receipt, McGregor Milling and Grain Co., to JFC, January 24, 1910, CvP.

40. J. H. Rainy to JFC, November 1917; advertisement, Cavitt Cotton Chopper and Schrieb Star Washing Machine; M. A. Jones to JFC, April 14, June 27, 1921; GC to JFC, January 11, 1911, CvP; Amsler, McGregor, 13–14.

CHAPTER 7

1. Obituary, *Waco Times Herald*, 1906, CP.
2. TC to JFC, January 14, 1910. Tuberculosis was commonly contracted by young men away at college due to the close quarters in the dormitories and the unpasteurized milk the students drank in their cafeterias.
3. Kathleen Caufield to Watson Caufield Arnold, June 11, 1973; Henry Clifton to JFC, May 23, 1921, CP.
4. Interview, Cavitt Caufield, CP; TC to JFC, September 19, 1919; Mrs. J. B. Rodgers to Mrs. Thomas Caufield, December 7, 1919, CP.
5. TC to JFC, September 19, 1919; Mrs. J. B. Rodgers to Mrs. Thomas Caufield, December 7, 1919; J. H. Caufield to Kathleen Caufield, June 11, 1973, CP; J. H. Caufield, *Caufield Heritage*, 109.
6. Webb, *Great Plains*, 425; GC, interview, CP; W. R. Poage, *After the Pioneers* (Waco: Texian Press, 1969), 151; CC, interview, CP; "Local Pioneer Dies," *Waco Times Herald*, June 10, 1908, CP; Conger, "Fencing," 129–37ff.
7. Interview, Cavitt Caufield; interview, George Caufield, CP.
8. Hollon, *The Southwest*, 242–67ff; Kelley, *The Handbook of Waco and McLennan County, Texas*, 52; HJC to WC, May 15, September 25, 1860, CP; Poage, *McLennan County*, 65, 69–72; Webb, *Great Plains*, 317. A well dug at the Wat Caufield house about 1888 has been in continuous use for more than one hundred years and is typical for those of the time and region. It is about fifty feet deep, lined with limestone, and connected to a windmill. It supplies water to an elevated metal water tank for indoor consumption and provides water pressure to indoor plumbing. The windmill also fills another stone tank for the animals. GC, interview, CP.
9. Interviews, Watson Arnold, Cavitt Caufield, George Caufield, CP.

10. Cavitt Caufield, Watson Arnold interview, CP. In 1910, Wat and Kate Caufield harvested three hundred bales of cotton on the 2,000 acres they owned. Cotton sold for 25 cents a pound or $125 a bale. They made $37,500 and netted one-third, or $12,500. That represents $625,000 in 2020 US dollars. They were rich indeed!

11. Interview, George Caufield Jr.; Kathleen Caufield to Watson Caufield Arnold, June 11, 1973; Mollie Caufield Cavitt to Mary Ann Young Foote, January 4, 1904, FP.

12. JFC to RA, March, 11, 1905; RA to JFC, December 24, 1906, January 25, 1907, March 2, 1910; JFC to RA, March, 31, 1910; W. T. Taliaferro to JFC, April 27, June 27, 1916, CvP.

13. Notes, J. B. Russ to JFC, August 1918; W. Rubert Smith to JFC, July 31, 1918, CvP.

14. JFC to RA, March, 31, 1910, CvP.

15. Deed of sale, to Clara Cavitt, November 11, 1904; JFC to estate of Harold Westcott, November 10, 1904; deed of trust for A. S. (Sid) Cavitt from Clara Cavitt to J. V. Cavitt, February, 21, 1905; Will Hickman, Tax Collector, San Angelo to JFC, December 8, 1909, CvP.

16. Jesse Scargile to JFC, October 29, 1917, CvP. Advertisement, *McGregor Mirror*, 1915; William Goode to JFC, April 13, 1906; account statements, First National Bank of McGregor, for C. J. Cavitt, 1909 to 1911.

17. John Cavitt to JFC, September 9, 1910; Clara Cavitt to JFC, January 27, 1916, CvP.

18. Receipt, Peterson Wool Merchants, to JFC, July 22, 1909; receipt, George Richardson Wool Merchant, San Angelo, to JFC, April 14, 1915; Norman Cavitt to JFC, December 7, 1911; Jesse Scargile to JFC, October 29, 1917, CvP.

19. Depositions, Mary Cavitt Washington, J. F. Cavitt, and John B. Cavitt, 1916; John B. Cavitt to J. J. Gallaher, Bank of Romney, October 26, 1920; Prescott HuideKoper to John B.

Cavitt, August 10, 1920, CvP.

20. John B. Cavitt to JFC, July 2, 1910, CvP.

21. J. V. Cavitt to JFC, June 17, 1906; J. Cavitt Jr. to JFC, November 21, 1911; Henry Mitchell to JFC, February 13, 1913; J. R. Case Company to JFC, October 10, 1911, CvP.

22. Advertisement, *McGregor Mirror*, 1915; William Goode to JFC, April 13, 1906; Lizzie Cavitt Goode to JFC, October 11, 1907; account statements, First National Bank of McGregor, for C. J. Cavitt, 1909 to 1911; JFC to W. T. Goode, April 25, 1907, CvP.

23. RA to JFC, January 28, 1907, February 19, 1908; JFC to Sattler and Arnold, attorneys, February 10, 1906, May 25, 1906, January 10, 1908; John Cavitt to Clara Cavitt, November 3, 1909, CvP.

24. Claim, JFC to St. Louis Southwestern Railroad, March 7, 1907; handwritten ledger statement, 1918; St. Louis Southwestern Railroad to JFC, April 19, 1911, CvP.

25. C. E. Stockburger, Tax Collector, Coryell County to JFC, April, 30, 1916, CvP; deed, McLennan County, February 1865, 477, CP.

26. JFC to Turner and Dinge, December 17, 1909; Sam Cavitt to JFC, May 11, 1908, CvP.

27. Statement, B. U. Sims, MD, for Mrs. Volney Cavitt, December 15, 1920; JFC to Clara Cavitt, December 28, 1907; estate estimate for Clara J. Cavitt (Mrs. Volney Cavitt), July 29, 1921; JFC to S. E. Cavitt, January 4, 1924, CvP.

CHAPTER 8

1. Wright, *Old South, New South* (New York: Basic Books, 1986), 233; Fred A. Shannon, *The Farmer's Last Frontier: Agriculture, 1860–1897* (New York: Farrar & Rinehart, 1945), 137–38ff, 144. Worster, *Dust Bowl*, 60–62ff.

2. Shannon, *The Farmer's Last Frontier*, 215. The combine is, as

the name implies, a combination of several machines into one large instrument. A combine harvests the grain, cuts and binds the stalks, and separates the grain from its husk. The whole family participated in the grain harvest, some driving the machine, some driving the mules pulling the binder, others bringing water for the engine, fuel for the fires, or food for the workers. The machines were pushed rather than pulled through the fields. A tractor or mules moving in front of the harvesting blades would crush the grain before it could be cut. Once the farmer harvested the grain, long leather belts connected the steam turbine to a thrasher, which separated the grain from the residual stalks and blew the stalks into giant haystacks. Shannon, *The Farmer's Last Frontier*, 137–38ff. For an excellent description of wheat farming on a grand scale, see McGregor, *Counting Sheep;* McBride, *The "Filosofer,"* 179. CC, interview, 1995, CP.

3. After World War II, motor-powered vehicles were faster and the numbers of tractors, motor trucks, and combines increased dramatically on all farms, but the number of mechanical cotton pickers and cultivators did not increase until the mid-1950s. Seth Shepard McKay, *Texas and the Fair Deal*, 1945–1952 (San Antonio: The Naylor Company, 1954), 45–76ff.

4. Ezell, *The South Since 1865*, 137; Sitton and Utley, *From Can See to Can't*, 9, 57.

5. Brown, *King Cotton in Modern America*, 131–33.

6. Sitton and Utley, *From Can See to Can't*, 10, 57.

7. Caufield paid $8,845 for 320 acres ($28 an acre). He borrowed $7,500 at 10 percent interest. By 1921 he had $12,800 ($40 an acre) invested in the farm, including a house valued at $1,000, a barn valued at $500, and $11,300 in land. He sold the land at a $5,000 loss, CP.

8. Partnership agreement, G. Caufield and T. A. Clifton, November 1, 1920, CP.

9. GC and CC interview, CP.

10. Gum Brothers Company to JFC, May 27, 1925; J. F. Cavitt to Volney Cavitt, February 12, 1928, CvP; Faulk, *Fort Hood*, 10–11.

11. GC and CC interviews, CP.

12. Fred Foote Jr. to Zelma Scott, family history, May 1946, FP.

13. Ibid.

14. AF to FF, April 11, July 10, 1882; E. A. Blount to AF, June 7, 1882; abstract for land title, Coryell County, Texas, June 7, 1882, FP.

15. Frances Foote to FF, March 29, 1883, FP; AF to FF, January 25, 1885, FP.

16. Faulk, *Fort Hood*, 8–9; Fred Foote Jr. to Zelma Scott, family history, May 1946, FP. See E. N. Fergus, Carsie Hammonds, and Hayden Rogers, *Southern Field Crop Management* (Chicago: J. B. Lippincott Company, 1944).

17. Agreement letter, January 2, 1911; list of expenses for G. Caufield, 1905–1908; entry, December 22, 1906, CP; Charles Smith to JFC, February 4, 1915, CvP; Provence, *The Citizens National Bank of Waco*, 35.

18. Watkins, *King Cotton*, 307; M. N. Williamson, Q. M. Morgan, and Ralph H. Rogers, "Economics of Mechanical Cotton Harvesting in the High Plains Cotton Area of Texas," *Texas Agricultural Experimental Station Bulletin* (1951), 735; Cyrus Lundell, *Agricultural Research at Renner, 1944–1966* (Renner: Texas Research Foundation, 1967); Nicholas Lemann, *The Promised Land: The Great Black Migration and How It Changed America* (New York: Vintage Books, 1991), 132.

19. Wright, *Old South, New South*, 233; Shannon, *The Farmer's Last Frontier*, 137–38ff, 144.

20. Street, *New Revolution*, 108–110ff; Fite, *Cotton Fields*; Williamson, *High Plains Cotton*, discussed in 17–80ff.

21. Brown, *King Cotton*, 57–58.

22. Street, *New Revolution*, 108–110ff ; Fite, *Cotton Fields*.

23. Williamson, *High Plains Cotton*, 170–80ff; Lundell, *Renner*, 735–40ff; Street, *New Revolution*, 136–43.

24. Watkins, *King Cotton*, 307; Street, *New Revolution*, 136–43ff; advertisement, CP.

25. For discussion of the transition of rural towns into urban cities, see John D. Hicks, "The Significance of the Small Town in American History," in *Reflections of Western Historians*, edited by John Alexander Carroll (Tucson: University of Arizona Press, 1969), 155–67; Edward L. Ayers, *The Promise of the New South: Life after Reconstruction* (Oxford: Oxford University Press, 1992); Robert L. Brandfon, *Cotton Kingdom of the New South: A History of the Yazoo Mississippi Delta from Reconstruction to the Twentieth Century* (Cambridge, MA: Harvard University Press, 1967); Brown, *King Cotton*, 22–23.

CONCLUSION

1. Sherman E. Johnson, "Changes in American Farming," miscellaneous publication no. 707, Washington, DC: U.S. Department of Agriculture, December 1949.

Bibliography

ARCHIVAL AND FAMILY COLLECTIONS OF PAPERS

Caufield Papers. Ledgers, letters, receipts, and accounts held by the Caufield family at the Caufield Ranch, McGregor, TX.

Cavitt Papers. Several file boxes containing the personal papers of Josephus Cavitt and George Caufield held by Cavitt Caufield in McGregor, TX.

Foote Papers. Annual account books, letters, receipts, and ledgers held by the Foote family at the Foote Ranch, Turnersville, TX.

Young Papers. Family papers, letters, and farm ledgers held by Frankie Glaze, Gatesville, TX.

INTERVIEWS

Cavitt Caufield, interview by W. C. Arnold, May 1995, McGregor, TX.

George Caufield Jr., interview by W. C. Arnold, December 9, 1995, Amarillo, TX.

Nathaniel (Sonny) Foote Jr., interview by W. C. Arnold, April 30,

2005, Foote Ranch, Turnersville, TX.

Watson Caufield Arnold, interview by W. C. Arnold, April 2001, Waco, TX.

ARTICLES AND CHAPTERS

Arnold, W. C. "Shetland Ponies on the Blackland Prairie." *Waco Heritage and History* 26, no. 1 (Fall 1996).

Conger, Roger N. "Fencing in McLennan County." In *Waco's Champion: Selections from the Papers of Roger Norman Conger*, edited by Marion Travis. Waco: Waco Historical Foundation, 1990.

———. "Waco: Cotton and Culture on the Brazos." *Southwestern Historical Quarterly* 75, no. 1 (July 1971).

Hicks, John D. "The Significance of the Small Town in American History." In *Reflections of Western Historians*, edited by John Alexander Carroll. Tucson: University of Arizona Press, 1969.

Lang, Aldon Socrates. "Financial History of the Public Lands in Texas." *Baylor Bulletin* 35, no. 3 (July 1932).

"Local Pioneer Dies." *Waco Times Herald*, June 10, 1908.

Lundell, Cyrus. *Agricultural Research at Renner*, 1944–1966. Renner: Texas Research Foundation, 1967.

McLean, Malcolm D. "Sarahville de Viesca." In *The New Handbook of Texas*, vol. 5, edited by Ron Tyler. Austin: Texas State Historical Association, 1996.

Roberts, Jim. "A Shetland—The Most Remarkable of All." *Pony Journal* (January–February 1995).

Sturtevant, G. "Old Circus Days in Texas." *Frontier Times* 9 (August 1932).

Syers, William Edward. "Molly Bailey and the Circus." *Off the Beaten Path*. Waco: Texian Press, 1971.

Thayer, Waldo. "Back in the Quiet Days Ponies Were Not Mean Like the One That Nipped Judge's Granddaughter." *El Paso*

Herald-Post, May 2, 1957.

Trowbridge, E. A. "Corn Versus Oats for Work Mules." University of Missouri, Agricultural Experimental Station, Columbia, MO. Circular 125 (July 1924).

Williamson, M. N., Q. M. Morgan, and Ralph H. Rogers. "Economics of Mechanical Cotton Harvesting in the High Plains Cotton Area of Texas." *Texas Agricultural Experimental Station Bulletin*. Bulletin 735 (1951).

GOVERNMENT DOCUMENTS

Bureau of Business Research. *Natural Fibers and Food Protein Production in Texas. An Economic Profile*. Austin: Texas Food and Fibers Commission, 1990.

Johnson, Sherman E. "Changes in American Farming." Miscellaneous publication no. 707. Washington, DC: US Department of Agriculture, December 1949.

McPhae, H. C., and D. A. Spencer. "Breeding Problems with Sheep." *Yearbook of the United States Department of Agriculture, 1936*. Washington, DC: U.S. Government Printing Office, 1937.

National Fibers Information Center. *The History of Cotton in Texas*. Austin: Bureau of Business Research, 1989.

Second Annual Report of the Agricultural Bureau, 1888–1889. Austin: State Printing Office, 1890.

Yearbook of the United States Department of Agriculture, 1895, 1898, 1900, 1901, 1903, 1909. Washington, DC: U.S. Government Printing Office, 1896, 1899, 1901, 1904, and 1910.

BOOKS AND DISSERTATIONS

Agee, James, and Walker Evans. *Let Us Now Praise Famous Men*. Boston: Houghton Mifflin Company, 1939.

Almaraz, Felix D. *The San Antonio Missions and Their System of Land Tenure*. Austin: University of Texas Press, 1989.

Ayers, Edward L. *The Promise of the New South: Life After Reconstruction.* New York: Oxford University Press, 1992.

Baker, D. C. *A Texas Scrapbook—1875.* Austin: Texas State Historical Association, 1991.

Block, W. T. *Cotton Bales, Keelboats and Sternwheelers: A History of the Sabine River and Trinity River Cotton Trades, 1837–1900.* Woodville, TX: Dogwood Press, 1995.

Bolton, Charles C. *Poor Whites of the Antebellum South: Tenants and Laborers in Central North Carolina and Northeast Mississippi.* Durham, NC: Duke University Press, 1994.

Brandfon, Robert L. *Cotton Kingdom of the New South: A History of the Yazoo Mississippi Delta from Reconstruction to the Twentieth Century.* Cambridge, MA: Harvard University Press, 1967.

Britton, Karen Gerhardt. *Bale o' Cotton: The Mechanical Art of Cotton Ginning.* College Station: Texas A&M University Press, 1992.

Brown, D. Clayton. *King Cotton in Modern America: A Cultural, Political and Economic History Since 1945.* Jackson: University Press of Mississippi, 2001.

Carlson, Paul H. *Texas Woollybacks: The Range Sheep and Goat Industry.* College Station: Texas A&M University Press, 1982.

Caro, Robert A. *The Years of Lyndon Johnson: The Path to Power.* New York: Alfred A. Knopf, 1982.

Caufield, Henry J. *Caufield Heritage.* Waco: n.p., 1976.

Cavitt, Ellen Burnett. *Some Tracings of Cavett-Cavitt Family History.* Waco: n.p. 1965.

Chapman, Paul W., and Wayne Dinsmore. *Livestock Farming.* Atlanta: Turner E. Smith and Co., 1947.

Clark, Thomas D. *Pills, Petticoats, and Plows: The Southern Country Store.* New York: Bobbs-Merrill, 1944.

Clegg, Luther Bryan. *The Empty School House: Memories of One-Room Texas Schools.* College Station: Texas A&M

University Press, 1997.

Conger, Roger. *A Pictorial History of Waco*. Waco: Texian Press, 1968.

Corder, Jim W. *Chronicle of a Small Town*. College Station: Texas A&M University Press, 1989.

Cox, A. B. *Cottonseed Crushing Industry of Texas in its Natural Setting*. Austin: University of Texas Press, 1949.

Crawford, M. D. C. *The Heritage of Cotton: The Fiber of Two Worlds and Many Ages*. New York: G. P. Putnam's Sons, 1924.

Crenshaw, Troy C. *Texas Blackland Heritage*. Waco: Texian Press, 1983.

Dale, Edward E. *The Range Cattle Industry: Ranching in the Great Plains from 1865 to 1925*. Norman: University of Oklahoma Press, 1960.

De Loach, R. J. H., and H. A. Phillips. *Progressive Sheep Raising*. Chicago: Armour's Bureau of Agricultural Research and Economics, 1948.

DeLoach, William G. *Plains Farmer: The Diary of William G. DeLoach, 1914–1964*. Edited by Janet N. Neugebauer. College Station: Texas A&M University Press, 1991.

Dobie, J. Frank. *The Longhorns*. Austin: University of Texas Press, 1990.

Dodge, Bertha S. *Cotton: The Plant That Would Be King*. Austin: University of Texas Press, 1984.

Dusenberry, William H. *The Mexican Mesta: The Administration of Ranching in Colonial Mexico*. Urbana: University of Illinois Press, 1963.

Erath, George Bernard. *Memoirs of Major George Bernard Erath*. Edited by Lucy Erath. Waco: n.p., 1885.

Ezell, John Samuel. *The South Since 1865*. New York: Macmillan, 1963.

Faulk, Odie B. *Fort Hood: The First Fifty Years*. Temple: Frank W. Mayborn Foundation, 1990.

Fergus, E. N., Carsie Hammonds, and Hayden Rogers. *Southern Field Crop Management.* Chicago: J. B. Lippincott, 1944.

Fite, Gilbert C. *Cotton Fields No More: Southern Agriculture, 1865–1980.* Lexington: University Press of Kentucky, 1984.

Flannery, Brendon. *The Irish Texans.* San Antonio: University of Texas Institute of Texan Cultures, 1980.

Foley, Neil. *The White Scourge: Mexicans, Blacks, and Poor Whites in the Texas Cotton Culture.* Berkeley: University of California Press, 1997.

Galloway, Mary Katherine Thompson, Mary Kathryn Spiller Briggs, and Marjorie de Maret Hicks. *The Irish of Staggers Point.* Robertson County, TX: n.p., 1973.

Goldfield, David. *Promised Land: The South Since 1945.* Arlington Heights, IL: Harlan Davidson, 1987.

Gould, Lewis L. *Progressives and Prohibitionists: Texas Democrats in the Wilson Era.* Austin: Texas State Historical Society, 1992.

Green, Ben. *Horse Trading.* New York: Alfred Knopf, 1977.

Haney, Robert L. *Milestones: Marking Ten Decades of Research.* Texas Agriculture Experiment Station. College Station: Texas A&M University Press, 1988.

Harris, Charles H. *A Mexican Family Empire: The Latifundia of the Sanchez-Navarros, 1765–1867.* Austin: University of Texas Press, 1975.

Herbert, Henry William. *Horses, Mules, and Ponies and How to Keep Them.* New York: Lyons Press, 2000.

Hollon, W. Eugene. *The Southwest: Old and New.* Lincoln: University of Nebraska Press, 1961.

Howard, Robert West. *The Horse in America.* Chicago: Follett Publishing Company, 1965.

Ivy, James D. *No Saloon in the Valley: The Southern Strategy of the Texas Prohibitionists in the 1880s.* Waco: Baylor University Press, 2003.

Johnson, Charles S., Edwin R. Embree, and W. W. Alexander.

The Collapse of Cotton Tenancy. Chapel Hill: University of North Carolina Press, 1935.

Jordan, Terry G. *Trails to Texas: Southern Roots of Western Cattle Ranching*. Lincoln: University of Nebraska Press, 1981.

Kelley, Dayton, ed. *The Handbook of Waco and McLennan County, Texas*. Waco: Texian Press, 1972.

Kelton, Steve. *Renderbrook: A Century Under the Spade Brand*. Fort Worth: Texas Christian University Press, 1989.

Kendall, George Wilkins. *Letters from a Texas Sheep Ranch*. Edited by Harry James Brown. Urbana: University of Illinois Press, 1959.

Krupper, Winifred. *The Golden Hoof: The Story of the Sheep of the Southwest*. New York: Alfred A. Knopf, 1945.

Lehman, V. W. *Forgotten Legions: Sheep in the Rio Grande Plain of Texas*. El Paso: Texas Western Press, 1969.

Lemann, Nicholas. *The Promised Land: The Great Black Migration and How It Changed America*. New York: Vintage Books, 1991.

Leyburn, James G. *The Scotch-Irish: A Social History*. Chapel Hill: University of North Carolina Press, 1962.

Lichtenstein, Jack. *Field to Fabric: The Story of American Cotton Growers*. Lubbock: Texas Tech University Press, 1990.

Long, William G. *Donkeys of the West*. New York: Ballantine Books, 1974.

Maharidge, Dale, and Michael Williamson. *And Their Children After Them*. New York: Pantheon, 1989.

Manning, Diane. *Hill County Teacher: Oral Histories from the One-Room School and Beyond*. Boston: Twayne, 1990.

Marshall, James. *Santa Fe: The Railroad That Built an Empire*. New York: Random House, 1945.

Matthews, Sallie Reynolds. *Interwoven: A Pioneer Chronicle*. College Station: Texas A&M University Press, 1982.

McBride, Alma McKethan. *The "Filosofer" of "Kukel-bur" Flat*. Waco: Texian Press, 1975.

McCallum, H. D. *The Wire That Fenced the West*. Norman: University of Oklahoma Press, 1956.

McGregor, Alexander Campbell. *Counting Sheep: From Open Range to Agribusiness on the Columbia Plateau*. Seattle: University of Washington, 1982.

McKay, Seth Shepard. *Texas and the Fair Deal, 1945–1952*. San Antonio: The Naylor Company, 1954.

McLean, Malcolm, ed. *Robertson's Colony*. 8 volumes, Arlington: University of Texas at Arlington Press, 1975–1995.

McLennan, Falls, Bell, and Coryell Counties, Texas. Chicago: Lewis Publishing Company, 1893.

Maudsley, Robert. *Texas Sheepman: The Reminiscences of Robert Maudsley*. Edited by Winifred Kupper. Austin: University of Texas Press, 1951.

Morgan, James Oscar. *Field Crops for the Cotton-Belt*. New York: Macmillan, 1918.

Myres, S. D., Jr., ed. *The Cotton Crisis*. Proceedings of the Second Conference, Institute of Public Affairs, 1935. Southern Methodist University. Dallas: George F. and Ora Nixon Arnold Foundation, 1935.

Nordyke, Lewis. *Cattle Empire*. New York: William Morrow, 1949.

O'Neal, Bill. *Cattlemen vs. Sheepherders*. Austin: Eakin Press, 1989.

Osgood, Ernest Staples. *The Day of the Cattleman*. Chicago: University of Chicago Press, 1929.

Parker, Richard Denny. *Historical Recollections of Robertson County, Texas*. Salado, TX: Anson Jones, 1955.

Perry, Garland. *An American Saga: William George Hughes, 1859–1902*. Boerne, TX: LEBCO Graphics, 1994.

Poage, W. R. *After the Pioneers*. Waco: Texian Press, 1969.

———. *McLennan County—Before 1980*. Waco: Texian Press, 1981.

Porter, Glenn, and Harold C. Livesay. *Merchants and Manufacturers: Studies in Changing Structure of Nineteenth-Century Marketing.* Baltimore: Johns Hopkins Press, 1971.

Powell, Roberta Blair. *A History of the Unity Presbyterian Church.* Turnersville, TX: n.p., 1972.

Provence, Harry. *The Citizens National Bank of Waco.* Waco: Republic Bank, 1982.

Rainbolt, Jo. *The Last Cowboys.* Helena, MT: American and World Geographic Publishing, 1992.

Reeve, Agnesa. *My Dear Mollie: Love Letters of a Texas Sheep Rancher.* Dallas: Hendrick-Long, 1990.

Rosengarten, Theodore. *Tombee: Portrait of a Cotton Planter.* New York: William Morrow, 1986.

Sage, Wayne. *Harris Creek Baptist Church.* Waco: n.p., 1979.

Schmitz, Joseph William. *Texas Culture in the Days of the Republic.* San Antonio: Naylor Company, 1960.

Self, Margaret Cabell. *Horses of Today.* New York: Duell, Sloan and Pierce, 1964.

Shannon, Fred A. *The Farmer's Last Frontier: Agriculture, 1860–1897.* New York: Farrar & Rinehart, 1945.

Sharpless, Rebecca. *Fertile Ground, Narrow Choices: Women on Texas Cotton Farms, 1900–1940.* Chapel Hill: University of North Carolina Press, 1999.

Silver, James W. *Mississippi: The Closed Society.* New York: Harcourt, Brace, & World, 1963.

Silverthorne, Elizabeth. *Plantation Life in Texas.* College Station: Texas A&M University Press, 1986.

Simmons, Frank E. *History of Coryell County.* Belton: *Coryell County News*, 1936.

Sitton, Thad. *Backwoodsmen: Stockmen and Hunters Along a Big Thicket River Valley.* Norman: University of Oklahoma Press, 1995.

Sitton, Thad, and Dan Utley. *From Can See to Can't*. Austin: University of Texas Press, 1997.

Sleeper, John, and J. C. Hutchins. *Waco and McLennan County, Texas*. Waco: J. W. Golledge, 1876.

Smith, David Paul. *Frontier Defense in the Civil War*. College Station: Texas A&M University Press, 1992.

Smith, Frank E. *The Yazoo River*. Jackson: University Press of Mississippi, 1954.

Smith, W. Broadus. *Pioneers of Brazos County, Texas, 1800–1850*. Brazos County: W. Broadus Smith, 1962.

Spratt, John Stickling. *The Road to Spindletop*. Austin: University of Texas Press, 1955.

Stearns, Monyene. *McGregor, Texas: Jewel of the Prairie*. McGregor: Monyene Stearns, 2000.

Strapac, Joseph A. *Cotton Belt Locomotives*. Huntington Beach, CA: Shade Tree Books, 1977.

Street, James H. *The New Revolution in the Cotton Economy: Mechanization and Its Consequences*. Chapel Hill: University of North Carolina Press, 1957.

Syers, William Edward. *Off the Beaten Track*. Waco: Texian Press, 1971.

Texas Almanac. Galveston: Richardson, 1856.

Thorp, Laura A. *Facts and Anecdotes of Turnersville, Texas*. Waco: Texian Press, 1973.

Wallace, Patricia Ward. *Our Land, Our Lives: A Pictorial History of McLennan County*. Norfolk, VA: Donning Company, 1986.

Waters, L. L. *Steel Trails to Santa Fe*. Lawrence: University Press of Kansas, 1950.

Watkins, James L. *King Cotton: A Historical and Statistical Review, 1790–1908*. New York: Negro Universities Press, 1908.

Webb, Walter Prescott. *The Great Plains*. New York: Grosset and Dunlap, 1931.

Wentworth, Edward Norris. *America's Sheep Trails*. Ames: Iowa

State College Press, 1948.

Whayne, Jeannie. *Shadows over Sunnyside: An Arkansas Plantation in Transition, 1830–1945*. Fayetteville: The University of Arkansas Press, 1993.

Williams, J. W. *Old Texas Trails*. Burnet, TX: Eakin Press, 1979.

Woodman, Harold D. *King Cotton and His Retainers: Financing and Marketing the Cotton Crop of the South, 1800–1925*. Lexington: University of Kentucky Press, 1968.

Woolfolk, George Ruble. *The Cotton Regency: The Northern Merchants and Reconstruction, 1865–1880*. New York: Bookman Associates, 1958.

Worcester, Don. *The Chisholm Trail: High Road of the Cattle Kingdom*. Lincoln: University of Nebraska Press, 1985.

Worster, Donald. *Dust Bowl: The Southern Plains in the 1930s*. New York: Oxford University Press, 1979.

Wright, Gavin. *Old South, New South: Revolutions in the Southern Economy Since the Civil War*. New York: Basic Books, 1986.

Yafa, Stephen. *Big Cotton: How a Humble Fiber Created Fortunes, Wrecked Civilizations and Put America on the Map*. New York: Viking, 2005.

Index

Watson C. Arnold has seen several incarnations of his career. A physician by training, he was the director of pediatric nephrology, dialysis, and transplantation at Cook Children's Medical Center in Fort Worth for twenty years. During that time, he earned a certificate in ranch management and a PhD in history from TCU. Arnold has taught in the pediatrics department of the University of Arkansas for Medical Sciences, and he has also taught in the history departments of TCU and Baylor. He is a member of the board of directors of the Texas State Historical Society.